a crooked smile

a crooked smile

a memoir

terri tate

SOUNDS TRUE
BOULDER, COLORADO

Sounds True
Boulder, CO 80306

Some names and identifying details have been changed to protect the privacy
of individuals.

Published 2016

Cover design by Rachael Murray
Book design by Beth Skelley

Printed in Canada

Library of Congress Cataloging-in-Publication Data
Names: Tate, Terri, author.
Title: Crooked smile : a memoir / Terri Tate.
Description: Boulder, CO : Sounds True, 2016.
Identifiers: LCCN 2016011240 (print) | LCCN 2016026322 (ebook) |
    ISBN 9781622037391 (hardcover) | ISBN 9781622037407
Subjects: LCSH: Tate, Terri,—Health. | Mouth—Cancer—Patients—Biography. |
    Cancer—Patients—Biography. | Mouth—Surgery.
Classification: LCC RC280.M6 T38 2016 (print) | LCC RC280.M6 (ebook) |
    DDC 616.99/4310092 [B]—dc23
LC record available at https://lccn.loc.gov/2016011240

Ebook ISBN 978-1-62203-740-7

10 9 8 7 6 5 4 3 2 1

For Eric, Justin & Georgie
*You give me reason to live.**

*From "You Can Leave Your Hat On," by Randy Newman

The privilege of a lifetime is to become who you truly are.

Carl G. Jung

foreword

The woman you are about to meet is a funny mix of corn-fed Midwest and California, tall and solid in a feather boa, a smart cookie, exuberant, ironic, and very game. She's the real thing—tough and sparkly as life, a lover, a fabulous complainer, an intellect, and an amazing writer. Her book is going to change your life.

I met Terri Tate twenty years ago in one of my writing workshops, and I grokked her immediately—she's that rare bird, a storyteller and healer, someone who has paid through the nose to stay alive, who now transmits layers of wisdom and truth, and yet exudes a great lightness and humor.

I wish you could meet her in person, but instead I'll try to describe her: She's big and tall, a billboard of coming through, with a wing-span so wide that she may just fly away. She moves with grace and ease and eagerness. Her long hands are pure power because she tells her stories with them, raised her sons with them, writes with them, touches you gently with them, smoothes her own soul and mind as if she is her own mother. She has very big green eyes like head-lights and thick, fancy rich-people's hair. Her fine cheekbones don't quite match, but if you don't insist on looking straight on, it doesn't matter. Her mouth has taken the brunt of the surgeries, but the stuff that comes out is so brilliant, loving, and hilarious. She has the great-est, most contagious laugh.

She's somewhat unusual looking because of all the surgeries, and quite beautiful. Symmetry is usually so important in the beauty canon, and this culture thinks appearance is everything, but she prevailed through it all with charm, skill, deep spiritual wisdom, and *joie de vivre*. And thus she sneakily found her own way to beauty, perma-nently damaged after so many surgeries, and even deformed. So she could no longer use an external mirror to assure herself that everything was okay—because it often wasn't. She found a truer one, the little powder compact in her heart.

She had to let go. And when you fall and all the guardians catch you, you find out that you are okay.

You will find in these pages that she has a huge appetite for life and living and food, and also a mouth that was rearranged by multiple surgeries for oral cancer. But because Terri writes like a dream, she describes dark material in a way that is totally honest yet also jaunty and visceral, and she makes it easy to read about. I laughed out loud while reading this book, over and over, and marked it up like a student.

She's a big solid clotheshorse of a woman with the longest legs and an open, questing self. She calls it like it is—how terrible she might feel sometimes, how hilariously annoying other people are, how embarrassing all of life can be—such dreck. And then she rises from it all, in sequins.

In this book we encounter a woman who is so well nourished on the inside that you would never know she was loved back to life after a diagnosis and recurrence that left her with only a slim chance of survival. It took her by the lapels and shook her like a rag doll. Miraculously, parts of her truest self rose up, two females you'll read about here—the Vile Bitch Upstairs and the Girl in the Closet. The Bitch said, "You are not paying attention, and that's going to kill us both." So she started paying attention. The Girl waited in terror for Terri to become safe, available, and brave. So Terri did. She got serious about healing and showing up for her life. She got real.

This brought her from hopelessness to vigor, which is the greatest story of all.

It's a true spiritual memoir. She learned to live in what can't always be seen, to give away love in order to fill up; she discovered that service is the path of fulfillment, and in practicing the radical self-love necessary to survive and thrive, she found the meaning of life.

All the things Terri thought were armatures of life—homes, a husband, fine conversations—turned out not to be, of course. So she set out to learn what was: love, the now, the truth of her spiritual identity.

This book is the story of her journey, the amazing people she met along the way, the quirky peace she has found. It's thrilling in its insight and first-rate storytelling. She's come through a mess, and like all great people you'd love to know better, she's a bit of a mess. So you want Terri to come sit next to you at the table and tell you her story—that the world did not scroll out the way it was supposed to. This book is a chance to sit with her for a while. What she found was what we all seek, the richest gift that life has to offer, and the reason we are here. She found and fell in love with her wild, divine, gorgeous, screwed-up, and deeply human self.

You can tell that I love her and love love love this book. They contain treasures. Come on in.

Anne Lamott
April 2016

may 2007

*O*uch!"

The make-up artist, a friend of mine, yanked another hair from my brow.

"This shaping is going to make you look so much better," Kathleena assured me. "Eyebrows make the face."

The pain was a welcome distraction from my anxiety. In fifteen minutes I was going to walk onto the stage of the most upscale venue I'd ever played to perform my solo show, *Shopping as a Spiritual Path*, for hundreds of people in San Francisco's Jewish Community Center. Dozens, hundreds, thousands, more—who knew?—would then watch the DVD in the privacy of their own homes.

"You know you want to look your best on TV," Kathleena added.

I couldn't argue the point, so I let her pluck away. "My best" was not what it used to be before cancer surgery rearranged my face, so I avoided the mirror as she worked. Moving on from my eyebrows, Kathleena applied bordello-worthy quantities of makeup, all the while assuring me that everyone needs this level of camouflage for video.

Except while awaiting biopsy results, I had never been this nervous. I tried to run my lines in my head and drew a complete blank. When I glanced at my script, the words swam on the page. None of them looked even remotely familiar.

Kathleena pronounced me done and passed me off to my friend Jo Anne, who was working wardrobe. Jo helped me slip into tapered black pants and a satiny bronze shirt over a sparkly, slinky bronze tank top. She said I looked great. As we left the green room, I allowed myself a glance at the full-length mirror. From a distance and without my glasses, I still looked pretty good: big green eyes sparkling between heavily blackened lashes; tall, thin-ish, and as my mother used to say, a body made for clothes.

Jo ushered me down the hall, her hand on my elbow so I couldn't bolt out a side door. We walked between thick ropes onto the stage. She positioned me behind the dense, maroon velvet curtain; gave me a quick, encouraging squeeze; and abandoned me. I could hear the expectant buzz of the crowd—one of my all-time favorite sounds. What was I so nervous about? I should be proud. I hadn't been expected to live, much less become a low-voltage star.

I reminded myself that this wasn't a life-or-death matter and did my best to replace my shallow panting with the deep breathing actors are trained to do. I told the voice that lives in my head—the one I call the Vile Bitch Upstairs—to shut up. I promised the inner child I call the Girl in the Closet that I wouldn't beat up on her no matter how it went. Then I whispered a prayer asking God to come with me and stepped out from between the curtains.

under my tongue

I am not in the habit of inspecting the underside of my tongue. But one blustery Michigan night in December 1990, I was brushing my teeth when a strange stinging sensation caused me to peek under there. Halfway back, on the left, I saw a raw spot about the size of a pencil eraser. I called my fiancé over to take a look.

"I get those all the time," Jeff said. "It'll go away in a few days."

Reassured, I crawled into our king-sized bed and went to sleep.

Jeff and I had just set a wedding date. He'd proposed to me the first time we went out together and, a few months later, slipped the engagement ring of my dreams onto my finger. The bold, asymmetrical design was clearly the work of my favorite jeweler whom I had taken Jeff to meet on our second date. The round-cut diamond was held aloft by a curved gold band on top and a zigzag band below into which a wedding band would someday fit. Or not. I gratefully accepted the ring but was in no hurry to wed. If I married Jeff, our wedding would be my third.

I married my first husband, Tom, when I was twenty. We had two wonderful sons. Then our union succumbed to the open marriage craze of the 1970s that hit Unitarians in Ann Arbor especially hard.

I took up with Michael at thirty. He was brilliantly funny, sexy, and brimming with potential. I knew from the start he was a bad boy. But I was certain that marriage to me would settle him down. That was one excruciating divorce.

Now, at forty-four, my new fiancé gave me reason for hope. Jeff was sweet and sensitive, and I had never dated anyone so good-looking. He had striking silver hair that shone in the sunlight, an almost-pretty face with well-defined, elegant features, and lively brown eyes that promised mischief, mystery, and wisdom. His soft, bronze skin was stunning to look at and luscious to the touch. Just walking beside him made me feel better about myself.

More important, Jeff was the first man I'd met who shared my somewhat quirky faith in God and my long-standing interest in spiritual exploration. Tom was an atheist. Michael vowed, and I think believed, that baseball was the path to the Godhead. Jeff had spent seven years in seminary and since then had pursued an even broader range of spiritual paths than I had.

Maybe this one could work. I agreed to marry him in a year.

We shared our happy news with my parents at a holiday gathering the week before Christmas. I knew Mom would be pleased. In our only conversation about sex, she had warned me against being one of those women who "gave the milk away for free." I was ten at the time and already confused by the pamphlet she had given me on the birds and the bees. I couldn't imagine what milk had to do with it. Now that I understood, I knew she would be glad that Jeff was going to "buy the cow."

Mom was sipping a martini and looking smashing in a white blouse with the collar turned up, black pants, and a red-and-black sweater. Mom could take an outfit from J. C. Penney and make it look like Prada. As usual, the ensemble showed off her black hair with its silver streaks, her jet-black eyes, and her year-round tan. Before my folks started spending winters in Florida, Mom spent many summertime hours holding aluminum foil under her chin to create a tan that lasted through the Michigan winter. My mother's mantra on a woman's appearance was "Do the best with what you have," and she practiced what she preached.

Mom inquired as to our wedding date.

"December 29 of next year," I said, beaming.

"I'll be dead by then," said my seventy-one-year-old mom, demonstrating both her signature optimism and her unfailing ability to make every conversation about her.

"Congratulations!" my blond, blue-eyed, movie-star-handsome father said, raising his cocktail glass in an effort to divert attention from Mom's prediction.

In the spirit of the evening, I decided not to mention that the shrimp cocktail burned the spot under my tongue.

Two days before Christmas, I was awakened by an automated voice from the Washtenaw County Jail asking if I would accept a call from my never-before-arrested, eighteen-year-old son. Fresh from his first semester at the University of Colorado, Justin and some high school buddies had celebrated their reunion by stealing a few items from an open car. The sunglasses that Justin took were worth more than five dollars, making his crime a felony. We spent Christmas Eve in court where we learned that the case wouldn't be resolved until March.

The first Gulf War and talk of a draft were looming. While being a felon might keep Justin safe, his twenty-two-year-old brother, Eric, was vulnerable. The war started the day Eric and Justin ended their Christmas visits to return to California and Colorado, respectively. It was harder than usual to watch their tall, lanky frames lope away from me.

I came from a long line of nervous mothers and had always worried about my kids. The oldest daughter, I began my role as a surrogate mom at four when my brother Greg was born. But I had never felt fully up to the job. My sense of being in over my head as a mother, struggling to keep everyone alive, well, and happy, never entirely went away. And these maternal shortcomings were confirmed when Greg took his own life at twenty-nine. Since then I had lived in fear that one of my kids might follow his example. Now, imagining my boys in combat or in jail made it easy to ignore my tongue.

With the holidays behind us, Jeff and I reclaimed our quiet lives in our sprawling house outside Ann Arbor. Less than a year after we met, we had pooled our resources to buy the place, which was so big and beautiful that we were still waiting for the real owners to show up. Evenings often found us soaking in the hot tub, our bodies heated to 104 degrees while our hair and eyebrows were frosted with snow. We held hands and gazed out over our apple orchard, blanketed in white with tiny lights glistening on bare branches. I had never had it so good.

By day, we returned to our careers in the helping professions. I had gone into nursing in large part because Mom wanted to be a nurse, but had never had the money for tuition. Once in the field, I discovered a deep aversion to gore and an even deeper interest in the workings of the human psyche, so specialized in psychiatric nursing. I earned a master's degree at the end of my marriage to Tom and spent a few years as a clinical specialist at the University of Michigan's Children's Psychiatric Hospital. But I felt confined by the structure of the large organization and ventured into business for myself as a therapist, hypnotherapist, speaker, and organizational consultant, becoming the first hypnotherapist in the Ann Arbor phone book.

Jeff had spent most of his career in the business world but now practiced Rolfing, an esoteric form of bodywork that involves aligning the body so it can heal itself. When we first got together, I didn't know much about Rolfing and, wanting to experience my new love's work, I agreed to be Rolfed. Jeff said I screamed louder than any client he'd ever had. But I was impressed. He was very skilled at the physical aspect of the treatments, but what really wowed me was his intuitive understanding of the emotional wounds that were released as he prodded my body into alignment.

During the month of January, I found myself having increasing difficulty concentrating on my job. Sitting in my peach velveteen recliner, listening to a client describe the weight problem she wanted to solve with hypnosis, my mind kept shifting to the pain under my tongue. Standing at the head of a conference table at Children's Hospital of Michigan in my navy suit, my tongue pulled my attention away from a subcommittee report. The pain was becoming undeniable. At the bathroom break, I rushed to the mirror. Was the lesion getting bigger? Was it redder than yesterday? Did it look a little deeper? I couldn't tell, but I knew that I needed to do something about it.

Years later, a malpractice lawyer would inform me that a sore in the mouth should be biopsied if it doesn't heal within seven to ten days. But when I saw my dentist he said, "It's probably just a tooth rubbing on that spot. I wouldn't worry about it."

His hygienist said, "The spot seems to have some white on it. I think I remember hearing something in hygiene school about cancer being white." Her words made my stomach spasm. I told myself that the dentist was the expert here. I decided to trust him.

And I did, for a while. The pain and the sore remained. So I consulted my chiropractor friend, who cracked my neck and prescribed B vitamins. I called the Unity Church twenty-four-hour prayer hotline and was assured that they would hold my sons and my tongue in prayer for thirty days. I wrote affirmations. I even visited a psychic body worker who put crystals on my chakras and interpreted my symptoms as indicators of past lives. The longer the pain continued in spite of my efforts, the less I was able to convince myself that it wasn't serious.

Toward the end of January, I saw an ear, nose, and throat surgeon who examined the spot and assured me that I didn't have the risk factors for oral cancer. I avoided asking what those factors were, as if being informed might make me more prone to it. "Come back in a month if it isn't gone," she said, smiling.

During that month, there were wedding plans to be made, and my correspondence with President Bush escalated along with the Gulf War. The list of things I couldn't comfortably eat was growing by the day: salad dressing, orange juice, tomato sauce, mustard, carbonated drinks. It was getting tough to have a conversation without mentioning my tongue. Like me, many of my friends were mental-health types, so theories of causation abounded. "Maybe your tongue is rebelling against saying 'I do' again," one colleague suggested. Another therapist friend, who knew that accessing and expressing anger weren't my strong suits, reminded me that repressed anger can cause illness. Someone else suspected family dynamics. Did I need to stand up to my mother? And what about my father, who was so seldom home when I was little that I really didn't know him? I had seen plenty of clients with physical issues rooted in their childhoods. Was my problem a metaphor for my neglected inner child biting her tongue? My new friend Sandy, a brilliant, dynamic woman who I'd met though my organizational development work, was in close contact with her rambunctious inner child. She'd named her Magic. Both Sandy and Magic wanted my inner child to come out and play. I found this all pretty silly but wanted to impress Sandy. Besides, if such a smart, successful woman needed to heal her inner child, I didn't have to be embarrassed about looking for mine. I read lots of John Bradshaw, watched videos on reclaiming your wounded inner child, and wrote with my left hand so "little Terri" could express herself. She didn't have much to say.

While I was busy plumbing my depths, one of my prayers was answered! The Gulf War ended. Knowing that my sons had been spared left me more time to obsess about my tongue. As far back as I could remember, the minute one worry was resolved, another popped up. The familiar toxic voice in my head was never at a loss for something to fear. Now it reminded me that it had been a month since that surgeon told me to come back if the spot didn't disappear. It hadn't, so I did. She said, "I think the lesion looks better."

I went to Jeff for a second opinion. He had a way of comforting me that I called our "You'll be fine" game. Whenever I felt afraid, I explained my fear to Jeff ending with, "But I'll be okay, right?" And he had to answer, "Yes, you'll be fine." While I knew that he couldn't see the future any better than I could, I somehow trusted his intuition more than my own. Even outside his Rolfing office, Jeff's intuitive powers had always dazzled me.

When we first started dating, I was eager to introduce my handsome new beau to all of my friends. Jeff showed an uncanny ability to read deep aspects of their characters after only brief or superficial interactions. I was very attracted to the possibility that someone might finally understand me. His depth was all the more appealing because my most recent husband, Michael, hadn't been at all interested in delving under the surface of things. Looking back, I suspect that Jeff understood me better than I understood myself.

But today he wasn't saying I'd be fine. Jeff was deep into a video game when I found him. He peered into my mouth and said, "I don't know. It looks about the same to me."

"Not what I want to hear," I said, sounding tough but shaking inside.

"I think you should see another doctor." I wanted to hear that even less, but I saw the fear in his eyes. A few months before we met, Jeff's wife of twenty-three years had died suddenly of unknown causes at the age of forty-three. He didn't want to take any chances with me.

"What about Dennis?" Jeff asked, referring to a colleague of his.

I made an appointment with Dennis Talley, an MD with a master's degree in public health and training in homeopathy. Dennis blends traditional with complementary medicine, and brilliance with humility. A recovering hippie, he has long gray-brown hair, a wild beard, and a spare frame. Dennis was that rare doctor who could use the words "I," "don't," and "know" in the same sentence.

"I don't know what it is, Terri," Dennis said. "But if I were you, I'd get it biopsied."

Two weeks later I sat in the oral surgeon's waiting room, silently chanting prayers and inspirational messages. *I'm sure this is nothing. No big deal. It'll be great to have it settled.*

"This needs to be biopsied," the surgeon said.

My heart thumped hard against my chest. "I have to give a speech in Kansas City on Thursday. Then I'm going to Boulder to visit my son."

"I don't care about speeches and trips," he said. "Get it biopsied *now.*"

I took the first available appointment and sped across town to Jeff's office.

"He says it has to be biopsied right away and I can tell he thinks it's really bad cancer and I hate all those assholes who have told me it was nothing," I blurted. I felt a sudden rush of anger, which was soon supplanted by fear.

Jeff gave me a quick hug. I wanted him to hold me longer, but his body was as stiff as mine. His voice tightened as he spoke. "Slow down. We don't know anything for sure. Just breathe."

"I have clients to see in an hour."

"You're in no shape for that," Jeff said gently. "Let me call and cancel your appointments."

"Oh no, you can't do that. They count on me." My mind raced. "Who knows how long I'll be able to work? We'll need money for medical bills."

"Your clients will understand. Forget about money right now," Jeff said calmly. "Let's cancel our sessions and go get coffee."

We sat at a round table in my favorite café, avoiding each other's eyes. Sipping my latte, I automatically assessed its impact on the spot under my tongue. Then I realized it was no longer up to me to diagnose the problem. Having medical science involved made the whole thing so much more real. This wasn't just my imagination, and it was probably going to take more than positive thinking to make it go away.

I caught Jeff staring at me. "What are you thinking?" I asked. I wondered if he felt like bolting before he had another dead wife on his hands.

"I was remembering what the dentist said about your tooth rubbing your tongue. And the ENT said it looked better. They could still be right." I appreciated his attempt to reassure me, but it wasn't working.

I had a week to get through before my biopsy. My keynote speech for the American Association of Diabetic Educators had been on the books for months. It took me days to crank up the nerve to cancel and even longer to call Eric and Justin. I asked Jeff to tell my sons that I might have cancer, and then I chatted with them as if it were no big deal.

My younger sister Valerie, who swings into action in a crisis, insisted that I get a second opinion from James Dudar, an ENT acquaintance of hers at the University of Michigan. Jeff came with me. "Terri White?" said a deep voice in a big hurry. "I'm Dr. Dudar."

We followed his white coat into an examining room, where he waved me into an unyielding stainless-steel chair, then stomped on a foot pedal, elevating me in jerky increments. He yanked my mouth open, scanned the spot in question, and spoke without hesitation.

"If it were my mouth, I'd have surgery and radiation. It's likely to recur, and you want to take every precaution," he said.

A thunderous screeching began in my head, drowning out the doctor's words. This icy man was, without benefit of a biopsy, telling me that I had cancer. Serious cancer that surgery alone couldn't cure. Cancer so bad that it would likely come back. How could this be obvious to him, when so many others had missed it? I tried to convince myself that he didn't know what he was talking about.

Years later, I learned that while I was tuning him out, Dr. Dudar told Jeff that if my cancer ever did recur, I would have a 2 percent chance of survival. I will always be grateful that Jeff kept this information to himself.

Through my fog of denial, I heard Dr. Dudar saying he'd use his clout to get me an appointment with the radiation oncologist the following Monday for a pre-biopsy assessment. Then I grabbed Jeff and fled the clinic as if escaping Dr. Dudar would erase his diagnosis.

Val took me to the appointment on Monday. I fixed my gaze on the back of her well-coiffed blonde head as I followed her into the reception area. My imagination was already offering up horrific pictures of what I might look like after treatment, so I plopped into a seat and buried my eyes in a magazine. Still, my peripheral vision glimpsed a room full of bald, burned, and emaciated people.

A nurse called my name and led Val and me into a sterile exam room. As we waited for the doctor, my cold hands and constricted throat let me know that I couldn't handle any more dire predictions. I wanted only enough facts to make treatment decisions. As a speaker on healthcare communication, I knew that male physicians give their patients an average of seventeen seconds airtime before interrupting. (Female doctors allow forty-five seconds.) So I talked fast as soon as the male resident, who looked younger than my paperboy, entered the room.

"You can examine this lesion so you'll know what it looks like before the biopsy," I told him. "Measure the spot, take pictures, and make notes. But don't tell me what might happen to me. The biopsy is tomorrow. I'll deal with it then."

The resident looked startled, but did as he was told and left. Val and I burst out laughing before the door was fully closed. "Do you suppose his mother drives him to work?" she asked.

"Yeah. I thought the toys in the waiting room were for patients."

Val and I made Doogie Howser jokes until the resident returned with the grown-up radiation oncologist, who interrupted me in less than seventeen seconds to ask, "Did you ever chew tobacco?"

"You didn't ask me that one," I said.

"I guess I made an assumption," Doogie said, blushing.

It hurt like hell as the elder doctor invaded my mouth with a tongue depressor and then he began citing odds. I tried to block his words as I had Dudar's, but it was clear from his tone that he didn't like my chances.

After the appointment, I went to my office to see a few clients, determined to pretend I was living my normal life. My officemate, Gretchen, a serene, beautiful woman I suspect is part angel, said, "I'm sure you're going to be okay. No matter what happens with this biopsy, you'll be fine." Her words had enhanced credibility because she'd been an ardent devotee of an Indian guru for twelve years, which I assumed gave her a direct line to Higher Truth. I wondered if she meant "fine" in the everything-happens-for-the-best-and-you're-fine-even-if-you're-dead way, but still I took comfort. Gretchen volunteered to write to the guru on my behalf, and I accepted her offer.

On the morning of the biopsy, friends gathered with Jeff and me at our round, claw-footed oak kitchen table overlooking the snowy orchard. We joined hands and our Unity-minister-in-training friend Dave led us in prayer, asking that the will of Mother-Father-God be done with regard to my health.

"Be more specific!" I told him. "Give God some clear instructions like, 'Make the biopsy negative.'"

"God knows what She/He is doing," he said with a hint of condescension. My faith in God was not fear-proof and given recent events, I wasn't entirely sure that I trusted Her/Him.

Jeff, Val, and Sandy came along for the biopsy because at this point in my career as a patient, I already knew the value of gathering all available troops when entering medical settings. My experiences with Dudar and Doogie had taught me that I needed multiple companions at each visit—some to talk to the doctor and remember the conversation, others to provide distraction. Traveling in the middle of the pack provided protection, and a posse helped equalize the power imbalance between the doctor and me.

As we pulled into the parking lot of the oral surgeon's office, I noticed the sign for the first time: Michigan Institute for Cosmetic Surgery. If only I were here for a nose job.

The redheaded receptionist said, "Wow, you have a big support team." I felt a little embarrassed for needing so many helpers, but was still glad to have my people with me. I was even more humiliated when Magic got tired of waiting and grew dissatisfied with the markers that Sandy had brought along. She marched up to the desk and, in her loud, faux-child voice, asked, "Do you have any better colors?"

After minutes masquerading as hours, a thin, white-coated woman came to lead me into the inner sanctum. I motioned for Jeff to follow, but as he stood up she said, "It's already too crowded in the treatment room. He can come in when we're done with the procedure."

"I'll be there as soon as they'll let me," Jeff said, kissing me good-bye. He looked relieved even if he did have to stay and play with Magic.

As promised, the room was jammed full of technicians and equipment. Why was all of this necessary for a simple biopsy of a tiny spot? Maybe things were worse than I had feared. I was told to sit very still in a tan vinyl reclining chair. After a brief hello, the oral surgeon stuck a needle into my tongue. I felt the poke and then a slow wave of numbness permeated the left side of my mouth.

With my eyes clenched shut and my tongue asleep, the surgeon's breath brushing my cheek was the only evidence that he was working in my mouth. My hands, resting on my stomach, held each other. I longed for Jeff's hand instead, and for general anesthesia. Although the room was warm enough, I was chilled through and through. My mind was frozen as well, and I couldn't gauge the passage of time. The doctor finally declared that he was done, but I kept my eyes closed until I heard Jeff's voice.

Walking us back to the waiting room, the surgeon said, "The results take seven to ten days. I'll be at a conference in Boston this week, so I'll call when I get back."

"Okay. Thanks," Jeff said politely. I stared down the hallway, eager for the exit.

The doctor paused then added, "You know, that spot didn't look so bad today. I'm not as concerned as I was. Maybe it's nothing."

maybe it's nothing

aybe it's nothing. Maybe it's nothing." As soon as the doctor uttered these words, they became my mantra. I got through the terror-filled days of waiting for the biopsy results by repeating that phrase and by surrounding myself with people who loved me. It helped that I was still swaddled in the belief that cancer was something that happened to other people. Even though I wasn't expecting to hear anything for seven to ten days, my heart froze every time the phone rang.

On Friday, Jeff took me out to breakfast and then delivered me to my crystals-on-your-chakras healer, whose cosmic assurances coupled with a massage left me more relaxed than I had been in weeks. Returning home, we opened the door to a ringing phone, which took a big bite out of that relaxation. "Will you answer it?" I asked Jeff, trying to sound just pitiful enough to get him to do it.

He hesitated, then picked up the phone. "Hello, doctor," he said. It could not be a good sign that the doctor was calling from his conference in Boston after only three days. Jeff's face confirmed my fears.

My heart raced and my gut froze. My skull felt too small to contain the deafening noise in my head.

Why is this happening to me? It's a mistake. The lab screwed up. I'm too young. I'm too nice. I don't have the risk factors. What the fuck happened to "Maybe it's nothing?" What is God thinking? What kind of god would let this happen? And after all I've done to help others! What about all the clients I've told, "You create your own reality"? I sure as hell didn't create this. What am I going to do?

Jeff hung up the phone. His lips barely moved as he said, "The cancer is too much for him. He wants you to see an ear, nose, and throat surgeon."

He began to cry. I stood stock still in the middle of the kitchen. I was too scared to cry in the same way that it is sometimes too cold to snow.

The past three months flashed before my eyes. Rage boiled in my belly as I realized that cancer had been growing in my mouth while I waited for a biopsy. My mind produced a dark, bloody opera in which my friend the medical malpractice lawyer cut out the tongues of all the experts who had placated and patronized me and told me it was nothing.

"He gave us the name of someone at St. Joe's," Jeff choked out. "I'll call him."

My mind was galloping through Elisabeth Kübler-Ross's phases of the grief process: denial, bargaining, anger, depression—everything except acceptance. Never, I thought. I'll never accept this.

Jeff was talking on the phone again. "The doctor we were referred to is out of town," he told me. "I got an appointment with some guy named Watson for Monday morning."

"What day is this?" I asked.

Jeff looked startled that I'd lost track of the days of the week. When we first met, Jeff used to marvel at how strong I was and seemed to be attracted to that strength. Now he was watching it drain away.

"I wonder if we should try to find somebody at the U of M hospital? Is it really better than St. Joe's? Oh God, I don't know."

"Let's call your sister," Jeff said in a wobbly voice.

Neither of us was especially long on organizational skills under the best of circumstances. We definitely needed Val's calm ability to manage complex situations.

My only sister managed a high-profile career in the business world like Dad's, a big house, a handsome husband, and three active, extroverted kids, all without appearing to break a sweat. She finished her Christmas shopping by August and needlepointed all her own ornaments. I was lucky to get my Christmas cards out by tax time. Val has perfect features and a casual elegance that make her look like she belonged in Grosse Pointe, the exclusive suburb where we grew up. She once briefly dated Edsel Ford II, a fact my parents couldn't help repeating for decades after the relationship went the way of the car bearing his name.

Ever since Dad started calling Val "my little princess," the critical voice in my head had used her success for ammunition. But now, none of that mattered. She dropped everything and came on board as the CEO of my health-care journey.

Understanding Val and Jeff's discussion of the pros and cons of St. Joseph's Mercy Hospital versus University Hospital required a level of cognitive functioning that far exceeded what I could manage. While they talked, I paced from the kitchen, down the hall, through the living room and dining room and back to the kitchen. As I walked, I hugged myself tightly to prevent my insides from spilling out.

Somehow I had to make it to Monday morning. Fortunately, a good friend was coming from Chicago for the weekend. For almost twenty-five years, Nan and I had carried on one of those conversations that resumed immediately, as if our words were separated by a comma rather than by years.

Jeff and I passed the hours until Nan's arrival in numb silence punctuated by muted exchanges about what we should do. He made phone calls. I listened to him tell one person after another our news. I wished that he would comfort me, but he was too busy handling the business end of cancer.

Nan's calming presence and quick wit provided relief that evening. Nan has dark-brown eyes that sparkle when she laughs, which she does a lot, especially at my jokes. She and I met when I was a young, mostly stay-at-home mother in Birmingham, Michigan. Nan was all that saved me from dying of boredom in that white-bread suburb that was way too much like Grosse Pointe for my taste.

Tom and I moved to Birmingham when Eric was six months old. Nan and her adorable one-year-old son Robbie, both olive-skinned and dark haired, showed up on our doorstep shortly after we arrived. She filled me in on all the neighbors over Amy Joy donuts and coffee.

Amy Joys became a staple, as did bologna sandwiches for lunch and beer with chips in the late afternoon. We were often reluctant to part and return to our respective husbands. Sometimes they would join us for a potluck dinner and more drinks. Nan and I each had another son at roughly the same time, and our four boys were best friends. She was always my favorite drinking buddy and stuck with me through all my marriages and divorces. Although she hadn't spent a lot of time with him, she got along well with Jeff.

Nan cooked dinner for all of us, and then she and I huddled on the couch, reminiscing about the great times we had when our boys were little. There were moments when I almost forgot my terror. But when she headed for the guest room, the arctic hollow in my gut returned, and I longed for physical consolation.

Jeff reluctantly agreed to come to bed with me. Our relationship was a bit unorthodox in that we usually slept in separate rooms. Jeff was a restless sleeper and preferred to sleep on a futon on his office floor. I sometimes felt deprived lying in bed alone, but told myself that he loved me in his way. I was embarrassed to tell people about our arrangement because it conjured up images of the sexless twin-bed marriages of fifties sitcoms. Even when we had sex, Jeff liked to sleep by himself afterward.

That night we crawled into bed together. His embrace was wooden, but his skin was soft. I rested my head in the crook of his arm and nestled up to him. After a few minutes, he started fidgeting and said, "Your head is too heavy." We attempted spooning, but he was soon inching away from me. Finally, my anger and sense of rejection outweighed my need for him to hold me.

"Leave me alone," I said. "Anything would be better than this."

I was wrong. Once he left me in that enormous bed, I had to deal with my fears and my fury. Why had I agreed to marry him? What was I doing with a man who couldn't cuddle and wouldn't sleep with me? That was bound to get old. Oh God, not another divorce! Then it dawned on me that this wasn't the ideal night to decide the fate of our relationship. I tried praying, but that didn't work, so I took half a Xanax and slept for a few hours.

Nan and I went out Saturday night with three of my nurse friends. I knew that the best way to get the real scoop on a doctor is to ask a nurse. They all gave Dr. Watson high marks.

Monday morning, Val, Jeff, Sandy, and I sat in Dr. Watson's waiting room, forcing "normal" conversation. I'd been spending a lot of time in doctors' offices, but this one seemed especially familiar. I realized it was also the office of the female ENT surgeon who only weeks ago had said that I didn't have the risk factors for oral cancer.

Finally, a nurse called my name. The four of us crammed into the tiny examining room where we waited some more. A trim, dark-haired man about my age entered looking like a conservative senator in a lab coat. He appeared stunned by the crowd, but managed to be pleasant. "I'm Dr. Watson. Who's the patient here?"

"I'm Terri White, and I'm very anxious. This is my fiancé. He's anxious, too. My sister and my friend are here to help us remember what you say."

Dr. Watson glanced through my chart. Then he gently inspected my mouth while asking me the now-familiar questions. "Are you a heavy smoker or drinker?"

"I smoked a pack a day for fifteen years, but I quit twelve years ago," I responded. "I quit drinking six months ago. Before that I was a social drinker. Possibly a little more social than most." Hypnotherapy had cured me of cigarettes, and Jeff and I had agreed to abstain from alcohol for a year to prove to ourselves we could do it. I would later learn that problem drinkers often quit temporarily to prove that they don't have a problem.

"Well, alcohol is a risk factor for oral cancer, but it doesn't sound like you drink enough to account for the disease," Watson said. This stemmed my guilt slightly. "The prototypical oral cancer patient is a sixty-five-year-old, chain-smoking, alcoholic man. If we catch the cancer early enough and the patient quits smoking and drinking, he stands a pretty good chance of survival. When oral cancer shows up in younger people without the obvious risk factors, the prognosis is not so good." I dug my fingernails into my palms, hoping the physical pain would distract me from my terror.

Watson continued, "You'll need surgery, and possibly radiation, although we'd like to avoid that if we can. Radiation to the oral cavity has horrible side effects. We'll remove the lesion and surrounding areas, as well as some of the lymph nodes in your neck, to see how far the cancer has spread. There's no way to know how much we'll have to take until we get in there. Surgery should be scheduled as soon as possible." He snapped my chart closed.

"Okay, if you don't have any more questions, just talk to my assistant about setting up the operation. Take care." And he left.

The tiny room seemed even smaller now. My pulse thudded in my ears. I'd been holding on to a sliver of hope that this doctor would discover that the others were wrong. We'd all chuckle about those silly lab results, and he'd give me some pills to solve the real problem with my tongue.

The four of us sat in stunned silence. Then we discussed Dr. Watson. He was nice for a surgeon, didn't talk down to us, and seemed to know what he was doing. We took a quick poll on whether we liked him enough to forgo checking out other doctors. We did.

The first opening in the operating room schedule was four days later, on Good Friday. Watson's pleasant assistant said, "Okay, so the surgery will be 11:00 a.m. Friday, March 29."

With the surgery set and Justin due home on Wednesday for his court hearing, it was time to face telling my sons that I had cancer. That felt much harder than dealing with it myself. How could I put them through this after the pain of two divorces? I rehearsed what I would say to them in my mind, wrote it in my journal, and practiced on Jeff. I put the calls off as long as I could, and then I dialed.

Eric answered on the third ring. I asked about his painting and his girlfriend before dropping the biopsy news. He started to cry. His sobs seared my chest, but I still had to tell Justin. He said, "You'll be fine, Mama," but his voice said, "I'm scared." Abandoning my kids would be the worst part of dying.

Since my diagnosis, the thought of dying had infiltrated my rare moments alone in the daytime and gone to bed with me each night. Its grip was especially powerful that night. At 2:00 a.m. I turned on the light and reached for my journal. Distressing, contradictory thoughts poured onto the page. Maybe some part of me did want to die. Did I really believe that we create our own reality? Perhaps my inner child was so angry that she wished me dead. I was raised to believe that good little girls didn't get mad or at least didn't show it. Mom's anger was so terrifying that I had swallowed mine. Maybe it was still in there.

I was flooded with shame that I hadn't done more, better, different work on myself. I railed against simplistic, patient-blaming New Age theories, and wondered at the same time if they might be true. With any luck, death would put an end to guilt, worry, relationship issues, and financial concerns. But by the time I dozed off, I was pretty sure I wanted to live.

Justin arrived from Boulder the next day, emanating his usual air of internal stability, especially under distressing circumstances. I felt comforted by his presence.

The following morning, my friend Lynn came in from St. Louis. I met Lynn on my first day at the University of Michigan. We liked each other right away even though we were a visual aid for "opposites attract." Lynn is short, has curly black hair, and is very cerebral while I'm tall, have wavy brown hair, and tend toward the emotional. While we were both from the Detroit area, our backgrounds were different. We were having ice cream at Blazo's on State Street a few weeks into our first semester when it hit me.

"You know," I said, "you are my first Jewish friend."

"That's funny," she replied, "you are my first gentile."

Lynn was my world traveler friend—together we cruised the Caribbean and went white-water rafting in Costa Rica. She introduced me to white asparagus in Paris and took me to a farmer's market in Nice where I ate a strawberry unlike any I'd known before, which remains the most delicious thing I've ever tasted. She insisted that we stay in a particular hotel in the south of France where we got very tipsy and then very hungover on fancy wine we bought with our winnings from Monaco. The bill for our one-night stay, dinner, and the wine was $950.

She was also my confidante. Lynn talked me down off a lot of emotional ledges with her calm, reasoned view of the world. We were in London together when Mount St. Helens erupted. I heard news stories about volcanic ash carrying long distances from the site and became concerned for my kids who were staying with their dad in Ann Arbor.

"Terri," Lynn said with a mix of patience and disdain, "you may not want to be married to Tom, but he has enough sense to bring the boys in out of the ash." She refrained from mentioning the odds of the volcanic ash making it to Michigan.

Lynn cooked spaghetti for the little party we had the night before my surgery. It was the last meal I would eat with a whole tongue. Val brought a Baskin-Robbins ice cream cake for Justin's nineteenth birthday. Sandy and Magic were there too. We sat around our kitchen table, Jeff jumping up every few minutes to answer the phone. "That was my son Dennis," he said after one call. "They're going to have a baby."

As much as I loved Jeff's kids, and as excited as I was to become a step-granny, anxiety over the next morning's events drowned out any reaction to the news. I excused myself to call the therapist I contacted in emergencies.

"Terri, I can hear the terror in your voice. You are so scared that you're leaving your body. Remember to breathe. That should help you get grounded."

I took a breath, still shallow, but deeper than the panting I'd been doing. An insight came with the inhalation: dying couldn't be any worse than the hell I had worked myself into. My religious training at the Grosse Pointe Woods Presbyterian Church had taught me that after death, the souls of the chosen departed go to heaven to enjoy God's glory and await their rewards and/or punishments. Though my faith wasn't helping much at the moment, I did still believe in God. But I had not been active in the church for a long time, which probably meant punishment. But even that sounded better than this. I relaxed a bit.

After a few more deep breaths, I went back to the party. I wanted to be a good hostess, to show my gratitude to my guests, and to entertain them so they'd keep coming back. I wanted to talk while I could, since my talking days might soon be over.

On Friday morning, Jeff and Lynn, who happens to be a lawyer, prepared to take a dressed-up, clean-shaven Justin to his 9:00 a.m. court hearing. Val and Sandy came to take me to the hospital. Lynn and Jeff would join us there when they were done in court. If he didn't go to jail, Justin would spend the day with Tom, his dad. I knew if he came to the hospital, I'd worry about him worrying about me. I couldn't bear his pain on top of my own.

Just as we were about to leave for the hospital, my officemate Gretchen called to tell me she was praying to the guru. The line beeped with another incoming call.

"They waived the felony charge," Jeff said. "He's getting the first-time-offender's reprieve, which means it won't even be on his record."

"Thank God!" This was the best possible outcome, and now I had less bad news to fear when I emerged from anesthesia.

Jeff and Lynn were already at St. Joseph's Mercy Hospital when Val, Sandy, and I arrived. Barb Hill, my dear friend and VP of patient care at St. Joe's, soon joined us. I'd met Barb at a gathering of child psych nurses in the seventies; in the course of our professional association, we'd become friends. We share abiding passions for Johnny Mathis and Dairy Queen. Barb is one of the kindest, most generous people I've ever met. And she's tough enough to handle surgeons. Because she was a big shot at St. Joe's, I asked her to accompany me into the operating room. Like me, Barb specialized in psychiatric nursing to avoid gore. She blanched at my request, her freckles more obvious against her pale skin, and said, "Do I have to stay for the surgery?"

"No, I just need you there until I'm knocked out."

Thirty years later I still harbored memories of my surgery rotation in nursing school: the steely matter-of-factness of the orthopedic surgeon removing the leg of a sixteen-year-old boy; a thoracic surgeon poised over the wide-open chest of an elderly woman barking, "Scalpel!" "Sponge!" If being an insignificant bystander in the O.R. made me lightheaded, I'd need a lot of support when I was the main event.

I had arranged to be hooked up to a tape recorder throughout the operation, listening to a relaxation tape made for me by a fellow hypnotherapist. Having done consulting projects with the American

Association of Operating Room Nurses, I knew that relations are not always cordial among surgical staff. Working long hours in a crowded room with no windows and no margin for error strains the social skills of even the best-intentioned caregivers. In the strict hierarchy of surgical departments, surgeons are often allowed to vent their frustrations on those "beneath" them. It doesn't help that the staff in most operating rooms consume gallons of coffee every day.

While Dr. Watson didn't seem the abusive type, I didn't want any tension among the operating team to leak through my anesthesia. And I wasn't eager to register comments like, "Oh my God, there's cancer everywhere." Research studies have linked patient outcome with the emotional tone in the operating room and with prognoses spoken aloud during surgery. It was bad enough to have my body open in that setting. At least my mind could be insulated by the soothing voice of my friend.

Yet another waiting room preceded the pre-op procedures. My team had to stay there while I was led into a cubicle to be stripped, gowned, labeled, poked, and interrogated. Only the promise of drugs kept me from screaming as the technician mined for blood in the veins on top of my hand.

Due to Barb's influence, my entire entourage got to join me in pre-op once I was prepared. Jeff quietly took my hand. Val got up close on my other side, chatting as if this conversation were taking place over a table in a fine restaurant. Sandy spoke even faster than usual, and Magic interjected comments like, "It sure is crowded in here," and "Tell your little girl it's going to be okay." Lynn, erect, grim, and silent, was having none of this inner child stuff. At one point, she backed up so far she was almost visiting the white-haired man in the next cubicle. After a few minutes, Barb came in, wearing a pale-green hat, mask, scrubs, and shoe covers that matched the curtains surrounding my cubicle.

"Is that Barb Hill? I barely recognize you in that get-up." I said it loudly enough for the staff within earshot to understand that I knew the boss.

A stream of residents, nurses, and anesthesiologists paraded through our congested compartment, all asking me the same questions. "Why can't these damned people talk to each other?" I asked. "I should have told the first guy to keep my answers to himself. The only thing that spreads through a hospital faster than a virus is a secret." I was as scared as I had ever been, but no amount of fear would keep me from trying to entertain my loyal supporters.

Finally, the anesthesiologist arrived, bearing a syringe. He injected something into my IV, and my thoughts became hazy.

Dr. Watson showed up, and I knew it was time to go. I said good-bye to Sandy, Lynn, and Val so Jeff and I could be alone.

Drugs slurred the last words I would speak with a whole tongue. "If I make it through this, I really will marry you." He squeezed my hand, kissed my cheek, and said, "Sure you will," his big, brown eyes brimming with tears.

With Barb in her booties shuffling beside my stretcher, I was wheeled down the hall to the operating room. I was out before we reached the doors.

are we taking the kids?

rom the beginning, I was hesitant to enter hospitals. I arrived, ass-first, at Mt. Carmel Hospital in Detroit on April 17, 1946, a full month after my St. Patrick's Day due date. Because I had tarried so long in the womb, I was born sans wrinkles and sporting a full head of brown, curly hair. The nurses tied bows in my locks and showed me off to visitors. Mom beamed as I put those bald, wizened little newborns to shame. By all accounts, our stay at Mt. Carmel was otherwise uneventful except for the noxious White Shoulders cologne of her roommate, which Mom would complain about for the rest of her life every time we visited a perfume aisle.

My arrival was especially momentous because Mom and Dad had been told that they would never have kids. Mom was twenty-six and Dad twenty-seven, old for first-time parents in those days. They had struggled with infertility issues for most of the five years they had been married. And then I made them wait another month.

But I was worth the wait—huge green eyes, fabulous thick hair, and perfect little features. Dad took tons of pictures, handed out his favorite cigars, and fashioned my birth announcement after the U.S. Army's Report of Shipment Form PDQ-9. Having served as a captain and ordnance department chief engineer during WWII, he knew the drill. White type on blue paper just like the Army did it: Consignee: Atkin residence; Contractor: Stork Productions; Description of Article: Infant, Female, Model A; Official Nomenclature: Terry Ellen;

Total Weight: 7 lb, 7 oz; Unit Cost: To be determined. My folks, Anne and Rupert, were listed as receiving inspectors.

And I wasn't just pretty; I was well behaved.

"You were such a good little thing," Mom was fond of telling me, especially when comparing me to subsequent siblings. "You were always a terrific eater, and you slept through the night really early. I loved to dress you up, and you never fussed."

Was I already trying to please her at that age? I've often claimed, at least partly in jest, that I was codependent *in utero*. While this is hard to prove, I never remember a time when my mother's happiness was not my first concern. My earliest memories are of trying to make her life easier especially during her frequent migraines, stomach troubles, and cancer scares.

A photo at around nine months shows me chubby-cheeked and sporting a white wool beret with a blue Scotty dog on the front. I was sitting in a card-table-sized precursor to the high chair. It's clear that I'd been dressed with care, but I'm wearing a troubled look and wringing my pudgy little hands. I've joked that my expression is like that of a CEO whose quarterly profits are way down, but in truth, it's nothing to joke about. I had already learned to worry.

I was not allowed to go along on Mom's next few trips to the hospital. She was rushed to the ER for a ruptured ectopic pregnancy when I was two. On April 12, 1950, she went back to Mt. Carmel to deliver my brother Greg. He was my birthday present the year I turned four, and Val, born two years later to the day, was my gift on turning six.

Now Mom and I really had our hands full! My visceral memories of that time are laden with maternal pride and responsibility rather than sibling rivalry. Greg was a rambunctious little guy, and I often had to protect him from Mom's wrath when he misbehaved. Val was a charmer—a cooperative baby whom Mom praised by saying, "I could leave her in the playpen for hours." In photos of that era, my little arms are always holding a baby or steadying a toddler. By the time I was seven, if Mom and Dad said we were going out to dinner, I asked, "Are we taking the kids?"

Bill came along when I was eleven and an experienced caregiver. Mom was pretty burned out by then, and Dad was not around much, so the role of primary parent was wide open. I could not have been more excited about our new baby.

While other preteens were gossiping about boys, I was sitting outside baby Billy's room singing him to sleep with the Mr. Clean jingle:

> Mr. Clean gets rid of dirt and grease and grime in just
> a minute.
> Mr. Clean will clean your whole house and everything
> that's in it.
> Mr. Clean, Mr. Clean, Mr. Clean.

I was a more typical teen when it came to sleeping in during summer vacations. I was still asleep at 10:30 one sunny July morning when I was fourteen. Mom burst into my room in a panic.

"Billy is missing! He told me he wanted to play golf and went outside with his little clubs. I figured he'd play in the yard like he always does. And now he's gone!"

I bolted out of bed and grabbed yesterday's clothes from the floor, without stopping for shoes. I hopped on my bike and pedaled furiously, heading first toward Lake St. Clair, where I often took Billy to watch the boats. Relieved not to see any sign of him or his miniature golf bag in the water, on the grassy shore, or in the middle of Lake Shore Drive, I rode up and down neighboring streets. My heart pounded, I could barely breathe, and my mind conjured hideous pictures of how this might end. And it would be my fault. I should have been up watching him.

Then it hit me. I pedaled as fast as I could in the direction of Lochmoor Country Club where Dad was a member. I wondered how Bill's little three-year-old legs could have traveled a half-mile in the time he'd been gone, but it was worth a try. I wasn't fazed by the looks of disdain directed my way from stuffy, bridge-playing matrons as I ran through the clubhouse violating all the dress codes. I screamed in relief when I saw his little form poised to sink a short putt on the club's putting green.

When Billy turned four, I threw a gala boy-girl dance party for him. I dressed him in a blue suit with short pants, matching tie, knee socks, and saddle shoes. He was unimpressed with the ensemble, but I was thrilled. This was like dressing my dolls only better. I had paid careful attention to the gender balance of the guest list so that everyone had a partner when it was time for the dancing. I made Bill dance with my friend Marcia's little sister. I still take partial credit for the fact that he's very smooth with the ladies.

Tending to Billy was a relatively pleasant method of helping Mom. Ministering to her and taking over her duties when she was ill were more stressful. There seemed to be a correlation between Dad's international travel and Mom's symptoms. I recall one night when Bill was a baby, a crying baby. Mom was writhing on the couch with an undiagnosed gastric ailment. Dad was in Brazil. Val and Greg were hungry, and I had homework to do. I had no idea how to reach Dad, nor did I know whether or how to call the doctor. My own stomach still clenches when I think about nights like that one.

Dad was seldom around because he was busy building a successful engineering career in the automotive industry during Detroit's heyday. Even if he was in residence when Mom took to her bed, I was more likely to fill in for her than he was. Dad's rare evenings at home were spent in his favorite living room chair surrounded by a protective moat of office work. If Mom wasn't sick, she'd spend most of the evening in the kitchen making a big production of cleaning up after dinner, or she might head down to the basement to iron. Wherever she went, she carried the yellow bathroom cup from which she'd been sipping since late afternoon. Although my folks had converted the pantry to a bar, which housed all manner of highball glasses, Mom always drank from those plastic cups—perhaps because they were opaque. The kids were in the den watching TV, and I was in my room doing homework. Dad might venture into the kitchen for another martini or to replenish his M&M supply, but otherwise he busied himself with important looking papers until he nodded off.

Unlike Mom, Dad was never sick. As far as I know, he never missed a day of work. I'm not sure if he was super healthy or just really didn't want to stay home.

And who could blame him? Mom would later claim that the happiest time of her life was when her kids were little, but I don't remember it that way. She often seemed overwhelmed and was, I now suspect, depressed. She would lash out at us for minor transgressions.

"Who left these damned books on my kitchen counter?"

On another day, the same books on the same counter did not bother her. She would inquire about our day at school and ask if we wanted a snack. When we did upset her, Mom blamed her symptoms on our misconduct.

"You friggin' kids have given me a lump in my throat the size of a golf ball." Or, "Now I have a headache; I hope you are happy."

Dad's absence was another causative factor. "Your goddamned father is so selfish! He's never here to help me. No wonder I have an ulcer." (I was ten before I realized that my parent's names weren't Mom and Your Goddamned Father.) When she talked to friends on the phone, she lamented, "I'm mother and father to four kids." I lurked in the dining room listening in the hope that she would add, "I couldn't do it without Terri," as she often did.

My mother taught by example that illness was the only legitimate way to avoid responsibility and to ask for what you needed without being selfish. Like her mother before her, Mom knew that medical attention was better than no attention at all. My maternal grandmother was the youngest of eleven kids in an impoverished family, where it took a lot to even be noticed. So Ma didn't have a great deal to give when she became a mother. Much of what she did have was washed away by grief when she lost her infant daughter, my aunt Mary Ellen, after whom I was named. I'm not sure when it started, but by the time I came along, my mom was taking care of her mom. And so it goes.

Mom soldiered through most of her ailments, telegraphing her distress via facial expressions, moans, and complaints. When things got bad enough, she took to her bed. And if she really needed a respite, there was the hospital. Mom seemed in her glory propped up in a hospital bed with validated symptoms and plenty of meds. She amused the staff with stories of her days as a nurse's aid and was everybody's favorite patient. This is not to say that I think Mom's pain wasn't real. Her illness-induced leisure came at a high price. Sometimes her stay involved surgery, which was painful, but her fears of cancer never materialized, so there was relief as well. I visited her in the hospital as often as I could while still managing things at home.

Mom was not just the recipient of care. She always rose to the occasion when we were under the weather. Legend has it that she once told the CEO of Chrysler to, "Move your fucking car," at a party because the babysitter had called to say that Greg had a fever. She wasn't that crazy about going out in general and going to Dad's business functions in particular, but she would never leave a sick kid. "You'll see when you are a mother," she often told me. "You always care more for the sick ones."

If we had a cold or the flu or chicken pox (which we all got at once), we were allowed to lie on the couch and watch TV for hours at a time. I still felt sort of guilty that I wasn't studying or setting the table, but I knew a good thing when I saw it, so I forced myself to nestle into the brown Naugahyde and watch *Our Miss Brooks*. Mom covered me with blankets, took my temperature, gave me medicine, and brought me Campbell's chicken noodle soup, Saltines, and Pepsi on a tray. When I had my tonsils out, ice cream was included, and I got to pick whatever I wanted from Jack, the Awrey Bakery man who visited us twice a week. I chose corn toasties and date bars. When pneumonia made me sicker than I'd ever been, Dad brought me yellow roses. Talk about worth it!

But my most serious illness as a child didn't buy me any time off. I was in first grade when a hard lump appeared on the right side of my neck. We went to see Dr. Margaret Zollicker as we always did when our symptoms exceeded what Mom could comfortably diagnose and treat. If she'd been born later, Mom would have been a doctor, and she seemed to relish her opportunities to practice on us. I am impressed that Mom took us to what I'm sure was the only female pediatrician in Grosse Pointe in 1952 and probably one of very few in the country. Dr. Zollicker was a little off-putting because she was what was then called "mannish," though to her credit, Mom never called her that. Our doctor was also kind and very thorough.

She and Mom consulted for months about my lump without figuring out the problem or how to fix it. They knew something was wrong with a cervical lymph node, but antibiotics didn't help. My tonsils and adenoids were removed, and the lump remained. I had to stay overnight in the hospital for that surgery and recall being caged in an oversized crib. I was terrified when Mom had to leave for the night. The smell of the ether was horrible and stayed with me for a long time. After a few more unsuccessful attempts to treat the lump, Dr. Zollicker referred me to an expert.

Dr. Paul Woolley was the chief of staff at Children's Hospital of Michigan. In order to get to his office, we had to walk through inpatient units filled with crib-cages like the one I'd inhabited. The whole scene was terrifying, and I didn't feel as brave as I acted while we waited for the doctor. But once I met him, with his Santa-like appearance and avuncular warmth, I relaxed a little. Dr. Woolley always told me how pretty I was and what lovely hair I had. It sounds kind of creepy now, but it felt good at the time.

I never minded going to Dr. Woolley, and it was a good thing because we saw a lot of each other before the lump was diagnosed. Several visits and a lot of tests revealed the culprit: bovine tuberculosis. This was not a common malady in Detroit, and it took a little doing to figure out how I had gotten it. Then Mom remembered the time, many months before, when we visited my paternal grandparents on their farm in Madison, Ohio. Dad's parents drank milk straight from their cows. As she always did, Mom had insisted we stop at the general store for Borden's milk on the way because she wasn't having her kids drink unpasteurized milk "like those goddamned farmers." Grandma saw this as a sign of snootiness from a city-slicker daughter-in-law who was never good enough for her Rupert in the first place.

One morning during our visit, I went downstairs while Mom was busy upstairs with baby Greg. Dad was off playing golf with his brothers. After asking me if I was hungry, Grandma served me cereal topped with "her" milk. Mom caught me in mid-bowl, inquired as to the type of milk and whisked the cereal away, her onyx eyes glaring at Grandma. It hadn't occurred to Mom to suspect that milk when my lump appeared.

By the time the TB was diagnosed, I was in the third grade. Mom insisted that I not mention the disease to my friends or they would assume that I had the highly contagious pulmonary tuberculosis. It was clear that this news could threaten my already tenuous popularity. My kind of TB was confined to one lymph node, and while there was apparently some danger that it might spread in my body, it didn't pose a risk to others. When asked why I had to go to the doctor so often or why I took so many pills, I was to say, "I have a chronic granuloma of the lymph gland." I'm a notoriously terrible liar and always felt guilty about this medical subterfuge.

My treatment consisted of three shots a week from Dr. Zollicker, twenty-one red-coated, foul-tasting sulfa pills a day, and periodic visits to a grumpy specialist. That icy doctor made me lie on a cold metal table while he stuck a huge needle into my neck to aspirate pus from the infected gland. This was the worst part of the ordeal, though I somehow managed to refrain from crying so as not to further upset Mom. I still have trouble accessing my tears.

After ten weeks of treatment, I was deemed cured. And then, two years later, the disease recurred. Since the sulfa dosage was based on weight, I now had to take twenty-six of the disgusting red pills every day. I visited the hideous needle doctor more often, but for some reason, the shots were omitted from this six-month-long round of treatment. I still had to keep my diagnosis from my friends, which was even harder now because they were smarter.

In addition to making a liar out of me, the TB and its treatment were painful, disgusting, and time consuming. And I was never actually sick enough to earn extended TV time. In fact, because Dr. Woolley told me to get plenty of sleep, I had to give up watching *December Bride* after *I Love Lucy* on Monday nights. Mom got me to bed early by saying, "Do you want to end up in Children's Hospital?" It always struck me as ironic that Children's Hospital was my biggest client when I became an organizational consultant thirty years later. The only upside of the whole ordeal was that I got alone time with Mom when we visited doctors, and she once bought me a fancy dress I wanted for taking all those pills. Even though his mother was to blame, Dad wasn't any more involved because I was sick. Between worrying about me, caring for the kids, and keeping the house spotless, it is no wonder that Mom was overwhelmed.

Even during the TB years, I tried to ease Mom's burden. I saved my babysitting money to buy her jewelry, threw surprise parties for her birthday, and wrapped the Christmas presents—sometimes even my own. The year I was nine, I hosted a surprise anniversary party for my folks. Mom had a headache and was too sick to attend.

Most of my decisions were aimed at pleasing Mom—even my career choice. At ten, I harbored a glimmer of hope that she might support my fantasies of a life on the stage. My wishful thinking was based on her enthusiastic response to my rendition of "The Yellow Rose of Texas"—the finale in a musical extravaganza that Linda Conway and I produced in her rec room. Mom attended all the plays I did in junior high and seemed to enjoy them. But my mother had always wanted to be a nurse. Her parents could not afford to send her to nursing school. As the first-born and a girl, it seemed I was destined to be a nurse before I could talk. I certainly had the caretaking background for the job.

Mom clearly articulated my career options. "You can be a nurse, a teacher, or a secretary. But you know what they say, 'Those who can't do, teach.' I've been a secretary and trust me, you don't want to do that." Mom had been a nurse's aid during World War II and loved it. Whenever I had doubts, Mom led me back to nursing with the same logic she used to convince Bill to be an undertaker. "You will never run out of clients." Her clincher was that I only had to be a nurse until I found a husband. And this way, that husband might be a doctor.

Nursing appealed to me for other reasons. I had always loved taking care of my dolls when they were sick. Rocking them, giving them bottles, and tucking them in made me feel safer. Besides, if I were a nurse, I wouldn't feel so helpless when Mom was ill. When Greg started to have problems in his teens, I had more reasons to become a nurse, a psychiatric nurse.

Next to the goody-two-shoes standard that I had set, Greg had always been mischievous, but he wasn't a bad kid. His behavior deteriorated in adolescence, but that was blamed in part on the severe back pain he suffered due to the spina bifida and spondylolisthesis that were diagnosed when he was seventeen. The orthopedic surgeon predicted that he would end up in a wheelchair. Drugs and alcohol were his answer to the fear and the pain. The suicide attempts began in his early twenties. One psychiatrist said he was schizophrenic and put him on psychotropic medications. We'll never know what combination of addiction, mental illness, and physical illness made his life unbearable. But in the end, even a summa cum laude master's degree in psychiatric nursing from the University of Michigan did not equip me to save him.

After many aborted attempts, Greg took his own life in October 1979. The belief that I might have kept him alive would haunt me for years. Ten days before he died, Greg left a message on my answering machine. I was thirty-three, recently engaged to Michael (who had just started law school), and frantically busy with my kids and my expanding role at the Children's Psychiatric Hospital. I was preparing for a huge project at work and decided to wait until it was over to call Greg back. Returning home after the successful presentation, I dropped my briefcase on the orange shag carpet and collapsed into the low-slung, leather chair in our living room. I kicked off my professional pumps and exhaled fully for the first time in months. Now I could relax. I was about to ask Michael and the kids if they wanted to go out to dinner to celebrate when the phone rang. It was my brother Bill.

"Greg . . . " he said slowly, in a broken voice. "He really did it this time."

We held a funeral for Greg at the Grosse Pointe Woods Presbyterian Church. I regret not bringing my kids, ages seven and eleven, but doubted I could take care of them while tending to Mom. People wanted to come by the house after the service, but she refused. "People aren't going to be partying here when my son is dead," she said.

Now that I had failed to save my "first kid," I became even more nervous about protecting the subsequent ones. Due in part to my early training around illness, I had always been anxious about the health of my boys. I was constantly dragging them to the doctor. Given my success in relationships with men, the most consistent male presence in my kids' lives was Howard Weinblatt, our pediatrician. I skipped one of my own rehearsal dinners to take Justin to see him for a sore throat. Howard waived his fee for that visit as a wedding present. Fortunately for all of us, my kids were pretty healthy.

And so was I. Since the TB, I had only had the occasional cold or bout of the flu. I did notice that these usually seemed to occur when I was on vacation. As a psych nurse, I understood that the body sometimes sends us the bill for living under too much stress as soon as we relax. Graduate school had also taught me all about using illness for "secondary gains" like attention and leisure. Being aware of these dynamics meant I could avoid them. I was determined not to follow in Mom's footsteps. However, here I was in the hospital with the big disease that even she had managed to avoid. But right now, the psychological underpinnings of my cancer were not my main concern. I just wanted the doctor to get rid of it.

blue skies and a black cloud

While my retinue sipped coffee in the hospital cafeteria and Dr. Watson excised part of my tongue and the adjoining lymph nodes, my unconscious mind absorbed soothing suggestions. "Picture yourself in your favorite place—the beach, a meadow, your favorite chair. Now, as I count down from ten, let yourself go deeper with each downward count. You are safe and relaxed. The surgeon's hands are guided by God to remove all the cancer. Your body is strong and healthy. You will recover quickly from this operation."

As I regained consciousness in the recovery room a few hours later, my first awareness was of my mouth, which seemed to be stuffed with cotton. I sank back into sleep. The next time I surfaced, Barb was leaning over my bed. She pulled the skinny blanket over my shoulders and said, "It went really well." I scanned her face for signs that she was lying, but was in no shape to interpret nonverbal cues.

My next bout of awareness was triggered by the sensation of movement. My drug-addled brain deduced that I was on a gurney with Val speed-walking alongside. Jeff trailed behind us, into and out of my view.

Two women in scrubs rolled me onto the firm, blue-pad-covered bed in my unadorned private room with its faded green walls and beige drapes. Jeff and Val made polite conversation and showed me gifts that had arrived for me, but didn't mention the surgery. I figured they'd already talked to Watson. The raccoon circles around Jeff's eyes could indicate a grim prognosis or might just be signs of exhaustion. My sister was so good at putting on a happy face that, even when I was fully conscious, I rarely knew how she felt. Groggy, afraid, and unable to talk, I decided to postpone actually asking them what had happened. I sank down in the bed and tried to rest.

Val spent the night in the hard, orange leatherette recliner near my bed. Prior to surgery, Dr. Watson had told me I wouldn't talk for at least a week post-op, and I knew that hospital call lights are not always answered promptly, especially on the midnight shift. The thought of being in a dark institutional room, alone and unable to communicate, scared me into inconveniencing people. Val and Jeff had generously agreed to cover all the shifts. This was a huge sacrifice for both of them: her because she was so busy and him because he abhorred hospitals.

Noise from the hallway made sleeping a challenge, but drugs helped me doze. Val gave up on sleeping and sat near my bed in a slim funnel of light, needlepointing a wall hanging for me. In beautiful gold letters, it said: "The only way out is through" and "Make light of the whole thing."

Early the next morning, I was surprised to receive a breakfast tray with my name on it. I couldn't imagine introducing any of the offerings into my sore, suture-filled mouth. I had assumed I'd be on IVs for days. But the aide told me to eat, so I chose yellow Jell-O from the array of hospital "health food," which also included sweetened apple juice, ginger ale, and coffee. I let a few cubes of cool gelatin melt in my ravaged mouth and trickle down my throat. Having achieved this feat, I signaled for my notebook and scribbled, "Tell Jeff to stop at McDonald's for coffee." If I was allowed coffee after a day without it, I wanted higher-quality brew than any I had found in a hospital. McDonald's coffee was my best bet in those days before there was a Starbucks on every corner.

Jeff arrived balancing cups adorned with golden arches. He searched my face for a safe place to kiss and pecked my forehead.

Feeling a tiny bit more normal with coffee in my hand, I signaled for my notebook and wrote, "What did Watson say?"

"He said it went well," Val said in typical no-nonsense fashion, her eyes locked on her needlepoint project. "They removed the tumor and the margins around it. They took about a third of your tongue on the left side and a sample of the lymph nodes down your neck. He didn't see any cancer beyond the tumor, but we won't know for sure if they got it all until we get the biopsy results."

"When will that be?" I wrote.

"Tuesday or Wednesday of next week," Jeff said, stirring his coffee and glancing at me to assess my response.

I was too worried about lurking cancer to grieve for the lost section of my tongue. I would deal with that later. Right now I had to figure out how I was going to keep it together for three or four days, knowing that everything hinged on those results. If the nodes and the margins were clear, I could skip radiation and still have a decent chance of staying alive. If not, I had the horror of a radiated mouth to look forward to and not much else.

"Will I be here that long?" I wrote in unsteady script. It was bad enough to cope with this uncertainty in the hospital. I panicked at the thought of being at home without heavy-duty chemicals while I waited for the call that would foretell my future or lack thereof.

"Probably not," Val said in a tone that suggested she knew what I was thinking.

"Justin said he'd be over later," Jeff said. I was aware that he was changing the subject, but lacked the energy to object.

"And brother Bill says he's coming tonight," Val added.

Armed with his science fiction book, Jeff took Val's place on the orange recliner as I tried to organize my fears and catch up on my rest.

Justin arrived that afternoon with a plastic slate for me to write on and his friend Joe for moral support. My son wore a bright blue-and-white knit hat with a White Castle logo over his light-brown curly hair. Even clouded by medication, I noticed that his skin was pale, his shoulders drawn up, and his voice uneven. I worried that it must be terrible for him to see me like this, especially after what he'd been through over the last few days. I tried to keep my notes on the slate cheerful.

Years later, Justin would tell me he'd seen light in my eyes that day, which led him to believe I would make it. I wasn't so certain. It saddened me that he was leaving for Colorado the next day, and I had no idea what kind of shape I'd be in when we saw each other again.

I felt a bit better by dinnertime when Bill arrived from Grand Ledge, a small town seventy-five miles west of Ann Arbor. My younger brother is more fun than might be expected of a funeral director, and the two of us create a little party whenever we get together. But that night, maintaining clever repartee by writing on my slate proved frustrating.

Easter Sunday brought a parade of visitors. By evening, my patience as a silent witness to lively conversations was spent. Bursting with words I couldn't say, I croaked, "eugh, aach," to insert my opinion into a discussion between Barb and her brother.

"She talked!" said Barb's brother.

"The doctors said she won't talk for at least a week, maybe ten days," Barb replied with authority.

"I'm telling you, she talked," he insisted.

Monday morning brought clusters of residents and interns on early rounds. After repeated examinations, they said the surgical sites were healing well and I could go home as soon as Dr. Watson finalized my discharge orders. By the time the doctor strolled in at 4:00 p.m., Val had joined us. In the midst of his post-discharge instructions, he casually mentioned, "The margins and nodes are clear."

None of us could believe what we had heard. Val said, "You mean the biopsy results are in?"

"Yes, one of the pathologists called me this afternoon. He said his wife is a client of Terri's and knew she'd be anxious to hear. The results are negative," he said with his usual reserve.

Val screamed. Jeff cheered. I went limp with relief. We all hugged.

"Well, it is good news," Dr. Watson said. "But remember, you'll have a black cloud hanging over your head for the next two years." What the hell was he talking about? I felt like I'd been kicked in the gut.

Watson went on to explain that 90 percent of oral cancer recurrences happen within the first two years.

Why in God's name was he telling me this now? My insides twisted with rage. Couldn't he allow us a moment's joy? I wanted to scream at him, but I couldn't even talk, so I grunted my loathing at Watson and waited for him to leave.

We pretended that he hadn't mentioned the cloud and went back to celebrating. I had no trouble accessing my faith at moments like this. With a fervent prayer of gratitude, I promised God that from that day forward, I would appreciate every moment. Cradling my flowers like Miss America, I was wheeled out of St. Joe's wearing the biggest smile my new, lopsided mouth could manage.

Our low thread-count sheets felt like silk after the scratchy ones in the hospital. I nestled my head into my favorite down pillow, Jeff tucked the comforter around me, and I finally felt safe. Thanks to endorphins and pain meds, I looked forward to my first restful sleep in months. I was about to doze off when I heard Mom and Dad arrive. They had come back early from their place in Florida. I hadn't seen them since Christmas and wondered why they weren't hurrying back to the bedroom to celebrate my good news. Finally, my mother appeared, carrying a pile of laundry she must have just folded.

"Where do you want these?" she asked, her gaze fastened on the clothes.

Laundry? The bile of resentment started to rise in my throat. Then I remembered all the other times when Mom had sought solace in housework and decided not to take it personally. Besides, I didn't have cancer. This was no time to complain. I pointed to the cupboard.

I pulled the down quilt tighter around me. Having neatly disposed of the clean clothes, Mom came over to the bed, brushed her fingers lightly over my forehead, and asked to see my incision. She was fascinated by everything medical—the gorier the better. She didn't flinch at the sight of my stitched-up partial tongue and swollen, inflamed mouth. When Dad finally joined us, he kept his gaze away from my surgical sites. They stayed a few minutes and then excused themselves "so I could sleep."

Relief that cancer and its treatment were behind me made my postsurgical liquid diet and low energy levels manageable. I spent the days visiting with friends, watching TV, staring at snow-dusted apple trees, and avoiding my face in the mirror. After an accidental glance revealed a swollen left cheek and misshapen mouth, I decided I wasn't ready for closer examination. But visitors said I looked good, much the same, and I took their word for it. I tried to enjoy the leisure I'd earned, while suppressing lingering concerns that the cancer might come back.

One afternoon, my officemate Gretchen and I curled up on the living room couch as she enthusiastically described a diet of grains and vegetables purported to help cancer patients.

"Grains + veggies too hard to chew," I printed on my trusty slate.

Gretchen grabbed the slate and wrote, "We can cook grains and put in blender or make soup or . . . " Then she caught herself, giggled like a little girl, her aquamarine eyes flashing and said, "Oh, I forgot, *I* can talk."

When you're diagnosed with cancer, everyone has a solution. I was inundated with books, tapes, meditations, diets, theories, workshops, therapists, and groups. I wanted to do all of them—and I didn't want to do anything that "cancer patients" did. While I had promised God I'd take better care of myself if He would remove the cancer, I didn't mean that in any cancer-specific way. I had had cancer, it had been removed, and that was that. It was time to get on with my real life.

I was getting stronger and gradually learning to talk with my newly configured mouth, but I lacked the diction and energy to go back to work. So Jeff and I decided to splurge on two weeks in a beachfront condo south of San Francisco where I could bask in the healing powers of the ocean and visit with Eric.

Our unit overlooked the Pacific through salt-sprayed windows. If I had felt better, I would have gotten out there with a bottle of Windex. Instead, I lounged on the couch and enjoyed the view through the film. We watched people on the beach and Fred Astaire movies, and we explored which foods I could eat and neighboring towns.

On April 17, 1991, my forty-fifth birthday, Jeff took me on a day-long romantic adventure: soft eggs at a fisherman's diner overlooking the Pacific, a spectacular drive down the coast, soup and flan at a quaint Carmel café, and shopping at I. Magnin. He patiently watched me peruse the sale rack and bought me a beautiful black dress at a deep discount. We wandered through art galleries and splurged on a Southwestern-style painting that matched our dining room. While I still couldn't talk well and had to rest frequently, we were content to be quiet and go slowly together—alive amid all that beauty.

But other days on that trip were not so idyllic. Alone together after weeks of being surrounded by supporters, Jeff and I spewed the rage we felt at cancer, at doctors, and at fate on each other. We had huge fights over which movie to watch first and whether to bake or barbecue the halibut. My characteristic need for control was now justified, I thought, because we were still in the cancer grace period, when the patient should get her way. Jeff also liked to be in control, and the recent caretaking extravaganza had exhausted his emotional reserves.

A few days into our oceanfront vacation, Jeff telegraphed hostility as he washed the juicer he'd bought because studies hinted that carrots might prevent recurrences of oral cancer. He banged metal parts against the sink, his unhappiness contagious.

"What's the matter?" I mumbled.

"Nothing," he replied before lapsing into prolonged silence.

With my lips coated with carrot juice, I hunkered down into my corner of the couch and began pouting back. Difficult as it was for me to talk, I was still no match for Jeff when it came to the silent treatment. I remained mute and sullen until I could no longer tolerate the tension, and then I thrust my notebook in his direction. "What's going on? Tell me. This is driving me nuts."

"I don't know," he said, his voice strained, his bronze hands clenched. "You have to let up on me. You expect too much. I just can't do it all."

"Oh yeah, like I'm sitting around eating bonbons. Like this has been easy on me," I wrote in angry script.

He stomped out the door to the beach. I felt like I had been slapped. I brooded over my plight, stuck thousands of miles from my support team with this selfish creep. How dare he walk out on me? His willingness to talk about our problems had always been one of Jeff's best qualities. I tried to understand his behavior, hoping that understanding might breed forgiveness. This had been hard on him too. Especially because he had already lost one wife. Maybe he was still afraid I might die, even though the doctor had gotten all the cancer.

With every minute Jeff was gone, my fledgling compassion dwindled. When he got back over an hour later, I was in the grip of cancer-amplified self-absorption and fury. It would be years before I would realize how scared Jeff had been, how hard it was for him to care for me, and to see the strong woman he'd come to depend on in such a fragile state. It took even longer to see the childlike neediness in my behavior.

Keeping our anger to ourselves, Jeff and I settled into living like civil roommates, engaging in an adult version of parallel play. This gave me a lot of time for myself, a gift I was not eager to receive. I took walks on the beach alone, trying to let the rhythmic pulsing of the surf, the warmth of the sun, and the smiles of the coppery-brown children settle my simmering insides. Instead, my fury drove me farther down the beach on each walk. At least I was building stamina.

I filled pages in my journal, trying to convince myself that these musings might someday make it into the inspirational memoir I had long wanted to write. Now that I'd had cancer, I had all the material I needed.

One day I remembered the suggestion of a fellow therapist that I enumerate the "benefits" of the cancer as a way to understand the experience. Though I was not feeling especially grateful, I started a list in the journal:

1. Jeff rose to the occasion and stuck with me.

2. Val was amazing, and we're closer and less competitive than ever.

3. My friends were so supportive.

4. I had to let my kids grow up in case I wasn't going to be around for long.

Then I got to thinking. If the cancer was useful to me, did that mean I had caused it? Was I turning into my mother after all? Did

I subconsciously want to be sick to cash in on benefits like avoiding responsibility and having license to be needy? Then again, I might have gotten cancer to disqualify me from the success contest with Val or to get out of having to support myself. Was my disease the result of some underlying loose screw that all my years of self-help had failed to tighten?

I wrote in my journal, "Why did I have to create something so awful as this cancer?" I wasn't really expecting an answer and was surprised when my hand took off on its own and wrote, "To slow down and love yourself." Who said that? It was not something I would have come up with on my own. Understanding that I had a lot to learn about self-love and slowing down, I focused on the content of the message and let the question of its source go unanswered for years. I'd read books by Louise Hay and knew that she attributed all emotional and physical problems to low self-esteem and saw self-love as the universal solution. I'd brought some of her tapes on the trip and started listening to them twice a day. Louise advised looking in the mirror and saying, "I love you" to the reflection. That didn't work for me.

Other women might rush to the mirror after an operation like mine to assess the damage. Not me. I'd removed my glasses before approaching mirrors since the surgery to ensure I had only the fuzziest notion of what I looked like. But now I was supposed to rub vitamin E on my suture line; Dr. Watson said it would reduce scarring. I approached the bathroom mirror with caution, gritted my teeth, and winced as I squeezed the oily vitamin out of the capsule onto the raised, red line on my neck. On my first close look, my face was still a little puffier on the left side, but otherwise not all that different than before. It wasn't a bad face, really, but it had always been too chubby and had too many freckles. I had never loved it and liked it even a little less now.

Midway into our two-week vacation, Eric came down from San Francisco, and I got to watch him paint an illustration for the cover of a beer magazine. He'd supported himself as an illustrator since he graduated from the Rhode Island School of Design. Eric's talent showed up when he was two and had astonished me ever since, but it had been many years since I was able to witness the process.

Two days later, as he was about to leave, Eric mentioned that he had let his health insurance lapse. This was the kind of news that would usually trigger full-scale panic in me. But my plan for healing myself included stepping down as the poster child for controlling mothers and I said, "I'm sorry to hear that. I'm sure you'll handle it."

"Wow! Have you changed!"

I didn't feel as calm as I was acting, but I applauded my progress.

Eric's presence served as a buffer between Jeff and me. Jeff's kindness toward my kids was one of his most endearing features. When he came into our lives, they opened their hearts to yet another potential stepfather. A friend once said that the only thing all of my husbands had in common was that they were nice to Eric and Justin.

After our time in the oceanfront condo, I was rested enough to return to a scaled-down version of real life. I continued to promise God that I would never work as hard as I had before cancer. I would exercise lots more, eat better, and keep my nose out of other people's business. By mid-May I was back to work almost full time.

I was feeling pretty good, although my energy level wasn't back to normal. A blood test in August revealed that I was anemic and needed a total gastrointestinal workup to rule out internal bleeding. Once you've had cancer, there is no such thing as a minor symptom, and even routine tests are terrifying.

Per instructions, I scheduled a gastroscopy and sigmoidoscopy with a Dr. Keinath at St. Joe's. He plumbed my upper G.I. tract with a gag-inducing tube down my throat and then explored the excretory end of my digestive system with an even larger tube. He chatted casually as he studied the intricacies of my colon, which were being projected onto a television screen that I, thank God, couldn't see. Curled on my left side in the fetal position, I attempted to respond to his friendly inquiries between gasps of pain.

When his banter stopped suddenly, I worried that Dr. Keinath was taking a closer look at some colonic anomaly, but it turned out that he was pausing to assemble his thoughts. "Did you ever teach a psychology class at U of M where you took the students to Ypsi State Hospital?"

I peered over my shoulder in disbelief. "Russell?"

My former student gave my G.I. tract a passing grade.

By then, my scars had healed and people who were unaware of my surgery didn't notice any change in my appearance or my speech. Those who knew what I'd been through continued to claim that they couldn't see a difference. I was thrilled to be successfully disguised as my former self.

three times a lady

Monthly checkups with Dr. Watson were a mandatory part of my postsurgery protocol. To my amazement, I didn't think about cancer much except during my weekly mouth self-exams and right before these monthly appointments. For the first six months, Watson failed to find more cancer. Once he'd sounded the "all clear" at each visit, we'd chat about everything from medicine to marriage. I was grateful to him for saving my life and for his careful handiwork on my neck and mouth.

One September evening six months after the surgery, I was conducting my routine mouth check when I noticed a tiny red spot on top of my tongue. In an instant, I went from being a woman with a future to a doomed soul. This was undoubtedly the recurrence that Dr. Dudar had predicted. My hands shook as I dialed Jeff's office number. No answer. He was probably with a client. I had to see him and although I did not feel up to driving, I leapt into the car and sped to his office.

I pounded on the door and rang the bell of the mauve Victorian-turned-holistic-health-center. No response. The place looked so dark that, had it not been for Jeff's car and one other in the parking lot, I would have assumed it was empty. How could I get his attention? On my hands and knees, I crawled under the bushes, peeking in the few illuminated windows until I spotted Jeff and began banging on the glass. He looked up at me, startled. His stocky, swarthy client was supine on the Rolfing table wearing only Jockey shorts and a surprised expression. Jeff quickly covered him with a sheet and met me at the front door. "What's going on?" he asked in an amazingly patient voice.

"Look," I shrieked, pointing to the spot.

"It looks like a broken blood vessel to me," he said. "I'm sure it's no big deal." His failure to panic reassured me even though the last spot he'd told me not to worry about had proved to be cancer. "Come on in," Jeff said. "I'll tell my client to wait a few minutes, and we can call Watson." Together we left a message on the doctor's machine. Then I left Jeff to his client and rushed home to wait for Watson's call.

"Cancer doesn't usually occur on top of the tongue," Dr. Watson said confidently an hour later. "When it does recur, it tends to do so near the original site." His words reassured me enough to wait two weeks until my next appointment. By then, the spot was gone, but Watson hypothesized on its causation, "Sounds like it might have been a broken blood vessel." Jeff smirked.

That little red dot was the first in a long series of cancer scares. Each one reminded me just how quickly the disease could change everything and how far I had strayed from my promises to take better care of myself. As I would with every future near miss, I expressed my gratitude to God, asked for forgiveness for breaking my vow of self-care, and recommitted to that promise.

To demonstrate my sincerity, I went for a walk. Striding down our dirt road on a gray September day, I noticed that I was obsessing about my kids' finances and attempted to put my overactive mind on pause for a Be Here Now moment. I inhaled the fragrance of the pines; listened to the serenading sparrows; and reveled in the oranges, golds, and reds of the few remaining leaves on the oaks and maples.

Most of the leaves were already on the ground. They crunched under my sneakers as I walked. The crackling sound triggered a picture in my mind. From out of nowhere, an image began to come into focus, fuzzy at first. Then a frail female figure emerged. Although I had done a lot of inner work, it was unusual for me to have a visual image. Most of what had happened in my head was expressed by a voice—not a very nice voice.

The figure was huddled in the corner of a dark closet. A woman-child of indeterminate age, she looked brittle, dehydrated, and sullen. She sat all hunched in on herself: legs drawn up to chest, emaciated arms twisted around knees, large sunken eyes staring blankly out at nothing in particular. She was as dry and brittle as the leaves underfoot, and her bones protruded like their spines did. She resembled those people in *Life* magazine who were discovered by the authorities after being locked in the family basement for years because they were a little too odd.

I called out, "Hello." There was no response. The vision began to blur. "Who are you?" I tried again. She was gone as quickly as she'd appeared. I attempted to recreate the picture but couldn't. Could my inner child really be in such sad shape?

That night, I wrote about the vision in my Writing from the Right Side of the Brain class. Reading my piece to my classmates, I named her the Girl in the Closet. Exposing her felt like taking off my clothes and standing naked before the group. The other writers encouraged me to pursue her, as this was the stuff of great memoirs.

But my ambivalence toward this self-indulgent inner child work was strong, and I became discouraged easily. I was beginning to think that protective services had put my inner child in a foster home due to neglect, and regaining custody would be more trouble than it was worth. The siren song of my current, real life was calling. I had better things to do.

Chief among my "better things to do" was planning a wedding while deciding whether or not to go through with it.

One of the speeches I gave to nurses was called "Empowerment: A Process for Creating the Impossible," in which I told the story of meeting Jeff to illustrate how the impossible—finding love after two failed marriages—had happened to me.

I met Jeff in 1988 at a self-discovery program called the Forum, a watered down version of Werner Erhard's est. Like the original est training, the Forum was a two-weekend seminar designed to free participants from their past and help them experience satisfaction in the present moment. The repackaged Forum was focused on "goal-oriented breakthroughs," and the ground rules weren't quite as stringent as est, but it still demanded absolute punctuality and prohibited watches, eating, or talking unless called upon. There were more frequent meal and bathroom breaks than in the original training, and the sessions were shorter—twelve to fifteen hours compared with fifteen to twenty. Two years earlier, I'd given Eric the workshop as a high school graduation present and had participated in it with him. When he came home from his second year at college, he asked me to do the Forum with him again.

"Only if I'll find the love of my life," I teased him.

Eric chuckled, assured me that I would, and then clinched the deal: "I want you to do it because I love you."

I was freshly divorced from Michael, whom I had considered the love of my life. We'd been separated for three years, and never one for being alone, I was ready to find a new candidate for the position. I told the Forum registrar that my intention in enrolling was to "prepare myself for a healthy relationship with a man."

The first tenet taught in the workshop was that our reality grows out of our belief system. To create what we want, we have to uncover our underlying assumptions, "clean up" any residual resentment, and substitute healthier beliefs. It didn't take much emotional excavation to unearth that my difficulties with men were connected to my distant relationship with my father. The first weekend of the seminar fell, significantly I thought, on Father's Day. I summoned all my courage and called Dad on a break.

"Happy Father's Day!"

"Thanks. What are you up to?"

Dad traveled a lot on business. He probably already feared running into me at an airport, dressed in orange robes handing out flowers. I didn't explain my whereabouts.

"Dad, I want you to know I forgive you for not being home much when I was a kid."

Because Dad was a well-mannered, Republican mechanical engineer, I wasn't surprised that he didn't delve into a deep discussion of feelings.

"Thank you," he said, then added, "your mother always said that was hard on you." I wasn't sure whether I was more surprised that Mom had noticed or that Dad knew what I was talking about. He even seemed to appreciate the call.

Now that I had fixed things with my father, I vowed to take full responsibility for my romantic relationships. In my journal, I wrote a detailed vision of my ideal mate. I had just learned that Michael had moved in with the paralegal he had been seeing before we separated, so trustworthiness, honesty, and a penchant for monogamy were high on my list. My vision also included: smart, spiritual, healthy, fun, open with feelings, great sense of humor, likes to travel, reasonably attractive, liberal, and of course loves my kids, and vice versa. I was also hoping for health insurance.

One afternoon of the Forum, I had a revelation. It hit me that deep down I had always believed I was unattractive to men. No amount of male attention could convince me otherwise. I knew that if I wanted a successful relationship, this belief would have to go.

The workshop leader began the second Saturday-morning session by asking, "What have you gotten out of the course so far?"

I raised my hand. Filled with trepidation in spite of my sexy black sundress, I stood to address the assembly. "I uncovered a deep belief that I am unattractive to men. I have decided to change that belief so I can change my reality. From now on, I will believe that I am attractive to all men and that the only thing that varies is their level of awareness of that attraction. So, if a man staggers down the street in a drunken stupor, I'll tell myself that he is attracted to me but is chemically incapable of realizing it."

The crowd laughed, and the leader praised my application of the theory to my life. I sat down, embarrassed but proud that I had revealed myself so openly.

Later that day when we returned from a break, I was directed to sit next to a great-looking, silver-haired man I'd noticed the previous weekend. He turned his head toward me and, without a second's hesitation said, "I am attracted to you, *and* I am aware of it."

"The feeling is mutual," I responded, shocked by my own chutzpah.

"My wife died three months ago," he said.

"Oh, I'm sorry," I said.

He's too needy, a voice in my head whispered.

I bumped into Jeff again the next night as the hundred-plus participants flocked toward the exits at the dinner break.

"Do you want to have dinner together?" I asked him, surprising myself again.

"I'm eating with my friends," Jeff said, obviously rattled, "but you're welcome to join us." He introduced me to his best friends, George and Dotty. As I climbed into their van, I felt as if the four of us had been going out for pizza together for years. We talked openly about Jeff's wife's sudden death. They told me how great she was and how close they had all been. They were understandably still in shock.

Jeff and I had our first real date the night after the Forum ended. Jeff arrived early, bearing flowers. We walked downtown through tree-lined streets and found a table at a sidewalk cafe on Main Street. Before we ordered, Jeff said, "Do you think it's too soon for me to get involved, since my wife just died?"

"No, I don't," I replied, "but my mother will."

Jeff threw back his head and laughed with his whole body. I loved his laugh.

After dinner, we walked all over town having the first of many long talks about the various paths we'd taken to get to God. Jeff told me about *A Course in Miracles,* a sacred text that was purported to be the channeled voice of Jesus. I had always had a personal connection to Jesus and would come to love the *Course* as much as Jeff did. We ended up under a willow tree on the bank of the Huron River, sharing stories of our lives.

"I have two sons," he said.

"Me too!" I said.

"I'm the oldest in my family," I said, tossing leaves into the river and watching them ride into the darkness.

"So am I," Jeff said.

"I'm the oldest of four, and I was the junior mother."

"I have eleven brothers and sisters," Jeff replied. "I've changed a lot of diapers in my day. When I got married, I told my wife that I didn't want kids right away, but she got pregnant and there I was dealing with diapers again."

I ignored his resentful tone and focused on what a sensitive guy he must be to have done all that nurturing. We sat listening to the crickets, quiet and comfortable with each other. I had never felt so at ease on a first date.

"You know," I said, "our kids will be on their own soon and we won't have anyone to take care of."

"That's hard to imagine," Jeff said. "But I guess you're right." Our eyes met. "Maybe it's time for us to have some fun."

And then he kissed me.

§

Despite the power and romance of our coming together and the fact that we had been engaged for three years, I still wasn't convinced that Jeff and I should marry. My internal debate went something like this:

You can trust him.

Don't you think it's weird that he won't sleep with you?

Yes. But he sure is good to your kids. And you love his boys. Together, you could create the beautiful, almost intact family you've always wanted.

He can be so goofy and impetuous and unpredictable.

Sometimes you find his childlike innocence charming.

He doesn't make much money and probably never will.

You own this fabulous house together!

He's very smart in his own way, and his intuition is amazing.

He's always playing with gadgets and coming up with weird inventions.

Barb said he was the best-looking guy you've ever been with.

Looks aren't that important. And the two of you fight quite a bit, especially after a few drinks.

He isn't intimidated by your strength or your career.

God knows you're no expert at marriage.

There are always going to be issues in a relationship. He's willing and able to deal with them directly.

This last selling point stood in sharp contrast to my marriage to Michael. I had to chase him around the house to get him to talk to me. While Jeff was a good communicator one to one, he was a strong introvert and often socially awkward. But we shared such a powerful spiritual connection. Most of all, he'd stuck with me throughout the horror of cancer. If the cancer came back, would I want to face it without him?

One gray morning, I approached Jeff while he was sitting at the kitchen table buried in the Sunday paper.

"Don't you ever have doubts about getting married?" I asked him.

"In my mind," he said, "we're already married."

§

It was the most picturesque of all my weddings. Afterward, a friend would ask, "Why would you have such a grand wedding if you weren't even sure you wanted to marry the guy?"

"I was ambivalent about the marriage, not the wedding," I answered.

It was December 29, 1991. The setting was pure Currier and Ives: a tiny, white-candle-lit church in the middle of a frozen field on a snowy evening. Jeff looked stunning in his black tuxedo. I caught a glimpse of him, flanked by his tuxedo-clad sons at the altar, as I began my third trip down the aisle, flanked by my own sons. All four boys are six-foot-three and gorgeous, but his were clean-shaven with short, tidy haircuts, and mine had lots of artsy hair on their heads and faces. My dress was long, slinky, and black with a huge white ruffle that plunged to a deep V in the back. My six nieces and nephews, ages three to ten, were our attendants in tiny tuxedos and black velvet dresses. Val and Barb did readings, and Bill sang a Johnny Mathis tune, "Long Ago and Far Away." (I'd refused his offer to sing "Three Times a Lady.")

Jeff and I didn't drink at our reception because we had extended our abstinence period since Watson told us about the connection between alcohol and oral cancer. On our honeymoon in Baja, we decided to allow ourselves six connubial "alcohol exceptions." That decision produced some fabulous evenings and some disasters, so we agreed to eliminate exceptions and stop drinking again when we got home.

§

March 29, 1992, was the big day—one year since my surgery with no sign of cancer. I was halfway out from under Dr. Watson's black cloud. I wanted to celebrate but was cautious. I envisioned the gala dinner party I would throw if I made it to March 29, 1993, and began planning the guest list and menu in secret to keep from jinxing the event.

§

In mid-August, we all gathered in Seattle for Jeff's older son's wedding. Brad was thoughtful enough to include Eric and Justin as his attendants. I hoped that someday I would be mother of the groom at my own sons' nuptials.

After the celebration, Jeff and I had one evening alone together before we went our separate ways. He was returning to Ann Arbor, and I was off to Taos, New Mexico, for a long-anticipated writing workshop with Natalie Goldberg. We sat at a small table in a tony Italian restaurant in downtown Seattle, still recovering from the previous evening's reinstated alcohol exception and sharing glasses of wine.

"Now that the kids are more or less on their own," I said, "I think it's time for us to have the fun we talked about on our first date."

"What do you have in mind?" Jeff asked.

"I want us to create a vision for our future," I said, my eagerness building with each sip of wine. "I'll start, okay?"

Jeff nodded slowly.

"I want to be healthy. I want to have a great marriage and sex life. I want to write a book that will help lots of people. I want to have a successful consulting practice. And I want to make enough money for us to travel and be generous with our kids and grandkids. I want to live somewhere besides Michigan at least part of the time."

Jeff was staring at me blankly. "What's *your* vision?" I asked him, hoping he'd hop on board.

"I don't really have one," he answered. "Things have a way of working out."

Jeff sounded defensive, but when I thought about his life, I realized he'd always belonged to the "see what happens" school of planning. When his hormones started to kick in after years in a Catholic seminary, he fled the cloistered life for a secular college, majoring in zoology. After graduation he took a job making bullets at a brass company. He worked his way up from the assembly line to district sales manager, earning an MBA while he was at it. Based on changes he'd seen in a friend who'd benefited from Rolfing, Jeff signed up for that brand of bodywork. After one session, he abandoned the security of the brass company a few months shy of qualifying for a pension, and became a Rolfer.

When we met, Jeff had a small Rolfing practice in his basement. A few months later we were doing our taxes together, and I asked him what a twelve-dollar entry in one of the columns referred to.

"That's what I earned last year. After expenses, of course," Jeff said, manifesting none of the shame I would have felt if my annual income were in the low two figures. I had earned eighty thousand dollars that year.

It dawned on me that Jeff had been living on his late wife's life insurance. Clearly I'd have to continue to support myself forever. I kicked myself for neglecting to put "financially stable" on my wish list.

Now, sitting in a Seattle restaurant, I started to see that I had been fooling myself. No wonder I was ambivalent about this marriage. Jeff just might not be cut out to be a full partner in the grand adventures I had planned. "How in the hell will you get what you want if you don't know what it is?" I blurted.

"I'll be okay with whatever happens."

I pouted for the rest of the evening, and we parted on less than cordial terms. I was glad to be going off to Taos by myself. I'd go after my dreams, whether my husband wanted to come along or not.

black clouds

The writing workshop took place at the Mabel Dodge Luhan House amid the purple majesty of the Taos Mountains. This was the most independent thing I'd ever done. I had never been away from home by myself for so long, and there was no one to take care of but me. After a couple of days, I realized that knowing what I wanted to do wasn't so easy after all. I couldn't even decide how to use my free time between classes. Did I write with a small group, visit the Taos Pueblo, browse the quaint shops, or explore the mesa? Maybe Jeff wasn't the only one who didn't know what he wanted.

The classes were pure joy. I devoured Natalie Goldberg's insights about writing and scrutinized my classmates for tips on how real writers talk, sit, read, and dress. My sense of not fitting in was less severe than usual. These writing types seemed to be as weird as I was. I felt at home, at last, among the misfits.

Natalie announced a final reading in which any student could have up to two minutes to share a piece they'd written. I was reluctant after hearing the polished products of the other students. But I vowed to participate despite the Vile Bitch's insistence that my work wouldn't measure up.

One of my life strategies has always been to buy the clothes I'd need if I got what I wanted. In the Taos town square, I bought a multicolored flowered skirt and a purple Lycra top that, unlike anything I'd worn before, managed to create the illusion of cleavage between my small breasts. The look was just right.

I decided to read my assignment from a guest teacher at the workshop, who'd told us to write a myth. He'd offered several possible scenarios; I chose "You're a patient in a mental hospital. Your sanity has been restored, but you've grown to like the institution. You don't want the staff to find out that you've recovered."

I approached the podium, emboldened by my sexy outfit. Holding my notebook in tremulous hands, I read:

Speechless

It is very dark in here. I squeak in a way that makes no sense. I used to be loud, clear, and articulate. They have cut out my tongue. The cancer ate it, and squeaking is my only option.

Using the slate with the red frame and stick pencil does not work. By the time I write an idea, the conversation has progressed and my thought is outdated. People grow impatient and save the really important conversations for later, after they leave me.

I write less on the slate. I do not work. Everything I used to do required talking: therapist, hypnotherapist, speaker, consultant. Friends thought of things I could do without a tongue, like those paralyzed people who paint with their mouths. Forget it. I am not eating. I will not watch videos. I stop reading.

They bring in my old therapists. They could only help me when I had a future. What will they do next? Prozac, Mellaril, Thorazine. I have no tongue under which to hide the pills so I learn to tuck them in the far-left corner of my mouth until the staff goes away. Then I hide them under my mattress. It is getting red, brown, blue, gooey under there, but I do not care.

I hardly move now, and the activity around me increases. I am losing weight—what I always wanted. Now opening my eyes is an effort. It is very dark.

I wake up. My bed has shrunk from king size to twin. The air smells. Is that urine? I hear shuffling, moaning, whistling, a TV in the distance. I have an IV in my left arm—a vicious plot to keep me alive.

They attempt to arouse me, feed me, talk to me, get me to pee, but I play dead. I am less and less aware of my surroundings. I begin to like it in here. It is quiet.

What would I have to do to get rid of this damned IV? Probably eat.

The nurse comes in. I squeak and signal for a drink. My hair must be a mess. I wonder who is paying for my hospitalization.

They disconnect the IV. I still do nothing. I do not want to raise their expectations. I have visions of occupational and recreational therapy, making lanyards and playing volleyball, coached by some well-meaning zealot asshole who does not know how dark it is in here. I don't want a skill. I don't want to support myself.

You have survived it all, they say, *a brother's suicide, alcoholism, divorces, TB, cancer. You can beat this too.*

Maybe you can write, my cosmic-new-age-always-looking-for-the-bright-side-there-is-a-reason-for-everything friends say. Fuck writing.

I am going to suck this green Jell-O through a straw and look out the window and watch the other crazy people shuffle around the circular drive. I don't make appointments, I don't answer calls or letters, and I don't care who is fucking whom.

The response surprised me. Everyone, including Natalie, liked it. The darkness of the piece surprised me, too. Where in the hell had that voice come from? I thought I was having a good time at the workshop; I was healed from the cancer. I could talk just fine. I had never looked better, my checkups were perfect, and I had a clear vision for the future, which now included a new career as a writer.

Unable to locate the origin of the negativity, I attributed the whole thing to an unconscious fluke and shifted my attention to replaying Natalie's compliments in my head. Buoyed by her feedback, I promised myself that I'd build regular writing practice into my schedule, no matter how busy it got.

By the time I got home, I was happy to see Jeff. Even if he didn't have a vision, I'd missed him.

I jumped into work. It felt like I'd finally made it as an organizational consultant. Other than a little Mexican vacation with Lynn in early November, I was booked solid until Christmas. I might even make enough money to get off the financial roller coaster I had ridden until then. My visioning was working.

My first project was to design and facilitate a retreat for the nursing leaders from one of my favorite client hospitals. As I stood before the group in the wood-paneled conference room in Detroit's Renaissance Center, I finally felt like a "good old girl."

After the first day, which had gone well, I had a little time to myself before dinner with the group. I was exhausted and wanted to go straight to bed, but the evening networking was a vital part of the project. Perhaps a walk would wake me up. As I pushed myself along the mazelike track atop the towering hotel, which overlooked the depressed city and the Detroit River, I sensed that something was not quite right in my body. I squashed the sensation and dressed for dinner.

Sure enough, I came down with the flu the next day. Despite my postcancer promises to put my health first, it was excruciating to back out on commitments. After two weeks of struggling to get well while maintaining my normally busy schedule, I called the doctor, who prescribed an antibiotic. I began to feel better.

As I recovered, I noticed a strange tingling in my tongue. It was intermittent at first, and I tried to ignore it, attributing it to my understandable hypervigilance.

The sensation persisted. My regular checkup with Dr. Watson was over a month away, so I scheduled the next available appointment.

Dr. Watson found nothing wrong and didn't seem concerned. He said the antibiotics could be causing the tongue symptoms and told me to come back in a month if they didn't clear up. Only later did I realize that this was the same advice I'd been given the first time I visited that office.

Jeff and I took a much-needed getaway weekend in northern Michigan. But my tongue often burned to the point of pain, so I could eat fewer and fewer foods, and it was hard for me to enjoy the fall colors or my husband. I was usually the conversation starter in our marriage, but I wasn't up to it. An awkward silence hung in the air as we browsed in the quaint fishing village of Leland. We hiked the beach near Northport while I tried to pull my thoughts back from grisly possibilities. Even at the quaint B&B overlooking the lake, semisnuggling with Jeff in a four-poster bed before a roaring fire, I couldn't get my mind out of my mouth.

Once home, I was sucked into a vortex of consulting projects. I vowed that as soon as they were completed I would take a month off to be quiet and write.

I tried to devise probable causes for the nonstop pain and tingling in my tongue. Jeff, on the other hand, knew that these symptoms likely signaled the recurrence that Dr. Dudar had predicted, the one with a 2 percent chance of survival. It became increasingly difficult for him to keep up his end of our "you're going to be fine" game.

The symptoms persisted. I returned to Dr. Watson's office in mid-October.

"I don't feel anything in there," he said. "It could be lichen planus, which is a fungus that causes symptoms like yours. Or maybe it's thrush," he said, sounding hopeful. I tried valiantly to lap up the alternatives he was offering. "I don't think it's cancer," he concluded.

I don't care what you think. It hurts like hell and I'm terrified. Do something! I thought. I politely suggested a biopsy or an MRI.

"I wouldn't know where to biopsy since there's no discernible lump. A physical exam is more effective than an MRI in diagnosing recurrences of oral cancer." I wondered how this could be true. Years later other doctors would disagree. "Let me run the test for thrush. Come back if it's not better in a couple of weeks."

The thrush test came back negative. I asked nurse friends about the symptoms of lichen planus and searched for similarities to my own. Dr. Watson's "I do not think it is cancer," played in my head as my new medical mantra. My willingness to pursue these flimsy possibilities was evidence of my desperate needs to please my doctor and to find a more benign explanation for my symptoms. Apparently, Dr. Watson didn't want to believe it was cancer any more than I did.

Another appointment with Dr. Watson was scheduled for early November, Election Day. It was a typical Ann Arbor almost-winter day—cold, barren, and gray. I stood in line for two hours waiting to vote, all the while reciting the Serenity Prayer to calm myself. "God grant me the serenity to accept the things I cannot change, the courage to change the things I can, and the wisdom to know the difference." Watching the other voters chatting casually to pass the time, I envied them their healthy tongues. I wished that I had time to pass casually. Voting meant having an opinion about the future, as if I might be around to care who was president.

After voting, I drove twenty miles to see Dr. Watson. My support team had had the audacity to return to their own lives, so for the first time in years I went to a doctor alone.

Every muscle stood at attention as I perched on the straight-backed chair in the waiting room. Fifteen minutes later, the doctor himself ushered me into the exam room—violating the usual protocol and deepening my suspicion.

Dr. Watson went right to examining my mouth, fixating on a spot under my tongue. I recalled his statement that if cancer recurred, it usually showed up near its original location. I stiffened as he poked that area, first with a cold, metal probe and then with his gloved fingers. He removed his hand from my mouth and raised his gaze to my eyes, looking chagrined.

"Well, there is something there," he said in a somber tone. Then, in a more upbeat voice, "But it doesn't feel like cancer. I think it's probably just an infection. I want you to take an antibiotic for ten days. If that doesn't resolve it, we will talk about doing a biopsy."

My whole body tightened, and I quivered inside. All the fear that had been straining at the portal of my awareness pushed through my denial and flooded me with full-on terror. Here was the black cloud that this asshole had predicted.

I could tell he wanted me to leave and take my pain and panic with me. I shared his desire to leave his office but wanted to take time to kill him before I left. "Even if it is cancer," he added, "another ten days won't matter."

What do you mean it won't matter, you shithead? How about the seven weeks you wasted while the goddamned cancer was eating my mouth and God knows what else? Suddenly it was easy to access my repressed anger.

I grabbed the antibiotic prescription out of his hand and ran, cursing myself for coming to see him alone. I had to talk to Jeff.

The pay phone in the cramped pharmacy downstairs was in use by an old guy in brown polyester. He looked close to eighty. I'd be lucky to make fifty. He hung up, and I called Jeff out of yet another Rolfing session to give him more bad news.

There was a pause on the other end of the line and then, in a flat voice, Jeff tried once again to calm me. "We'll get through this. Watson could be right. It may just be an infection."

I drove to Ann Arbor on autopilot, pummeled by dark thoughts. *My time is up. Why didn't I enjoy those cancer-free months more?*

Jeff was waiting outside his office looking lost and cold. I couldn't feel very much, but his stiff hug helped. As exhausted as he was and knowing what he knew, it was a wonder that he could console me at all. While I appreciated the effort he was making, I also took him for granted.

That night Jeff tucked me in then left me to go to his bedroom. At 2:00 a.m., I turned on the TV to see Bill, Hillary, Al, and Tipper dancing around the portico outside the State House in Little Rock, singing "Happy Days Are Here Again." Instead of the elation I normally would have shared with them, I felt sadness that I probably wouldn't be around to see Bill and Al finish their term.

I was boxed in on all sides by bad options. If I followed Watson's plan, it would be at least two weeks before I saw him and a month until I got a biopsy. Meanwhile, cancer was almost certainly gaining more of a foothold, and anxiety was obscuring useful thoughts. Starting over with another doctor seemed more than I could manage and, as Val had pointed out, "What will you do if a new doctor gives you conflicting advice?" I even considered returning to Dr. Dudar at U of M but wasn't quite desperate enough to do that. Maybe I didn't want to give him the satisfaction of being right. And as long as I held on to Dr. Watson, I could cling to the thin strand of hope that one of his wild-ass theories might be true.

The day after Watson found the lump, I conducted a daylong retreat for a troubled nursing unit at Children's Hospital. Two days later, I led a conflict resolution workshop for two hundred nurses from U of M. Then I went home and collapsed. I canceled the trip I'd been planning for months to Mexico City for the Day of the Dead celebration. Lynn and I had been trying to get to this event for years, but right now travel in general and this holiday in particular held little appeal. Still, not going left me empty. It felt like I was dropping out of life. I was no longer capable of work. Plagued with guilt at disappointing my clients again, I was sure I would slide from my brief moment of success to becoming a penniless, tongueless bag lady.

I spent my days trying to wrest support from busy people and flailing from one possible remedy to another. As my despair increased, so did my openness to alternative therapies; the traditional medical system was clearly letting me down. Jeff spent endless hours hunched over his computer researching healing methods.

My writing teacher knew someone who'd beaten cancer with Ayurveda, the five-thousand-year-old Hindu art of prolonging life. She referred me to a practitioner in Pontiac, a dying auto town forty miles from home. I was as depressed as the surroundings when I pulled into the parking lot of the run-down office building. The waiting room was furnished in dilapidated, East Indian, hippie style. Behind the receptionist were shelves stacked high with "products," which I would soon learn were not only essential to my survival but also very expensive.

The cheerful receptionist, obviously high on "products," led me to a smaller, but equally dreary, room to listen to an introductory tape about Ayurveda. She said there were two such tapes, one each for people with and without cancer, and wondered out loud which one to play for me. She went to check with the doctor. "Please God, make her give me the normal one." She returned and inserted the "with cancer" tape into the boom box. I hadn't even met this doctor. How in the hell did she know I had cancer? Did the ancient Hindus diagnose through walls? I wanted to bolt. Only good manners and a molecule of hope that some part of this weirdness might save me kept my trembling body in the hard folding chair.

Finally, I was escorted in to see the doctor. She took my "pulses," pressing her twig-like fingers firmly on parts of my body that I never knew were pulsing. She went on to describe the massive lifestyle overhaul necessary for me to achieve health. Not only would my eating habits have to be totally revamped to fit my "pitta" body type, I must also eliminate coffee and alcohol. I was to start each day with an hour of yoga, do Transcendental Meditation for twenty minutes twice a day, gargle with sesame oil, use an Ayurvedic tongue scraper and, of course, take plenty of products. It would also be highly desirable for me to attend a week-long session at Maharishi Ayurveda Health Center for *panchakarma*, a program of detoxification and rejuvenation. While the doctor did not come right out and say that she thought I had cancer, her treatment plan implied it. She handed me a pink, loose-leaf binder stuffed with eighty pages detailing my revised life and ushered me back through the curtain of purple plastic beads into the waiting room. Relieved of $369, arms laden with products, I headed for the parking lot in tears.

At home I waded through the pink notebook and tried to convince myself that I could integrate all these new habits, while wondering why I would want to waste what little time was left on this crap. But I pushed myself to practice yogic sun salutes, straining to stretch my tight body into the pictured poses. I called the Transcendental Meditation Center to see if my instructor from eight years ago was still there, in hopes of retrieving the mantra for which I once paid $400. The next day, she refreshed my memory and stressed the importance of regular practice. I promised compliance, wondering how I would ever manage to sit still.

And what luck! The Ayurvedic retreat center closest to Ann Arbor had an opening in its panchakarma cleansing camp for the week before my next appointment with Dr. Watson. It cost $1,200, but any chance that the exotic treatments could remove the lump and the pain, which the antibiotics had not touched, made it worth every penny. Wouldn't it be something if I could march into Dr. Watson's office cured? Even as I entertained this fantasy, deeper down I doubted that this ancient system of Indian medicine would actually help me. But the program would give me something to do besides waiting for the biopsy and monitoring my mouth.

The thought of driving the 375 miles to the retreat center north of Toronto by myself was too depressing to contemplate. Jeff, bless his heart, agreed to take me. When we set out from Ann Arbor, we stopped for coffee as we always did on our road trips. But we knew this wasn't just another road trip. It was a desperate, last-ditch attempt to save my life, so the charade didn't even last as far as Detroit. We tried to make casual conversation, but what was there to say? By the time we approached the center, Jeff's beautiful hands gripped the steering wheel tightly, and he glared at the monotonous highway in grim silence. Knowing that I was facing a week alone in a strange place, my insides were as frozen as the surroundings.

The beige, bleak, barracks-like center was located on a small lake. Dreading the long drive home and eager to escape, Jeff deposited me quickly and headed for the parking lot. I wanted to chase after him and beg him not to leave me in this God-forsaken outpost. It reminded me of the time my parents tried to leave me at summer camp and I instantly generated the nausea, fever, and chills necessary to get them to take me home. There were no symptoms that would get me back into the car this time.

My room resembled the cheapest room at a Motel 6: dingy white walls, a less than comfortable twin bed, a molded plastic nightstand with a metal lamp, and a pseudowood desk and chair near the window overlooking the frozen lake. The small, worn throw rug in the middle of the tile floor was gray like everything else. I felt like I had stepped into a black-and-white movie.

A white-clad attendant informed me that except for a few scheduled activities each day, I was to stay in my room by myself, meditating and practicing yoga. I avoided solitude even when I felt well, why would I want it now?

At dinner that night I faced down a bowl of brown-green paste, spiced beyond the tolerance of my tender mouth. After that I ate rice and oats at every meal. Most of the other diners were as somber as the surroundings, but one lively woman in her mid-fifties with brown, tousled hair and a warm smile stood out. "I just got diagnosed with cancer for the fourth time, and I'm not afraid anymore," she said nonchalantly while eating her gruel. Stunned, I just nodded. I knew I'd never face cancer without fear. I would think of this woman often in the months ahead.

Some treatments were quite pleasant, such as *shirodhara*, which involved warm oil being poured over my "third eye" to soothe my nervous system, massages, and hours wrapped in a blanket listening to chanting Hindu monks. The endless enemas I could have done without.

Many evenings were spent in another grim room with fellow inmates listening to Deepak Chopra explain the tenets of Ayurveda. In his sonorous voice with the perfect Indian accent, he urged us to "fall into the gap between your thoughts where you can access the field of infinite possibility and create healing." There *were* no gaps between my thoughts. Each day seemed endless, the loneliness lethal.

I was almost certain I could feel something growing under my tongue. I called Dr. Watson from the rickety pay phone in the cold, desolate hallway to ask if he could do the biopsy before December 1. He said he was too busy. I thought again about finding another doctor, but what could I do from here?

I did schedule an appointment with the center's staff doctor, a reserved young fellow whose calm demeanor was a compelling advertisement for meditation. He listened respectfully to my whole story, nodding at appropriate junctures, and said, "Your symptoms could be indicative of a lot of conditions other than cancer." Praise Maharishi! "I think these problems could be linked to the TB you had as a child," he said. "The massive doses of antibiotics you took may have destroyed helpful bacteria as well as the disease, leaving you with a compromised immune system." He mapped a complicated regimen to strengthen my immune system. Burdened with the weight of more suggestions I knew I would not implement, I returned to my room.

What if the TB I had as a child really was to blame for all my problems? I sat at the rickety desk and stared, unseeing, toward the ice-covered lake recalling how I contracted bovine tuberculosis. Replaying this saga, I realized the similarities between that time and my current crisis. Had my mother been as scared during her months of not knowing the cause of that lump as I felt now? Recently, after my father's death, I discovered a small scrap of paper among my share of his belongings while preparing for his memorial. On one side of the paper a clever homily was printed and on the other, in Mom's hand-writing, "The lump under Terri's chin won't be a problem." She must have written it in 1952, which meant that the tiny fragment had been through six moves in sixty-three years and traveled five thousand miles without being detected. Who knew that my Mom was the Louise Hay of the fifties? Finding the affirmation made me feel very close to Mom and showed me how concerned she must have been.

Maybe my present problems were just an opportunity to relive and release leftover emotions from that childhood trauma. As much as I believed in the power of unresolved emotions, I couldn't buy that explanation for long and soon fell back into full-scale terror. On Friday, Jeff arrived to retrieve me. I'd never been so glad to see him.

I called Dr. Watson the moment I got home. He emphatically repeated that he didn't have time to do the biopsy before December 1. I was still furious with him and couldn't believe that someone I had seen as a friend could let me down this way. I thought I was special to him. How could he treat me like just another patient?

With nothing but time and fear on my hands for the next ten days, I continued to stalk every possible path to a cure. Jeff was still my richest source of alternative approaches to healing. He introduced me to a client of his who had vanquished a uterine tumor with a macrobiotic diet. The woman was thin, beautiful, and appeared vibrantly healthy. She was also more than generous with dietary details. While I couldn't argue with her results, I was not sure I could handle the arduous process. I had trouble reducing my coffee intake on a good day. How was

I going to change all my eating habits while a tumor was growing in my mouth?

One night in late November, Jeff came home all excited because another client of his was entertaining a world-renowned healer. Jeff said if we were lucky, we might be able to get an appointment before he returned to Europe. We were lucky.

The next day, Jeff and I entered a drab apartment building in the neighboring town of Ypsilanti and met the healer. He spoke no English, but from his translator I gleaned that he was a retired Czechoslovakian sea captain. I'm no stickler for credentials, but as a nurse, I would have preferred some relevant training.

The captain showed us into a beige room, empty except for one folding chair. Jeff sat on the floor and I perched on the hard seat, staring at the faded wall while the captain waved his rough, gnarled hands in circles a few inches from my body. I felt nothing.

"Doesn't he have great energy?" Jeff asked me on our way home.

"Uh, yeah, I guess so."

"You know he makes house calls?"

"Really."

The next morning, the captain was sailing from one end of our house to the other, "assessing invisible energy currents." Through the translator, he announced that an evil stream flowed under the place where I lay my head every night. I did have cancer again, he said, and would go through a lot, but that ultimately I would be okay. I began to relax. Then I realized that I was taking solace and advice from a washed-up sailor I knew nothing about in a language I didn't understand.

Still, we moved the bed.

§

I was having an increasingly hard time convincing myself that my worsening symptoms were anything but cancer. And although Jeff continued to spare me the specific statistic, I was pretty sure that a recurrence would almost certainly be fatal. Applying the lessons of the

Forum, I had been directing my energy to creating a vision of myself free of cancer. It was definitely time to envision a healthy future self, even if I did have cancer now.

One night a few days before the biopsy, I dressed all in black, except for the red trim on my lizard cowboy boots. I wore black stirrup pants, black turtleneck, and a large, abstract silver cross necklace that Jeff had bought me on our honeymoon. I put on the raccoon coat that I never dared wear in Ann Arbor and struck a Wonder Woman pose—head thrown back, chest out, hands on hips, and feet firmly planted in defiance. I told Jeff to take my picture. Then I asked him to take me to A Moveable Feast, a restaurant as pretentious as its name and, thanks to a raft of analgesics, I enjoyed a sumptuous dinner. On the way home, I indulged the extravagance that impending death allows and got the film developed at the One-Hour Photo. In those snapshots, I looked strong and healthy. I posted them on the refrigerator, the bathroom mirror, and beside my bed. Whenever I caught sight of myself, I could almost believe in a future for that powerful woman.

But my mind was more often mired in grim predictions and the fear they produced. Jeff was running low on reassurance. I was afraid to ask him if I would be okay. He still complied with my wishes and met my needs, but he did so slowly and without enthusiasm. Sex was pretty much a thing of the past, and conversations were strained. Apparently all that cooperation was building a stockpile of resentment in him. His unspoken fears and grievances were creating a wedge between us when we needed each other the most.

§

The biopsy, which was conducted in St. Joe's outpatient clinic under general anesthesia, was a much bigger deal than the one I'd had in the oral surgeon's office almost two years before. Moving in and out of a fog on my way back to consciousness, I strained to interpret Val and Jeff's moods as an indication of my prognosis.

"Watson says it doesn't look bad in there," Val lied.

"He says he's hopeful," said Jeff.

In truth, Dr. Watson was anything but hopeful. My husband and sister had decided to let me hold on to hope until the results were official. Jeff and I took great pride in our openness with each other. The fact that he could pull off a scam of this magnitude showed my level of distraction and the distance between us.

Well intentioned as their deception was, the waiting was torture. I tried praying, reading *A Course in Miracles*, calling the Silent Unity prayer ministry. None of my usual methods for consoling myself were working. I made one last-ditch attempt to connect with God by writing, "Please don't let this be cancer!" on a slip of paper and putting it in my "God Box," symbolically turning it over to something larger than myself.

By the time Dr. Watson called three days later, I was in bed with a pillow over my head to block out the ringing of the phone. Jeff appeared at the bedroom door. His ashen face, drained of all expression, communicated the verdict. Thrusting the portable phone in my direction, he asked, "Do you want to talk to Watson?"

"Hell no!"

"We'll call you back," I heard Jeff tell the doctor. Now expert at handling bad biopsy news, he called Val and Barb and asked them to come over. Unlike the first time he learned that I had cancer, when Jeff's tears had flowed freely, he now appeared as frozen as I felt.

Horrible questions pounded in my brain. How much of my tongue would they take this time? Would I be able to talk when they were done? Where had the cancer spread while I was getting enemas from Hindus and energy from a Czechoslovakian sea captain? Was it in my brain, my jaw, my lungs, my larynx? Where was I going to find the money, help, and fortitude for a long, painful death? And even if by some miracle I did survive, what kind of life would it be, sitting around all hacked up waiting for cancer to come back?

Why didn't that Watson son of a bitch listen to me? I would pay for his mistake with my life while he was out playing tennis, driving his little red Miata, and going on ski vacations at his fancy Vail condo. Not only had he failed me in his professional capacity, he had betrayed our friendship. I never wanted to see that bastard again, but knew I had to keep our appointment that evening where we would "discuss the options." I already knew that my options did not include having Dr. Watson on my team. Still, I fretted about hurting his feelings if I dismissed him. Mine was indeed a terminal case of needing to please.

I didn't have to worry about rejecting Dr. Watson. He rejected me first.

"Your condition is beyond my experience," he said, looking at the floor. "Let me tell you about a pair of doctors I recommend at Ohio State's hospital."

Oh great! my mind railed. *Not only is the cancer so out of control that he can't deal with it, it's so bad I need tag-team surgeons!*

As we left the office, Barb said, "Do you want to go Christmas tree shopping in the morning?" I didn't feel up to our annual tree-seeking ritual but figured if this was to be my last Christmas, I'd better have a tree.

Jeff engaged in his usual good-humored grumbling as he dragged tree after tree out of the prickly piles at Leveret's Farm Market so Barb and I could conduct our three-hundred-and-sixty-degree inspections of the fifteen-foot specimens. By the time we'd selected our favorites, Jeff's hands were scratched and his grumbling was not so playful. There was something comforting in playing our familiar roles—me bossy, him begrudging—at a time when nothing else in our lives was familiar.

While we were perusing evergreens, my indefatigable sister was researching the most respected treatment centers for metastasized oral cancer. Within two days, she had appointments for me at the University of Michigan, Ohio State, and Sloan Kettering. She had even called her most famous friend, Harry Smith of *CBS This Morning,* who tracked down television's Dr. Art Ulene in Bangladesh to get the referral at Sloan Kettering in New York.

Our first stop was Dr. Lambe, head of the U of M Otolaryngology Department. Appearing slightly bored by having to repeat information he had obviously delivered hundreds of times, he explained what the operation to remove my cancer might entail.

"If it looks like the cancer has infiltrated the jaw," he said, keeping his gaze on Jeff or Val, "we will have to remove at least half of that bone. We'd replace it with a titanium bar, which is attached to the left ear, then screwed into the remaining jaw on the right." Dr. Lambe pointed to his own body as he described how he would bring tissue from my neck and chest up into my mouth to form a flap over the titanium bar. "This procedure is called a pectoralis flap, and it works well because the vessels stay connected at the point of origin, so the reconstructed area has an adequate blood supply." He paused briefly then added, "If her condition necessitates this procedure, we will have to perform a tracheotomy, cutting a hole in the throat to maintain an airway during and after surgery."

I felt my stomach spasm and acid rise in my throat. I was stunned. And angry. Very angry.

No one had ever told me that I might lose my jaw! And a tracheotomy—dear God in heaven! Val and Jeff looked on in horror as I attempted to process these possibilities. I looked at them with suspicion. Had they heard this stuff before? Val quickly filled the silence with questions.

I didn't hear the answers. I was back in nursing school, suctioning a tracheotomy. The wrinkled, gray-faced man writhed in pain as I inserted a brown rubber tube into the opening in his throat to remove built-up secretions. It was not clear which one of us was more terrified. The image of that same man smoking a cigarette through the tracheotomy hole flashed through my mind. The next memory jolted me back into present time. That patient with the trach couldn't talk.

"The tracheotomy would only be temporary, right?" I managed.

"Oh yes," Dr. Lambe replied and went back to answering Val's questions.

And then it occurred to me that even if the tracheotomy didn't permanently silence me, removing my jaw and more of my tongue might.

"Will I be able to talk?" I asked, not sure I wanted an answer.

"You'll be able to talk," Dr. Lambe assured me, "but I don't know how well your speech will go over in business settings." He proceeded to do what turned out to be a very accurate imitation of how I would sound after surgery. He sounded tongue-tied or "mentally challenged" or both.

Covering my devastation with false bravado, I automatically reverted to my glib self-defense mode, "Well, disabled is in. I'll use it for a marketing advantage."

"How well you do," Dr. Lambe concluded my appointment, "will be up to you and me and God." I appreciated his bringing God into the picture and his awareness that he was not Him.

My next stop was Columbus, Ohio, to meet with Drs. Prescott and Gilbert at the James Cancer Center of the Ohio State University Hospitals. Columbus is my mother's birthplace, home of my father's alma mater, and final resting-place of my brother Greg. Val and Bill volunteered to make the sentimental medical journey with Jeff and me. We gratefully accepted.

Driving through the dark Ohio night in my brother's van gave us a rare opportunity for serious sibling conversation. We delved into usually verboten topics like our marriages, our sex lives, and our dead brother. Both Val and Bill opened up about marital challenges. This was the kind of closeness I'd always wanted with my family.

"I guess this cancer stuff is taking a toll on our marriage too," I ventured.

Jeff sat up straighter. "That's for sure," he said.

I felt a little jolt of surprise at how adamant he sounded.

At the Holiday Inn on Ohio State's campus, we opened the door between our adjoining rooms and told jokes into the wee hours, as if we were having a slumber party. At last, I got to be one of the kids, rather than the assistant-mother.

The next morning, the four of us camped out in a corner of the crowded waiting room of Dr. Prescott's clinic. After an hour, a perky young woman stuck her head out from behind the clinic door. "Dr. Prescott is running about two hours behind schedule today."

Bill and Jeff headed for the cafeteria. Val worked on a needlepoint belt for Dad. I tried and failed to avoid seeing the faces of my fellow patients—like the middle-aged man who'd lost much of the right side of his face. The skin between his nose and his neck was a mass of leathery scar tissue. Would that be me?

After a ninety-minute wait, my name was called, and we were escorted to another, smaller, more crowded waiting room for forty minutes more. When we were finally pried from the throng, I was weighed and measured and, at long last, parked in an examining room with my entourage.

For the next hour, I was probed and prodded and asked to tell my cancer saga to a parade of residents, interns, and medical students, all of whom felt free to discuss my case in front of me. "A tumor that size . . ." "Radiation during or after the surgery . . ." ". . . wonder about bone involvement." These "baby doctors," as Val called them, were talking as if I had cancer and plenty of it.

Denial dies hard. Until that moment I'd managed to sustain the fantasy that this whole cancer thing was some kind of mistake. Sitting in that stiff chair listening to commentary about my cancer, my body crumbled as if denial had been the only thing holding me up.

After a brief discussion of our respective football loyalties (Dr. Prescott, Ohio State; me, Michigan) and a brief examination of my mouth, Dr. Prescott made it clear that he, too, believed I was loaded with cancer. He referred to the disease as if it were our opponent in the Rose Bowl and we were mapping our offensive strategy. "We're going for a cure here," he said with conviction. I let out the breath I felt like I'd been holding for weeks.

Dr. Prescott was the first and last expert to mention a "cure," my new favorite four-letter word. I was convinced that my odds of surviving were greater with a doctor who thought I might do it. Years later, research supports that belief.

The doctor explained how he would do the surgery: he'd remove the cancer and the surrounding tissue, possibly including part of my jaw. Then he'd hand me off to his partner, Dr. Gilbert, for reconstruction. He told us that Ohio State was one of the few hospitals equipped to do intra-operative radiation—administering the treatment during surgery. Since I'd need radiation at some point, it would hasten my recovery to have it during the operation. Dr. Prescott shook each of our hands, nodded for his team to follow, and left us in the barren room to await Dr. Gilbert.

Robert Gilbert was trained in otolaryngological and plastic surgery at the University of Michigan, where he was revered by his colleagues, not only for his clinical prowess but also because he was "one hell of a nice guy." Dr. Gilbert was nationally recognized for his success with "free-flap" reconstruction following the removal of oral cancer—fashioning a new jaw from the patient's hipbone. All of Val's research showed this approach to be superior to the pectoralis flap that U of M's Dr. Lambe had touted in terms of postoperative eating, talking, and appearance.

Dr. Gilbert looked like he had just stepped out of an ad in *Gentleman's Quarterly*. It struck me as ironic that someone so perfect saved people's lives by making them look like the patients in the waiting room. I couldn't help wondering if he had any idea what it felt like to live behind the faces he created.

When I met someone who looked as good as he did, my insecurity usually provoked me to search for hidden flaws. As advertised, Dr. Gilbert was a nice guy, and I liked him right away. He acted as if he had nothing better to do than to chat with us. He examined me gently. Jeff and I both lacked the mental capacity to generate intelligible questions at that point, but he responded in great detail to Val and Bill's queries.

Val told Dr. Gilbert we'd think about our next steps and let him know what we decided. My brother and sister gathered up Jeff and me and led us out of the clinic.

In hopes of lightening the mood, we stopped at the café in Lazarus, a department store in downtown Columbus, for one of my favorite foods. The high point of my childhood visits to Columbus had been riding the bus down High Street with Ma, my maternal grandmother, for a heaping plate of "stuffing," made of dried breadcrumbs and covered in gelatinous yellow gravy. When my serving arrived, Bill said, "We came here for this?" He had a point. The "stuffing" wasn't as delicious as I remembered it to be. Even the elaborate Christmas decorations failed to stir my usual excitement. We talked about visiting Greg's grave, but decided we weren't up for another emotional excursion.

Val and I were scheduled to fly to New York the next day for my evaluation at Sloan Kettering. A big winter storm was predicted. I knew I really should explore all my options, but braving ice, snow, and Sloan Kettering's infamously cold doctors was beyond me. Exhaustion triumphed. I decided to be treated at Ohio State.

we need a little christmas

*T*he morning after we got home from Columbus, I was lying in bed, trying to recover from the assaults of that trip, when Jeff came into my room with the phone in his hand.

"It's Ohio State," he said. "There's a cancellation in the O.R. schedule for December 15. Do you want to take it?"

"Jesus," I said, still groggy from the sedative that hadn't helped me sleep. "How the hell do I know what I want? Ask Val. Tell them we'll call them back." Jeff cut me and my bad attitude some slack and did as he was told.

I wanted to postpone the surgery forever, and I wanted to get it over with as soon as possible. After a quick consultation with our team, Jeff called OSU and made the appointment. My surgery was now five days away.

My preoperative preparations were focused on spending every possible minute with my kids, Jeff, and other loved ones to feed my soul before I reentered the hospital where my body would be the focus of attention. I knew my kids were concerned, so we tried to keep things light around them. In spite of the beautifully decorated Christmas tree towering in our high-ceilinged living room, this was not going to be much of a Christmas. When I was a kid, Mom's holiday mantra was, "I'll be so goddamned glad when these friggin' holidays are over." As a mother, I was hell bent on creating magical Christmases for my boys. But this year they got one present each instead of a dozen, and we only listened to a couple of my fifty Christmas CDs. I steered clear of Johnny Mathis albums, my favorite, because he made me cry. Anxiety rather than holiday spirit filled the air.

Jeff was a calming, stabilizing presence in the background for all of us. When I awoke in the middle of the night with a jolt to the reality of my situation, I shuffled into his room like a kid with nightmares. I'd whisper, "Jeff," "honey," "hey," and he'd lift the covers, inviting me to join him on his futon on the floor. The strain on Jeff was beginning to show in the dark circles under his eyes and the shortness of his temper, but he never directly complained and he did his best to comfort me.

December 13 was a gray, brittle Sunday. Jeff, Justin, Eric, and I headed for Columbus caravan style. We stopped for dinner at Frisch's Big Boy outside Findlay, Ohio. Giddy with terror, we joked about the blue Jell-O under the plastic sneeze guard at the soup 'n' salad bar. I bought my kids each a kitschy Big Boy bank, not that they would need souvenirs to remember this trip. Although my lanky, bearded sons in their artsy, city attire could not be mistaken for Findlay locals, we probably looked like a happy family enjoying holiday travel.

As we settled into our "suite" at the Columbus Marriott Residence Inn where my family was about to become regulars, my connection with the conversation grew tenuous. Grateful as I was to have my husband and children with me, I felt unspeakably sad that my time with them might be limited.

Before bed, I tried to read from my favorite spiritual reader, *Daily Word*. I picked a passage on trusting God and staying in the present moment, but my mind kept wandering into the future.

The next morning, Jeff sprang into action at the 6:00 a.m. beep of the alarm.

"Come on," he urged me out of bed. "We have to be at the hospital by 7:30."

First, there was a meal to have, my last with an almost normal mouth. We sat across from each other in a diner booth, eating greasy grits and drinking bad coffee with little to say. I looked at Jeff's sad, beautiful face and wondered how he could stick with me through this. It occurred to me that I was asking too much of him, but there was nothing to do about that today.

§

The solemn, officious woman in the admissions department at the James Cancer Center of The Ohio State University Hospital wanted the facts. Who was I? Where did I come from? Who would do what if I died or became a vegetable? And, most important, who was going to pay for all this?

The Vile Bitch Upstairs, always poised and ready to point out new things to be afraid of, leapt on this question. *You forgot about that! What if the insurance doesn't cover this? Why the hell didn't you read the policy more carefully, or at all, for that matter?* Try as I might to convince myself that this was no time to worry about money, financial ruin joined the other horrible outcomes performing a macabre ballet in my mind.

We spent the rest of the day in the bowels of the James Cancer Center where I was scanned, examined, questioned, x-rayed, MRIed, and bloodletted. Justin and Eric, looking tense and pale, were waiting in my room when we returned. Per my request, they'd hung a wide circle of white paper on the wall with the words "Healing Circle" in blue marker. I planned to have all my caregivers sign their names, in the hope that this connection might make them more careful with me.

The first hospital employee to enter my room was an elderly, stooped black man pushing a mop.

"Would you like to sign my Healing Circle?" I asked him.

His brow knit with confusion, as if my noticing him at all, let alone speaking to him, was most unorthodox.

"I'm going to have everyone who takes care of me sign it. I'd like you to be the first."

He propped his mop in its mobile bucket, took the pen that Justin offered and wrote, "Otis Johnston" in tiny script at the very bottom of the circle.

"Thanks so much. I really appreciate your help," I said.

"It's about time someone wanted to know my name," Otis said.

I thought of all the times that I'd tried to explain to hospital administrators how the treatment of every employee, from the top to the bottom of the organizational ladder, impacts the creation of a healing milieu. If I ever got back to work, I vowed, I'd do whatever I could to help hospitals make people like Otis feel acknowledged.

Val and Barb showed up and, at my insistence, Eric and Justin drove back to Ann Arbor. A radiologist with hair like steel wool bustled into the room to evaluate me for intra-operative radiation. He peered into my mouth and immediately declared, "Oh no, you aren't a candidate for our procedure. It won't work on a tumor the size and location of that one."

I thought I was as afraid as I could get, but his words injected me with even more terror. Not only did his pronouncement confirm that the tumor was really nasty, but also that I faced weeks of radiation, with its horrible side effects, after recovering from the surgery. Had I known that I wouldn't qualify for intra-operative radiation, I might have searched beyond Lambe to find a doctor at U of M so I didn't have to drag everyone to Columbus. But it was too late now. I'd never been so scared and depressed. Picking a hospital had been one of the biggest decisions of my life, and I'd blown it. Now shame compounded my fears about whether I'd make it through this surgery and what would be left of me if I did.

§

Early Tuesday morning, I was awakened by a flurry of activity. It took a moment to register where I was and what I was doing there. Jeff, Barb, and Val chatted nervously as they trailed alongside my gurney. The only comfort I felt came from their presence, so I convinced the nurse to let them all into the preoperative area. I noticed that the patient parked beside me had a bigger crowd of well-wishers than I did. What was this, junior high? Even in the face of disfigurement and possible death, I wanted to be popular.

After somber farewells to Val and Barb, I kissed Jeff good-bye. I would have kissed him longer and better if I'd known I would never again be able to kiss him properly.

The anesthesiologist started the IV drip, and I took a groggy ride to the operating room, which was very bright, the way I pictured the tunnels in those near-death experiences. I heard distant voices, smelled antiseptics that reminded me of nursing school. And then I faded away.

§

I cannot breathe. I cannot breathe.

I cannot talk or move to tell anyone that I cannot breathe.

Everything is blurry.

Why are those tall metal shelves full of supplies towering above me? They could topple over on me.

Where am I?

I have to let someone know that I cannot breathe.

Gagging, I try to force an audible grunt. I can see people in the distance. *HELP! HELP!* The words form in my head, but I cannot get them out.

I cannot breathe.

Finally, a nurse notices my writhing and comes to my bedside. "Don't worry," she says. "This machine is breathing for you. Just relax." She disappears.

I still can't breathe. What machine is she talking about? What if it isn't working? It doesn't feel like I'm breathing.

Suddenly, there are people all around me. A male voice is calling my name. "Terri, Terri! Can you hear me? The operation failed. We have to take you back to surgery." Somewhere in my fuzzy consciousness floats the question: how long can a person survive under anesthesia? More anesthetic washes this question away, along with my foggy awareness, as I'm whisked back to the operating room.

§

Again, I woke up, and again, I could not breathe. I assumed I was back in the ICU, although I was not lucid enough to be sure.

There's my sister. Barb. And Jeff. Is that my brother? This guy looks like my brother-in-law, Peter. What are Bill and Peter doing here? They weren't supposed to come for days. This can't be good.

My parents drift by as if on a surrealistic conveyor belt like those moving walkways in airports. Numb horror freezes my mother's face. *Mom and Dad weren't planning to visit so soon. Is this the chaplain? He looks like Ichabod Crane. Is he talking about dying?*

§

It was several days before I heard the stories and began to understand what had happened while I was outside awareness.

After seeing me off to the operating room, Jeff had joined Barb and Val in the "surgical waiting area," which was actually just the lobby of the James Cancer Center. My team sat, benched in silence. Val stitched her current project, Barb addressed Christmas cards, and Jeff stared at his book or straight ahead, seeing nothing. Occasionally, one of them wondered out loud why my surgery was taking so long.

About six hours later, a woman in scrubs appeared, called Jeff's name, and said, as if announcing a business meeting, "Dr. Prescott needs to talk to you. Please pick up the white phone."

Jeff, his stomach careening, lifted the receiver to hear Dr. Prescott's voice saying, "The cancer was even more advanced than we anticipated. We just removed a tumor the size of a golf ball. I need your consent to be more aggressive than we had planned. There is a good chance that the cancer has infiltrated her jawbone and if we don't remove that bone, it will kill your wife. Do I have your permission for more radical surgery?"

Jeff sat motionless, numb, imagining me wide open on the operating table while he pondered the options and my future. When Val could no longer tolerate not understanding the horror flashing across Jeff's face, she grabbed the phone out of his hand. Dr. Prescott repeated the questions with growing urgency. Could he remove more than half of my lower jaw? Could he remove the floor of my mouth on the left side? What about the lymph nodes all down my neck? Val shoved the phone back at Jeff and said, "Just say yes."

Jeff knew that there was no choice, but paused under the weight of a decision that would dramatically alter the rest of my life. "Okay, go ahead," he said and collapsed back into his chair.

"How the shit did Watson miss a tumor the size of a golf ball?" Jeff blurted to no one in particular. We would all have that question, but it was never answered.

Val recalled how sometimes, when Mom was upset, she'd say, "You kids are making me so nervous I have a lump in my throat the size of a golf ball."

They debated whether to share that description with me and decided to defer telling me for the foreseeable future. By the time I heard the phrase, I was incredulous but too busy trying to stay alive to have much reaction.

My crew knew it would take a while for Dr. Prescott to remove all those body parts and for Dr. Gilbert to create a flap. From where they sat, they could see cancer patients with IV poles huddled against the biting cold outside, smoking. They took turns getting tasteless food from the cafeteria.

At 10:00 p.m., Jeff could no longer stand the silence. He called the operating room. "She's still in surgery," was all that he learned. Midnight came and went. No one even thought of sleeping.

At 3:00 a.m., twenty hours after it had started, Dr. Gilbert arrived to say that the operation was over. "We finally got the free-flap to work," he said. "It took seven attempts. We replaced more than half of her lower jaw with the iliac crest of her left hip and rebuilt her mouth with tissue and vessels from the hip area."

"Why did it take so many attempts?" Val asked.

"The vessels were the problem," the doctor sounded apologetic. "We kept attaching the veins and arteries, and then they would collapse. We ended up having to take vessels from her left ankle after the ones from her hip failed. But it all seems to be working now, and she's in the ICU. Do you want to see her?"

The central feature in all descriptions of what I looked like was the size of my head. Val said that it had inflated to twice its normal size, due to all the IV fluid I'd taken on during surgery. Then there was the "hole in my throat" for the ventilator. And the myriad tubes and monitors.

Jeff recoiled when he saw me. He later said that he flashed back to the radiant, sexy woman he had met less than five years before. Now repulsed, he had to force himself to look at me. His stolen glimpses convinced him that I would certainly die. Barb's nursing background brought her to a similar conclusion. She was struck by the glassiness of my eyes. Val said she saw terror in those eyes and felt it in my viselike grip on her arm.

Stunned and spent, Jeff nevertheless manned the ICU waiting room, while Val and Barb went back to the hotel for a brief rest. A few hours later, they returned to relieve him. During the changing of the guard, Mom, Dad, and my brother Bill arrived. They *had* arrived sooner than planned because of my condition. Jeff left for the Residence Inn, and the rest of my family went to lunch, leaving Barb as the waiting room point person.

Minutes into Barb's watch, Dr. Gilbert rushed into the waiting room, looking for Jeff. "I have to talk to him. The vessels in the free-flap have collapsed again. I need his permission to do the pectoralis flap."

The red light was blinking on the hotel phone when Jeff walked into the room. Once again, he had to choose for me between further disfigurement and dysfunction or death. And, once again, all he could say was, "Yeah, go ahead." With a longing glance at the bed, Jeff turned and drove back to the hospital.

Meanwhile at the restaurant, Val was trying to prepare our parents for what I looked like, so they wouldn't keel over at the sight. In the process, she began to cry. It was the first time our family had seen her cry since Greg died.

Barb stayed in the hospital lobby, rehearsing how she was going to tell my family about my return to surgery. She remembered a conversation I had had with her recently, during which I'd told her that I wasn't sure I wanted to live if I couldn't talk. In tears, she prayed that if, as she now suspected, I was not to speak again, I would die during this operation rather than linger in speechless agony.

"Terri is back in surgery," she said to my returning clan. Bill burst out sobbing and ran to the men's room. Val pressed for details. My parents looked on helplessly.

The second operation, the pectoralis flap that I could have had back in Ann Arbor, lasted for four hours. Dr. Gilbert took tissue from my left breast, chest, and neck, somehow pulled it up into my mouth with the vessels still attached to their original location and wrapped it around a jaw-shaped titanium bar which had been screwed onto my remaining jawbone. Then I was returned to the ICU.

Over time, I have come to understand most of the fuzzy perceptions I had during my five days in ICU. I had felt as if I couldn't breathe because I was on a ventilator, which no one had thought to tell me about beforehand. The activity I sensed to my right was focused on the popular patient I had seen in the preoperative area. She died, which explained why she was getting so much attention. It had been horror on my mother's face. And the hospital chaplain had, in fact, paid a call to talk to me about death. I never did find out if he looked like Ichabod Crane.

Later, people asked me if I thought I was going to die during my time in the hospital. I never knew how to answer them. I did feel disconnected from life as I'd known it. And if I'd been able to step back and evaluate my situation, I would have seen that death was a very real possibility. There were many moments when I couldn't imagine how I'd ever leave the hospital alive. But most of the time, clenched as I was in the cold, tinny embrace of medical technology, my senses dulled by chemicals, it was all I could do to get over the mountain of one minute and get ready to climb the next.

By Sunday, December 20, five days after the surgery, I was off the ventilator and ready to be moved to the head and neck cancer unit. I had an IV in each hand, a catheter draining urine, a nasogastric tube for feeding, oxygen piped into my nostrils, a tracheotomy at the base of my throat, and five chest tubes draining from the incision sites into a big bottle on the floor. The nurse who admitted me to the unit said, "I've never seen anyone with so many chest tubes." Surgical staples marched along the entire left side of my body, from mouth to ankle.

Settling into room 933, I saw through blurred vision that Val had covered all the mirrors in my room with pictures, affirmations, and get-well cards. Even the shiny paper towel dispenser was covered. My Healing Circle hung in the corner with several signatures surrounding Otis's.

Val directed my intermittent attention to the decorations that brightened the otherwise drab room. She had thought of everything. A miniature gold tree bearing blue lights violated the hospital's policy of no Christmas lights, flaunting Michigan's colors deep in Ohio State territory. On a shelf near my bed, Val had placed big pictures of Jeff and our boys. My kids had hung handmade signs reminding me to breathe on the walls and ceiling. Flash cards were neatly stacked on the bedside stand. On them, Val had printed commonly used phrases like "I love you," "Raise my bed," and "More drugs, please."

Also included in Val's guided tour were two floral arrangements— artificial, because the fragile immune systems of patients at the James Cancer Center couldn't tolerate the real thing. Val named the friends who had sent the first bouquet and then hesitated. Even in my stupor, I could sense her squirming as she said, "These are from Dr. Watson. The card says, 'Wishing you all the best.'" With IV-encumbered hand gestures, I signaled Val to get those flowers out of my room.

I attempted to settle into my new surroundings. Lying on my back with the head of the bed elevated was my only option due to the multiple tubes that tethered me. I felt like Mr. Duffy who, according to James Joyce, "lived a short distance from his body." None of it seemed to belong to me anymore. I was connected to my body only by pain and the inability to find a comfortable position.

My mouth was a swollen mass of sutures. I could barely open it; the tracheotomy precluded talking. My thinking and vision were too cloudy for writing, and I couldn't sit up to reach my flash cards, so I needed someone with me all the time.

Val and other visitors covered the day shift. Jeff valiantly suppressed his loathing of hospitals enough to spend every night huddled on the floor of my room on a thin, egg-crate-foam mattress. Each evening before "bedtime" (as if I had any other kind of time), Jeff helped the nurse position me with piles of pillows, then retired to his corner. We tried to grab minutes of sleep between intrusions but had to stay on guard to stop aides from sticking thermometers into my mouth and to keep my IV from running dry. The respiratory therapist decided that 2:00 a.m. was the ideal time to change the oxygen tank. Sometimes, even when no one else was bothering us, I would grunt for Jeff's attention just to be sure he could hear me. He responded with a gruff "What?" and then I pantomimed realigning my pillows or getting a pain shot.

If we did manage to drift off to sleep, we had to wake ourselves up before 5:30. Otherwise, the clamoring herd of doctors on rounds would startle us awake. The chief resident, Dr. Wilson, whom Val had nicknamed "Dr. Loud," led the pack.

"How are you doing?" he bellowed that first morning as he proceeded to rip off covers and bandages to answer his own question. Even if I could have talked, I would have been stunned into silence by his brusque approach.

Dr. Loud pointed out various interesting features of my revised anatomy to his protégés, and then they exited as rapidly and noisily as they had appeared.

Sleep was impossible after Dr. Loud and his entourage left. The lab technician drew my blood. Then the daytime nursing staff trickled in to repeat everything that had been done on the midnight shift and then some. My temperature, pulse, and respirations had to be measured regularly. Five times each day, a nurse uncorked the brown rubber tube hanging from my nose and poured Ensure down it for my dining pleasure. And my tracheotomy needed suctioning several times a day. This was the most physically painful process of the whole ordeal. A nurse would insert a tube in the hole in my throat and command me to "cough" to bring up any postoperative gunk lurking in my lungs. The searing agony of the procedure never failed to remind me of that poor trach patient back in nursing school and to make me wish I had given him more drugs.

At some point each morning, I had to be "bathed," which meant that someone ran a wet washcloth over the few areas of my skin that had not been stitched, stapled, or punctured.

I was even less enthusiastic about the next activity on my agenda—getting weighed. It took three people to prop my fluid-bloated body and its accoutrements onto the scale long enough to determine that I was still twelve pounds heavier than I was before surgery.

I hated being at the mercy of the hospital's inexorable routine. And I still felt awkward being so dependent. I was the helper, the nurse, trained and experienced in putting the needs of others before my own. Even with all the practice I'd now had, the loss of identity and control that went with being the helpee rankled me. It was bad enough to have to rely on hospital staff. At least they were getting paid.

Being a burden on my husband came with a price of a different sort. After we'd been there a week, Jeff started to grow surly. He was slow to answer my requests and eagerly watched the door for his replacement at the end of his shift. I was hurt that he was in such a hurry to leave.

Even as I began to be able to write what I needed, I was still terrified to be by myself. And even with constant company, I felt deeply alone.

§

Visitors came from all over. Many of them said, "You don't look as bad as I thought you would." Always a sucker for flattery, I was consoled by this. Although my appearance was a low priority, I thought that looking better than expected might mean I could surprise people by surviving as well.

The passage of time was meaningless. My life was measured in the space between pain shots. I was learning to love the morphine derivative Roxicet, which, according to the *Physician's Desk Reference,* claims "euphoria" as a side effect. Euphoria was elusive, but the medication offered me brief respites from pain and fear. Tempting as it was to ride the high and drift off into another world, my earthly moorings felt too tenuous to risk letting go. And there were a lot of down-to-earth activities on my agenda such as twice daily "ambulation."

"Come on dear, let's walk!" By the time the nurse had disconnected my tubes, hooked my IV to the walker and the catheter bag to my leg, and put on my slippers and robe, I was ready to go back to bed.

I hunched over the walker, gripping its metal frame with blanched knuckles. With the physical therapist on my left arm and Jeff on the right, I slowly pushed one foot in front of the other, tentatively testing my iliac-crest-free left hip. Eric and Justin often led the cheering section, with backup provided by miscellaneous staff: "Way to go, Mom." "Nice work, Terri." When I made it all the way around the nursing station, a distance of at least forty feet, I got accolades worthy of Diana Nyad when she swam around Manhattan.

These outings increased in frequency, but I still spent most of my time in bed or, when coerced, sitting up in a chair. The pain was diminishing a little, but getting comfortable in my body was a relentless challenge. When my mouth wasn't producing disgusting surgical residue, it was horribly dry. I had never imagined thirst so profound. The hospital's solution to this problem, lemon glycerin swabs, provided very temporary relief and a lingering pseudocitrus taste. I was thrilled when a nurse finally allowed me a few ice chips, although they came with a warning. "Be careful that you don't swallow these. You could choke, you know."

I had no control over my remodeled mouth. How could I keep from swallowing? But the cool drip of that first melting ice chip down my parched throat was worth the risk. I sucked ice every chance I got. Even so, my throat was increasingly sore. The doctors didn't seem concerned, saying the nasogastric tube could be causing irritation. I was convinced that they had overlooked a rampant case of throat cancer and none of my efforts to get well would matter in the long run.

The doctors were similarly unimpressed with the fact that my eyesight wasn't improving. "Blurred vision" was high on my list of complaints to Dr. Loud for several mornings before he responded. Finally he shipped me over to the ophthalmology clinic where I was diagnosed with a "glaucoma-like" malady that the doctor there assured me was unrelated to my current condition and could be rectified with a "little laser surgery."

My inner screecher let loose, *What do you mean a "little surgery"? No one is shooting any goddamned lasers into my eyes!* I scrawled, "Get me out of here," to Val and Jeff on my spiral pad.

Later that day, Val began loading my medical appendages and me into a wheelchair and pushing us down the hall as if we were late for an important meeting. I signaled for my notebook and wrote, "What day is it and where are we going?"

"It's Christmas Eve, and we're going to the lobby to see my kids. They're too young to come up to the unit." I dreaded my nieces' and nephew's reaction to my appearance, but Val was on a mission, so there was no turning back.

The sterile lobby of the James Cancer Center left a lot to be desired as the setting for a cozy family Christmas gathering. Instead of carols, we heard, "Paging Dr. Sullivan. Dr. Daniel Sullivan, call the ICU STAT." And in lieu of the bustle of holiday shoppers, we were surrounded by the contagious despair of people rushing to see loved ones in various stages of cancer hell.

Apparently, Val had prepared her kids because there wasn't any obvious flinching. My nieces Kaitlyn and Kendall managed tentative embraces, tubes and all. Seven-year-old Ben scurried over for a quick hug and then returned to his mother and whispered, "Auntie's in there," with relief. Given the circumstances and lacking my usual contributions, the conversation was stilted. After one especially long silence, Val prompted Kait to hand me a Federal Express envelope. I had noticed the envelope and thought it typical of Val to have some major business deal pending on Christmas Eve. The package was addressed to her and it was from Harry Smith. Why, I wondered, would Val give me a present she got from her most renowned friend?

Peeking into the envelope, all I could see was plastic bubble wrap. My family knew how I loved to pop that stuff, so I figured that might be the gift. Closer inspection revealed the real present, a CD, *Christmas Eve with Johnny Mathis*. I looked up, smiling as well as I could. Johnny had been my idol since I was fourteen. Val said, "There's more."

Further digging unearthed an off-white envelope, with "For Terri" written on it. The words "Johnny" and "Mathis" were embossed in bold letters on the stationery. The message, handwritten in brown ink, was out of focus for me, so I handed the note to Kait, who read:

For Terri—
Sorry to hear that you are not feeling well. My biggest wish for this holiday season is for you to hurry and get better! You're in my thoughts.

Luv, John

A slow tear rolled down my cheek and got absorbed by a bandage. I grunted and groaned in gratitude. I tried to say "Thank You" with my eyes, but in case it wasn't working, I wrote a note of thanks to Val. Then I scribbled a message to Jeff, begging him to go out into the bitter Ohio night in search of an appliance store that hadn't closed early on Christmas Eve. He returned triumphant with the last portable CD player Radio Shack had in stock.

Back in room 933, I had an elegant Ensure dinner via my NG tube. Jeff pushed my bed over by the window so I could see the hazy but colorful lights of downtown Columbus. I ordered a shot of Roxicet. Jeff sat closer to my bed than usual and reached through the side rail to hold my hand as we listened to my new best friend sing "We Need a Little Christmas."

get me out of here

t 4:00 a.m. on Christmas morning, Nancy, a lithe, effervescent RN who accomplished more in an hour than most of her colleagues did in a shift, bounded into my room. If the James Cancer Center had a cheerleading squad, she would be its captain. In spite of my usual disdain for this level of exuberance, I had come to like Nancy ever since the night she'd put Jeff in bed with me.

"You know, honey," she said to him as I struggled to get comfortable for sleep one night early in my stay, "I was in the hospital recently, and my boyfriend crawled right into bed with me."

Jeff's aversion to cuddling was vastly intensified by the thought of snuggling up to my tubes, bottles, and wounds. He tried to inch away, but Nancy corralled him, putting her arms around his not insignificant body and forcefully coaxing him onto the bed, where she positioned us for maximal skin-to-skin contact. I wished he'd been more enthusiastic, but I appreciated his willingness to stay with me anyway. The warmth of his body made me feel safer than I'd felt in the hospital, and I managed to get my first decent night's sleep.

Early on Christmas morning, Nancy decided to shampoo my hair as a Christmas present. I was filled with dread at the thought of dragging my puffed-up body with its unwieldy attachments to the sink at that ungodly hour. I'd also almost forgotten that I had hair. But I didn't want to offend my best nurse, so I allowed myself to be painfully draped over the sink while Nancy zealously scrubbed my scalp.

"I want to finish my work so I can go home and play Santa before my daughter wakes up," she said, smoothing strawberry-scented suds away from my eyes. I envied her, remembering how much I had loved creating gala displays of Christmas presents for my kids.

Nancy propped me up in bed and surveyed her handiwork. "You look great!" she enthused. "Your Christmas guests will be so surprised." She was one of many who would say that I looked great, and though I hadn't seen myself, I didn't believe any of them.

Val and Jeff came by. Val was anxious to get back to the Residence Inn, where she was preparing a traditional holiday feast in a kitchen suitable for making microwave popcorn. Her kids had been less than thrilled about transporting Christmas to Columbus, but Val was firm. "When you're grown up," she told them, "all the other Christmases will blur together. But you will always remember this one."

Justin and Eric arrived before Val left. The kids had planned to take in a movie that afternoon, but Val informed them that they were on mom duty. Eric gave me a beautiful stuffed angel that he hung over my bed to provide protection. Justin had written me a poem, "Ode to Mom," which moved me as much as I could be moved. My physical deficits left little room for emotion.

Grim as my condition was, I did my best to make it less devastating for them. I wrote upbeat notes on my slate asking about their friends and their drive from Ann Arbor. I insisted they leave during my dressing change. By the time they came back to my room, I was exhausted and woozy on Roxicet. Justin put on my new Johnny Mathis CD, and they played Scrabble while I floated in and out, riding on the music. Being with my kids, Johnny, and the painkillers made for a better than expected Christmas.

On December 26, one of Jeff's five sisters and her husband arrived from Iowa. Later, she'd describe how, even though my body was mangled, "your eyes reached out to us, and your spirit seemed to grab onto us." What with all the attention focused on my body, I had very little sense of my spirit while I was in the hospital. It felt as if God, Jesus, and my soul had all deserted me. I was desperate to latch on to the life force of those around me and let it pull me through.

The next day, a nurse's aide announced that I had special guests. With great fanfare, Barb and my friend and client Doris England, VP at Children's Hospital, marched into my room sporting white nurse's uniforms and caps, singing Christmas carols, and bearing balloons, gifts, and decorated bedpans. Barb and Doris asked how they could help, and I asked them to shave my legs and armpits. As they very carefully shaved around sutures and tubes, I jotted on my pad, "I'm getting some pretty expensive nursing care."

"You deserve it," Doris said.

"Yes you do," added Barb. "You make even this feel like a party."

That afternoon I was resting after all that activity when a woman in a white lab coat came in and pulled up a chair. "Hi. I'm Kim, a clinical nurse specialist." Jeff closed his book, jumped up, and eagerly excused himself, "so you and Kim can talk."

"How are you feeling?" Kim asked in a quiet, even tone.

Uncertain as to what kind of feelings she was fishing for, I wrote, "I'm okay, all things considered."

"How are you dealing with all of this? You've been through quite a bit," she said. "It would be normal for you to feel a little depressed." Kim was the first and would be the last health-care provider to ask about my feelings. I was very grateful but wasn't ready to explore them with a stranger when I couldn't talk. I would have liked for her to just sit with me and let me write what I could about my emotions. Instead, she talked for me.

"Your surgery is going to affect your appearance and your body image, as well as your ability to eat and to talk. Maybe even your work," she added. "What kind of work did you do?"

Frightened by her use of the past tense, I printed, "Therapist, hypnotherapist, workshops, speaker."

"Oh, my goodness," she said, thumbing nervously through my record. "Then I guess this *will* have an impact on your career. You're probably concerned about supporting yourself." Apparently, Kim was attempting to mirror my deepest fears so I'd know they were normal. I appreciated her concern. And I wanted to strangle her with my tubing.

I scribbled, "I'm trying not to think about that right now."

"Oh, that's a good idea," she said, gathering her papers and backing out the door. "I'll come back later." I never saw her again.

While I had been trying not to think about my career if I were to survive, worry was always lurking; the fact that I couldn't talk had not silenced the vile voice in my head. The well-meaning nurse had also catapulted financial concerns to the front of my mind. I knew Jeff would help all he could, but he didn't make enough to support us both when he devoted himself to his practice. Now his full-time job was caring for me. Like a dog with a chew toy, I wrestled with visions of fiscal ruin. But no one was asking me to pay any bills today. I needed to get well first.

Where was Jeff? I wanted him to come back and settle me down. He would say, "Don't worry about money. We've always been fine, and we'll always be fine." His reassurance still meant more than my own. I watched the door for him with increasing agitation. My fear of disaster began to generalize beyond money. I checked all my body parts and attached equipment. Sure enough, one of my IV bottles was almost empty. Nursing school had taught me that air bubbles in veins kill people.

I pushed the call button. After a few moments, a female voice said, "Can I help you?"

I tried to say "Nurse."

"Can I help you?" the voice repeated, less cordially.

I made another attempt, which still came out "nnuuh."

"What did you say?"

I went for "Help," which sounded like "eeuhll."

"I can't understand you," the woman said.

I screamed at her in my head and then gave up on trying. Wouldn't you think they'd be used to people with imperfect diction on a head and neck cancer unit?

When at last Jeff returned, I wrote him an angry note about my suffering in his absence. I felt a little nasty taking it out on him, but who else was I going to blame? He grimaced, looking guilty and resentful at the same time. "Hold on," he said gruffly, "I'll get the nurse."

Since my condition was improving, I had begun to feel that I should ask less of him. But now it was clear that my claim of needing constant supervision had been vindicated, and there weren't a lot of other volunteers. I knew I'd be deeply indebted to him when this was over but decided I'd make it up to him if the time came. Whatever was going on beneath the surface, we agreed that it wasn't safe for me to be there alone, and Jeff agreed to stay.

Except for protecting my kids, I was utterly and necessarily self-absorbed throughout my hospitalization. I spent my energy seeking a comfortable position on scratchy sheets, performing the endless required routines, and attempting to wedge an optimistic thought or two between my mental horrors.

Luckily, others were having positive thoughts for me. Cards and letters arrived every day—one aide said she'd never seen a patient get so much mail. Some were from people I didn't know, conveying prayers, affirmations, and healing energy. All the major religions were invoked; deities and gurus I'd never heard of were solicited on my behalf. I didn't know it then, but a significant body of research has shown that patients benefit from long-distance prayer. The patient doesn't need to know about it, and the type of prayer doesn't matter. Even without scientific proof of their efficacy, I was grateful for the prayers.

I usually turned to God and Jesus in tight spots, but my faith was hard to access while I was in the hospital. It felt like getting well was up to me, and I wasn't sure I was up to the job. I remembered hearing a guru say that we humans can only see 5 percent of what is really going on in the universe. The fraction of reality that I could see was making me wonder what God was up to. Jeff assured me that it would take years for any of this to make sense, so I postponed trying to figure it out.

By December 27, most of the equipment had been removed from my body. The chest tubes were gone, I was down to one IV, and I was peeing on my own. The nurses still suctioned my tracheotomy, but my "blowhole," as Val called it, was starting to heal, and I could breathe better through my mouth. The doctors were encouraging me to talk. Easy for them to say! Speaking involved holding a gauze pad over the blowhole, which felt really creepy. Over time, their urgings and my difficulty communicating in writing won me over. My first spoken word was "Roxicet."

I still had the nasogastric tube in my nose, and my throat was very sore. I cherished ice chips, which provided fleeting relief to my parched mouth. I'd also begun to lust for wilder pleasures. I dreamed of tuna fish sandwiches like the ones at Schettler's drug store and iced tea. As a little girl, I sometimes got to go with Mom to her doctor's appointments in the beautiful Fisher Building, and afterward we ate at the counter at Schettler's. It was just the two of us so those were very special times. Despite the current assault on my senses, I could almost conjure the smell of that tuna. I didn't believe Dr. Loud when he assured me that, eventually, I would be able to eat many foods. "Well, you may not be able to eat steak," he said, chortling with his cohorts as if the idea of me eating steak was terribly amusing, "but you should be able to handle most other stuff."

My ambulation was progressing nicely, and now it was time to relearn walking up and down stairs with my amended anatomy. I regretted how much I used to take my body for granted. I had always "lived in my head" and treated my body as if its only purpose was to keep my brain from dragging on the sidewalk. It scared me to realize how little control my mind currently had over its carrying case. I grudgingly cooperated and practiced basic stair climbing on the three wooden steps the bubbly physical therapist provided, feeling like a toddler doing it for the first time.

These signs of progress meant I was inching my way toward discharge, but my excitement about being released was diminished by the way I felt. I was so weak and tired, and my body so fragile and so "other." How could I make my body cooperate in the real world? Also, there was a problem under my chin.

One morning before Christmas, Pat, the plump, redheaded nurse who cared for me most often, had been conducting her rapid routine inspection of my wounds. Midway through scanning the incision under my chin, she paused—the same way Watson had paused when he discovered the lump in my mouth. I held my breath, waiting for her to explain the problem, but she left hurriedly, and I exhaled.

Later that day, Dr. Loud paid me an unexpected visit. His attention went immediately to the area Pat had surveyed so carefully. He too went silent. Then Pat returned bearing a megadose of antibiotics. "It's a good thing I found that infection. The doctors must have missed it. You could have been in big trouble if it went untreated much longer."

Apparently, big trouble was still a possibility. The infection lingered for several days. I wondered how my poor body would defend itself against this complication with all the other work it had to do. The doctors kept asking me if I could taste the medication they were applying externally. That would mean I had a hole in my chin, which went through to my mouth, and all the reconstruction in my mouth was in jeopardy. They looked worried when I wrote, "All kinds of weird tastes in there—metallic, bitter—I don't know." Three times each day, a doctor or nurse cleaned and medicated the wound, then repacked the opening with Betadine-soaked gauze. I held my breath each time, in part because it hurt like hell, but more because I was so afraid of what they might see.

Thank God I couldn't see the wound! I found the whole business unspeakably gross, which intensified my estrangement from my body.

One morning two weeks after my admission to the James Cancer Center, Dr. Loud completed the dressing change and said, "The wound is looking a little better. Pretty soon, you won't need hospital care for it, but you'll need to learn to change the dressings yourself. The nurse will be in to teach you how to do it."

My eyes bulged, and I grabbed for my notebook so fast the pages fluttered like the wings of a hummingbird.

"Are you KIDDING me?" I scribbled, "NO WAY I am going to look at that disgusting mess, much less touch it! I have to stay here til it heals."

A girl can dream. Given the trend toward drive-through health care, staying in the hospital long enough for the wound to heal was not an option. How ironic to get kicked out with an infection that was probably caused by the germs that run rampant through the place, many of which are resistant to antibiotics thanks to the overuse of those drugs. I'm glad that I wasn't aware then that hospital-acquired infections are a leading cause of death in the United States.

Alternatives were discussed: home health aides, visiting nurses, schlepping me to an outpatient clinic. None of these seemed practical because the dressing needed to be changed at least twice a day.

"Perhaps your husband could do it," Dr. Loud suggested.

Jeff stared blankly at Dr. Loud while the rest of us looked at him expectantly. It would take many years for him to be able to tell me what had gone through his mind: *I didn't sign up for this. We were supposed to have fun. I thought she was strong and I could rely on her. This is too disgusting! I don't want to look at that hideous hole in her chin. I hate hospitals, and I hate this whole mess. Get me the hell out of here.* As much as he wanted to run, he knew that he would feel worse if he did. Taking a step closer to me, he said, "I guess I could try."

I knew this was a huge sacrifice. Would I be as noble if our roles were reversed? Jeff overcame revulsion and nausea and became a student of dressing changing. Thanks to him, I was a step closer to going home. No matter how angry I got with him after that, the picture of him leaning over my chin with tweezers and a serious expression filled me with forgiveness.

Jeff and I were up early on the morning of December 29, our first wedding anniversary. Dr. Loud woke us up saying, "Terri, you're going to have to learn to eat unless you want to go home with the NG tube. We'll bring you a breakfast tray of clear liquids and see how you do. When you can eat on your own, we'll take out the tube."

While the prospect of eating was extremely appealing, the thought of getting food past the hazards in my mouth and the tube in my throat was terrifying. A friendly dietitian appeared with a booklet, *Learning to Eat after Surgery.* The manual warned: "Be very careful to avoid aspirating food or liquids into your lungs because your epiglottis, which usually prevents such aspiration, has been removed." Without control over what happened in my mouth, how on earth could I make liquids roll down my throat and into my stomach instead of down my trachea into my lungs? The book suggested several techniques, which all appeared impossible. Death through aspiration seemed a certainty.

My breakfast tray arrived bearing Ensure, Coke, grape juice, and horrible-smelling coffee. Nurse Pat demonstrated how I was supposed to "eat." She attached an eight-inch long, skinny red rubber tube to the tip of a 60 cc syringe. "You suction the fluid into the syringe," she explained. "Place the end of the tube on the back of your tongue on the right side, push the plunger, and squirt a few drops down your throat."

I gave her a look intended to say, "Are you crazy?" She was giving me instructions for suicide. Hadn't she read the booklet? And didn't she know that my tongue only had a right side?

"Here," she continued in her no-nonsense tone, as she handed me the syringe containing a thimble-sized dose of Coke. "Try it." Jeff looked on, mouth agape.

With trembling hands, I took the syringe and attempted to direct the serpentine tube to the proper spot. I inserted. I squirted. I coughed. I choked. I gagged. Jeff leapt up and pounded me on the back. I quit.

"Come on, you have to do this," Pat said. "You'll get the hang of it. Keep practicing. I'll be back in a few minutes to see how you're doing."

Jeff looked about as enthusiastic for this project as I felt. I wrote him a note: "I hope we'll have better anniversaries." He nodded, pulled his chair closer to my over-the-bed table and said, "Okay, let's give it a try." I sat up in bed and grabbed the syringe. Coke dribbled from its tip, and I let a few drops fall onto my tongue. The taste was excitingly familiar. The wetness was divine. It trickled down my throat. I looked up smiling to see tears in Jeff's eyes. He cheered. The next effort ended in choking, but we persevered. When Pat returned, Jeff proudly told her that I had imbibed almost twenty-five cc's.

"Oh, that will never do," she said coolly. "You have to take in at least five hundred cc's per meal before we can pull the NG tube."

Now I was in tears. I had failed and would have to go home with the tube in my nose. Motioning for Pat to take the tray, I crawled back under the blankets in defeat.

An hour later, the dietitian returned to see how I had done with breakfast. Jeff described our paltry success and how intimidated I had been by the "no epiglottis" warning in the booklet she had given us.

"Oh," she said smiling broadly, "you don't have to worry about that. You still have your epiglottis. We just gave you that booklet because it comes the closest of any we have to fitting your situation."

Rage and relief competed for my limited emotional space. Knowing that my epiglottis was intact, I choked down almost two hundred cc's from my lunch tray. Dinner measured four hundred and thirty. Dr. Loud stopped in after dinner to check my progress.

"Well, what do you think? Are you ready for us to pull the tube? Of course, if we take it out and you don't eat enough, we'll have to put another one down."

The decision was too complicated for me. I hesitated. Apparently, Dr. Loud took my silence as assent. Before I could answer, he and his assistant were at my nose, clipping and yanking. I felt the tube scraping against my insides as they yanked—like they were pulling a plunger out of my throat. I gagged, feeling like I might vomit. But then, fresh air rushed through my nostrils unfettered for the first time in over two weeks. I had never known such freedom. *Maybe God is here with me after all.* I promised Him that no matter what happened in my life, I would appreciate every unobstructed breath.

Over the next few hours, the rawness in my throat diminished, and I could swallow without pain. Maybe I didn't have throat cancer after all. As Jeff kissed me good night, I was flush with gratitude for the way he'd stood by me. While we both harbored plenty of feelings that would have to be dealt with later, we had made it through one hell of a first year as husband and wife. It had not been such a bad anniversary after all.

§

"How'd you like to go home today?" Dr. Loud asked me on the second to the last day of 1992.

I nodded eagerly and muttered, "Eehhs."

Jeff hurried to tell my brother Bill to come get us in his van. He was there in a few hours, and the guys packed up my accumulated supplies, including seven thermometers, five bottles of Betadine, four emesis basins, twelve rolls of tape, and a lifetime supply of gauze squares. A long lifetime.

Jeff took down the decorations in my room, and I caught a hazy reflection of my misshapen face as I was wheeled past the mirror. I turned away, not at all ready to encounter my new look.

As Jeff pushed me through the hospital doors into the gray Columbus day, a frosty mist washed over my face, and I took huge, grateful breaths of the brisk air. Jeff and Bill lifted me onto the backseat and positioned me amid a pile of Ohio State University pillows. Looking out the window at the boring highway thrilled me. We pulled into a Burger King, and it felt fabulous to be just another all-American family at the drive-through window. Bill and Jeff wolfed down Whoppers, fries, Cokes, and coffee. I sucked vanilla milkshake through my syringe all the way to Toledo.

welcome home

ear God, I was glad to be home.

Jeff and Bill lifted me down from the van, and each took an arm as I slowly hobbled toward the house. Eric and Justin appeared at the front door, looking happy to see me, but not quite sure what to do with me now that I was there. In the foyer, I paused to absorb the sights, sounds, and smells of home. I couldn't be sure, but I seemed to be inhaling sawdust.

Standing in the front hall, I surveyed what looked like a construction site. Our Christmas tree rose from a sea of drop cloths, icicles of white paint hung from its boughs, and the whole scene was blanketed with sawdust.

"We went ahead with the loft," Jeff said, sounding like a little boy with a big surprise.

Before cancer, we'd been talking about finishing the loft over the living room so I'd have a special place to write. I had assumed that the project had been scrapped. But Jeff had secretly decided to proceed, perhaps to increase the odds that I would live to use it. Justin and Eric had been overseeing construction while we were in Columbus. I took a brief tour, doing my best to articulate my gratitude. I'd deal with healing amidst ongoing construction later.

I sucked up a Roxicet nightcap and reveled in my reunion with my bed.

It was great to wake up of my own accord, instead of to the invasion of Dr. Loud and his brigade. It was New Year's Eve; 1992 could not end too soon for me. When the year began, my biggest concern had been how well our new marriage would work. Now, here I was, only part way through the hell of treatment with no guarantee that it would keep me alive throughout 1993. Our marriage was the least of my problems.

I told myself to stop brooding. I'd made it back to my beautiful home. I needed to get busy getting well. My good friend Marge was coming from Louisville today. Since she was in medical school, she could give Jeff a reprieve in the patient care department.

Marge had been married to Michael's best friend, and the four of us logged a lot of great times. Marge and Elliot lived in Florida, and our visits there centered on the "ponies." Our husbands were convinced that, with sufficient beer-fueled analysis of the racing form, they could uncover the algorithm for winning at the track. Usually, after pulling an all-nighter, Michael and Elliot were still hard at work when Marge and I woke up. We all downed lots of coffee and headed for Hialeah. In the car, I picked horses in each race based on the names I liked and gave Michael twenty dollars to bet for me. Marge and I dropped the guys at the track and went shopping. It never sat well with the men when my horses out-won theirs.

When I was still devastated several months after Michael left, Marge, a big proponent of moving on, decided I needed to get away. She and another friend met me in New York for a long weekend. When Marge saw what a mess I was, she immediately arrived at a diagnosis: "What you need is to get laid!" Getting laid is Marge's solution to every problem, and she created a treatment plan in the form of a tall, mocha-skinned jazz-pianist social worker who entertained us during a champagne brunch in Hell's Kitchen. My friends vetted the amorous musician by searching his apartment until they found the DSM-III and were satisfied that he really was a social worker.

Marge, a petite, compact bundle of energy took charge the minute she arrived. Like all my other long-term friends, Marge had adjusted nicely to my new husband, so they teamed up and dove right in to changing my dressing. Jeff removed the bandages from the wound under my chin and the unhealed suture on my chest. Marge's eyes lit up, and she stuck her head in between his body and my surgical sites.

"Now, let's see what they've done here. Oh my God—this is amazing! I've never seen anything like this!" Marge peered under my chin. "What's going on with this infection site?" They chatted excitedly as they worked on my wounds.

I waved my arms and signaled for my notebook. I wrote, "STOP!" in giant letters. "Go somewhere else to talk this crap!"

Marge put clean bandages on me, and they hurried into the living room to discuss what a medical marvel I was.

The first day of 1993 held a number of firsts for me. Marge insisted on giving me a bath. The warm water soothed my desolate body, but I was nervous that it might wander into my wounds. Another impediment to relaxation was seeing my new naked body at close range for the first time. I had no desire to look at what was left of me: my left hip, which now bulged where my small waist had been, my stub of a left breast with its pigeon-toed nipple, and a highway of sutures traversing my left side. I tried to share Marge's awe at the surgical achievements but felt only revulsion.

Soaking and surveying the extent of my losses, I was too numb to begin to grieve. I flashed back to nursing school, where I learned about the psychological impact of major surgery on body image. Fascinating theories, but I had way too much to deal with at the moment to apply them to myself. It would take decades for me to realize how lovely I had once been and to come to grips with the loss of my beautiful, symmetrical face and body. Now all I could do was motion for Marge to wash me so I could seek cover in the clean, pink nightgown that waited on the counter. Getting out of the tub, I caught a quick glimpse of my reflection in the large bathroom mirror. My left cheek looked like a chipmunk's, but my fuzzy vision kept me from discerning other details of my appearance, so I could postpone mourning my straight white teeth, full lips, and long, elegant neck. I was still scared about the problem with my eyes, but it was coming in handy.

Clean and exhausted, I was propped up in bed to watch my Michigan Wolverines play the Washington Huskies in the Rose Bowl. It felt great to be doing something normal, something that reminded me of my previous life. I had trouble believing that I had ever had the enthusiasm to be one of those screaming fans. Marge and Jeff retreated to the kitchen. Jeff was not a sports fan, and Marge was a recent refugee from her marriage to Elliot who, like Michael, was a sports-aholic. I didn't really mind. I had fun by myself.

During halftime, I granted myself an alcohol exception and sucked a Heineken through my syringe, savoring each bubble. My vision was clear enough to see a bad call in the fourth quarter, which deprived Michigan of a much-needed touchdown. Anger at a referee was a lot more fun than fear of death. Michigan won, and I took it as an omen. I made my maiden cane-free walk from the bedroom all the way to the kitchen for a postgame dinner with Marge, Justin, and Jeff. Eric had already returned to San Francisco. In my first attempt at eating without the syringe, I downed a tiny serving of Häagen-Dazs vanilla with a baby spoon. I went to bed triumphant on the first day of the new year.

The triumph was transitory. My recuperation fantasy had me lounging in bed in a silk gown between percale sheets, surrounded by flowers and blue Tiffany boxes, watching videos while others waited on me and anticipated my every need. The day-to-day business of recovery bore no resemblance to my vision.

I was surrounded by people spouting ideas on how to heal. "It's good for you to get up and move around." "Why don't you get dressed? That'll perk you up." "Do those exercises; they'll get your arm working again." "What you really need is some rest." "Time to do your mouth stretches." "Take your homeopathic remedies." "Listen to this hypnosis tape three times a day." "Watch this video on the nutritional causes of cancer."

"LEAVE ME ALONE!" I wanted to scream. Before cancer, I was doing well to floss once a week. Now I was supposed to be the queen of self-care. Many days I was too depressed to do anything beyond staying in bed feeling sorry for myself. I wanted to take Roxicet and enjoy the fleeting moment of euphoria, to stay up late and watch David Letterman, then sleep all day. I was deeply envious of the people making all the suggestions. I wanted to scream, "You're out there in the world looking gorgeous, earning money, eating in restaurants, cross-country skiing, biting into bagels, having sex, shopping, talking to friends. I'll never do any of that again. How the hell do you know what will make me feel better?"

It was as though I was a contestant in a cosmic round of *Let's Make a Deal.* Monty Hall described each book, diet, herb, pill, or crystal, touting every option while reminding me that only one door led to the grand prize of survival. Terrified of picking the wrong door, I tried to do it all. But I could never do enough to squelch the relentless nagging of the Vile Bitch Upstairs. Her "not-enoughness" message was nothing new, but it was intensified because the stakes were so high.

As far back as I could remember, and long before I named her, the toxic voice of the Vile Bitch dominated my mental airways. When I was a child, she hounded me with incessant demands to be a better daughter, a better student, a better piano player, a better Brownie, a better girl. The content varied, but the theme was clear. I was not enough.

As I got older and moved out into the world, the Bitch expanded her horizons. I'd never be the quality nurse she expected me to be. When I got divorced again and again, she had fodder to last a lifetime. *You are such a loser. You can't keep a husband to save your life. And look at what your antics have done to those kids.* She awoke before I did every morning and sat on the side of the bed, ready to pounce the moment I opened my eyes. Before I figured out what day it was, she had recounted all the things that needed worrying about that day. Once awake, I did everything I could to avoid her noxious litany. I stayed busy and surrounded myself with people. I kept my focus outside myself, caring for and attempting to "fix" others. Whenever I picked up a glass of wine, it was to shut her up. Now that my life was on the line, the pressure to please her was at an all-time high.

My list of "shoulds" far exceeded the time available. There were the mouth exercises: rolling a licorice whip around on my tongue in a particular pattern, doing tongue calisthenics, and opening my mouth as far as possible to bite on increasing numbers of tongue depressors for increasing lengths of time. These activities were intended to prevent my jaw from permanently closing up and my tongue from stiffening. Because of the pectoralis flap, my chest was a lot like that of a post-mastectomy patient. The doctors warned that if I wanted full use of my left arm, I had to pull strips of rubber sheeting as far as my arms could stretch, and I had to crawl my left arm painfully up the wall. Also, jumping on the miniature trampoline was good for my immune system.

When attempting to nap between activities, I was haunted by the mounting stack of books on healing beside my bed: *Love, Medicine and Miracles* by Bernie Siegel, *Heal Your Body* by Louise Hay, inspirational stories about cancer survivors, *Anatomy of an Illness* by Norman Cousins, *Getting Well Again* by O. Carl Simonton. Then there were the Bible and *A Course in Miracles* along with a host of other spiritual books and daily readers. Maybe I had lost touch with God, but I should at least read up on Him. Balanced on top of the books were the cassettes on beating cancer, preparing for radiation, as well as personalized post-op tapes from my hypnotherapist friend. I knew I ought to be using these things, or at least writing thank-you notes for them. Maybe I should write some healing affirmations. No, it was time to eat.

Eating took up most of my day. What to eat and how to eat it would prove one of the biggest challenges of life in my new body. By the time I left the hospital, the fluid retained during surgery had dissipated, and I weighed less than I had on admission. The doctors urged me to gain weight and strength in preparation for radiation, which was due to start in a few weeks and would further impair my eating ability. Back when I worried about dimpled thighs, I longed for permission to eat whatever I wanted. Now that my prayers had been answered, I realized I should have been more specific about the circumstances.

On a typical morning that January, I would drag myself out of bed around 9:00 a.m., put on my ancient red velveteen robe, and hobble to the kitchen in search of breakfast. At first the selections were limited to bland liquids that would pass through the syringe and tubing—juice, Ensure, or a milkshake of some kind. Then I added cooked cereal to my repertoire. Made milky enough, I could suck it up. I conducted periodic experiments in eating with a spoon, being careful not to disturb the delicate architecture of my new mouth. Because my tongue no longer worked to move food where it needed to be, I had to manually adjust the mush to get it into position for swallowing. Then I would squirt in some liquid to expedite the ride down. Toward the end of the month, I began the messy process of learning to drink from a cup. Soon all my nightgowns, T-shirts, and sweaters displayed colorful abstract retrospectives of recently consumed food and drink.

Regardless of the method of ingestion, breakfast took a couple of hours. I recorded every drop that actually made it to my mouth on my daily calorie chart. Often I returned to bed right after breakfast. Just as I was starting to get comfortable snuggling into my down pillows and comforter, it was time for lunch.

The hospital dietitian had advised loading up on protein to facilitate healing but said that getting the requisite 2,500 calories per day was more important than the type of food I chose. Even Marge, who was a health food zealot until medical school cured her of her interest in nutrition, told me to forgo food groups and concentrate on calories. So I might consider having some melted ice cream for lunch. Then I would recall what I'd read regarding nutritional theories of cancer causation: "White sugar feeds tumors." "The Institute for Cancer Research recommends that less than 20 percent of the daily diet come from fat." Jeff tried to interest me in carrot juice, reminding me of its purported benefits in the prevention of oral cancer, but the raw vegetables stung my sensitive mouth. Desperate, I would ignore the fat warning, squirt some Campbell's cream of celery, and call it lunch.

Friends brought real food, which I couldn't eat in its original state. But with the help of a food processor and a blender, almost anything could be liquefied, including the elegant salmon dinner provided one evening by a former client who was a gourmet cook. Jeff ground it up and served it to me in a tall glass as I sat, still in my stained nightgown, at the kitchen table. It was astounding to discover how much of the pleasure I used to derive from food involved its texture. The salmon-flavored gruel was not a significant improvement over the milkshake I'd had for breakfast.

That night, Jeff sat next to me and began to devour his perfectly formed food. His shoulders curled with fatigue or depression or both. A nicer person would have felt only empathy for him, but my compassion was riddled with envy at his ability to gobble up that fabulous meal. He offered to pulverize the cherry tarts a friend had brought. I declined, so he ate them. Exhausted long before I was full, I had an extra-strength Ensure for dessert, which, even at a whopping 355 calories per eight-ounce can, only brought my daily total to 1,850. I caught myself feeling nostalgic for the NG tube.

One evening, Barb came over for dinner, and we ordered Chinese food as a special treat. It would be my first grown-up restaurant food since my operation, a major step from the baby mush I'd been gumming. As I consumed the warm, salty, overly yellow egg drop soup via my red tube, I noticed that my nose was running. Closer inspection revealed that this was no ordinary runny nose. The soup was trickling from my nostrils. Evidently, the surgery had created a little detour between my mouth and my stomach, which this particular fluid had, for reasons of its own, decided to take. How could I ever eat in a restaurant?

Barb assured me this was a temporary situation. Writing on my slate, I called myself a Chinese soup-breathing dragon and then worked to savor the soup that didn't end up in my napkin.

As a child, I was known as a "good eater." In adulthood, only my guilt kept me from being an all-out hedonist. Now it was clear that the pleasure of eating was forever lost to me. I mourned this new loss as I would the death of a friend. A good friend.

The only variety in my daily routine consisted of doctor's appointments. Val and Jeff went with me to an ophthalmologist who specialized in glaucoma; I was terrified of what the doctor might say about my still-fuzzy eyesight. If he said I needed more surgery, even "just a little laser surgery," or if my vision was threatened, that would spell the end of my already overtaxed coping mechanisms.

The three of us ran through our faux cheerfulness routine in yet another sterile waiting room. My gut clenched when the nurse called my name. As I stood to follow her, a young blonde woman who'd been sitting behind us came up to me and said, "Are you Terri White?"

"Yeth," I tried to enunciate.

"I recognized your voice. I heard your speech at U of M's Pediatric Nursing Department last November. You were wonderful!"

It was great that she had liked my speech—my last one before surgery, maybe my last one ever. The fact that she'd recognized my voice was even better.

The ophthalmologist assured me that blurred vision was an expected side effect of the amount of anesthesia necessary for twenty-four hours of surgery. Why didn't the bastards in Ohio know that? My new favorite doctor predicted that my eyesight would return to normal and, over time, it did. Leaving his office, the three of us cheered and hugged as if we'd won the lottery.

The last doctor I wanted to see was Watson, but he was the only ENT surgeon in Ann Arbor who knew my case, and I wasn't strong enough to travel to Columbus. On the way to St. Joe's with Jeff and Val, we discussed what, if anything, I should say to Watson about how long he took to find my recurrence. We agreed to defer confrontation until I felt stronger.

The doctor's demeanor was muted as he surveyed the results of his delayed diagnosis. I showed him the section of the suture line next to my left nipple to determine why it wasn't healing. He seemed especially chagrined at what little remained of my left breast, blanching as he examined the area.

"It isn't clear what's going on here," he said. "Maybe there's a stitch inside trying to get out. Irrigate the opening with saline three times a day and then apply antibiotic cream. It should close up in time." This would prove to be the first in a long line of contradictory but equally ineffective prescriptions for the stubborn wound near my heart. He paused and then said, "We could rebuild this breast with plastic surgery. We would just . . ."

He began to detail his plan for reviving my breast. Oh yeah, right! Sign me up. Like I'm going to let you anywhere near my body with a scalpel!

". . . and it could look quite natural," he concluded.

I slowly shook my head.

By way of preparing me for my forthcoming radiation, Dr. Watson said, "If you think you feel bad now, wait until you've had a few of those treatments."

My anger swelled as we left his office for the last time. Friends had suggested suing Dr. Watson for taking so long to discover my recurrence. With barely enough energy to deal with the medical system, I was in no shape to tackle the legal system, too.

§

Next on the agenda was a visit to the maxillofacial prosthodontist, a dentist who specializes in radiated mouths. A tiny, fast-moving person whom Jeff named "that bumblebee woman," Dr. Mason was kind and attentive, but her message was bleak. She warned that if my oral hygiene was less than perfect, I could get an infection in my remaining jaw, which would require that it, too, be removed. Her warning would forever haunt me when I brushed, flossed, or cleansed my mouth—and when I didn't. I had no doubt that I would choose dying over going through that surgery again.

Dr. Mason held a mirror to my mouth to show me the correct method for mopping up around my seven surviving lower teeth, forcing me to look inside my mouth for the first time. It was red, slimy, and swollen, reminiscent of the insides of frogs we dissected in seventh-grade biology. I had been careful to avoid peeking in there and was stunned that others had done so without getting sick. They either had strong stomachs or love really was blind. No wonder Jeff only kissed me on the cheek. I was impressed that he dared to come near me at all.

Jeff denied that the changes in my appearance bothered him. "I can see your inner beauty, and that's all that matters to me." I believe this was true for him then, and I *had* to believe it at the time. His words fit the denial I was building about my new appearance. But he was clearly growing more resentful when he had to "do my chin and chest," which was code for changing my dressings. Several times, I saw him wince mid-procedure. He was more reluctant than ever to touch me. He was terrified of disturbing my new structure by hugging or kissing me too hard. Jeff later admitted that it made him feel superficial to admit that he was grieving my lost beauty. If he started to feel self-pity, he'd say to himself, "How can I complain? I've got it easy compared to her."

Jeff's physical distancing was part of a general withdrawal. He was having a much harder time than I'd realized. Always a loner, all this togetherness was taking its toll on him. There was the pressure of balancing full-time caretaking with reviving his Rolfing practice to pay our mounting bills. And perhaps worst of all, the independent woman he had fallen in love with had turned into a misshapen, clingy lump.

The unspoken thoughts and feelings between us kept us apart. We were still physically together much of the time, but we lived in separate worlds, each slogging through the details of our day. Every once in a while, we took tiny breaks from the relentless routine and let ourselves watch a video or play our favorite dice game. These respites were usually Roxicet-reinforced for me. Later Jeff confessed that he had dipped into my drug supply a few times to relax. Though he still slept on the futon in his room, once in a while we had a careful cuddle before he tucked me in.

Whatever our problems, Jeff was my main source of human contact because I seldom left the house. At first, I stayed home because I lacked energy. The shortest excursion could exhaust a whole day's supply. Even as I got a little stronger, I was too disconnected from life to have any place to go. During my long hours at the kitchen table squirting or gingerly spooning a meal, I fantasized about going out someday. Everyone said I looked much better since my head had returned to its normal size. There were still plenty of wounds and swelling at the surgical sites, and I was gaunt from not eating, but those who had seen me through it all said my appearance was getting better all the time. New visitors still often greeted me with, "You don't look nearly as bad as I thought you would."

But what if I were out in public and ran into someone who knew me but hadn't heard about my cancer? I saw myself standing in the checkout line at Kroger's, fidgeting while old friends or clients rearranged their faces to create socially appropriate responses to the way I looked. I would have to take a normal-looking person with me to explain. And what would I do about strangers? I envisioned small children poking their mothers and asking, "Mommy, what's wrong with that lady?" The mother would shush the kid and smile weakly at me, pretending her darling hadn't said a word.

If going to the store was fraught with danger, working seemed impossible. Why on earth would anyone hire me with this face? Even on the days when I thought I might have a future, I didn't like to picture what it would look like. I had completely lost touch with the presurgical vision of myself as Wonder Woman, though her image was still displayed all over the house.

All I could do was stay home and worry. A skilled fretter from birth, cancer was expanding my worrying vistas exponentially. While my time was focused on practical concerns like eating and talking and fears that these functions might be further diminished by radiation, the specter of dying was always lurking in the background. What if my wounds didn't heal?

And what list of cares would be complete without anxiety about my kids? When all else failed, I agonized about money. My office rent was $1,000 a month, my disability insurance wouldn't kick in until May, and then it wouldn't begin to cover my expenses. I was capable of brooding about finances, even though whenever I thought I was dying and reviewed my life for regrets, the only one I found was having wasted a moment worrying about money. And in those moments when death seemed nearby, I was always glad that I had let Lynn talk me into that expensive hotel in the south of France.

I tried to defer concern about the future and focus on the daily details in front of me. I continued to search for faith to help me through the days, but God still seemed out of reach. I tried reading my favorite line from *A Course in Miracles,* "There is no order of difficulty in miracles," but I failed to feel the thrill that principle usually inspired. Writing in my journal took too much effort. Throughout my convalescence, the members of our Mastermind group drove all the way to our house to include Jeff and me in weekly meetings. Mastermind prayer groups are founded on Jesus's promise that "Where two or three are gathered in my name, there am I in the midst of them" (Matthew 18:20). The spiritual connection and having my friends pray for my healing felt wonderful, but within a few hours the glow wore off and I felt alone again. Like an injured and abandoned child, I could only look to external sources for comfort. It was as if all of my internal resources had been used up and I was unable to nurture myself in any way.

The better I got physically, the more I was left alone. Jeff was spending increasing amounts of time at the office. I suspected he was padding his time away with stops at bookstores and coffee shops. I was so needy and self-centered that I begrudged him even that. My other regulars were also running low on care-giving energy, eager to return to the world outside the sickroom. I could hear Val's voice tense up when I called, as if she were afraid I'd ask for yet another favor. Barb was trying to adopt a baby from Mexico, so she was even busier than usual. I still had visitors, but not enough to provide the kind of assistance I needed: cooking, bathing, exercising, and getting to doctors and to the upcoming daily radiation treatments.

Conversations about how to handle my "excessive needs" were held in my presence. I sat on the sidelines of the discussions experiencing a paradoxical assortment of emotions. I was ashamed to be such a burden to those around me. I knew I had been extraordinarily blessed by the amount of support I had received throughout my illness. Some friends did way more than I would have expected. And while some did less, no one bolted, as I know is common during cancer and its protracted convalescence. Val, Barb, and Jeff had been amazing. While I was deeply grateful for all this incredible help and recognized its role in my survival, I also felt abandoned. I suspect that the withdrawal of my caregivers triggered childhood memories of Mom redirecting her attention to a sicker sibling when I showed the first signs of recovery. My best self could not have expected more from my exhausted friends and family, but at times the needy part of me wished they could limp a mile in my slippers.

The answer to the nursing shortage arrived in the form of Kathy, an acquaintance of my parents who had recently separated from her husband and needed money and a place to stay. Neither Jeff nor I were thrilled to have a roommate, especially one we didn't know, but there were no other volunteers, so Kathy moved into our lower level at the end of January. A slim, nervous woman of about fifty, she was quite concerned about her appearance and couldn't understand my lack of interest in mine. Kathy fussed over me constantly, sometimes teasing my hair while I ate. We explained that we weren't eating much meat, but Kathy cooked beef soups, meat loaf, and one night, a steak. I looked at her in disbelief, my eyes as big as the bone in the tenderloin. I was too exhausted to deal with her, so I handed back the tray and slid down in my bed to sulk.

Kathy shuffled around in fuzzy pink slippers and often startled me by speaking from inches away when I had not heard her approaching. I found myself straining to entertain her, hoping to keep her happy. Also, she smoked. We asked her to refrain from lighting up in the house and for a few days she did. During the second week of her stay, smoke began filtering up the stairs and through the vents into my bedroom. The smell made me sick and knowing that smoking is the major risk factor for oral cancer, I had no desire to inhale the second-hand variety. When Jeff confronted her, Kathy assured him that she only smoked outside, but our noses told us otherwise.

Having Kathy in the house made going out more attractive. So when Barb was notified of a baby girl born in December who might be available for adoption, I suggested a shopping spree. My reasoning was that the child, whom we tentatively called Maria Elena, might be waiting to see what kind of wardrobe went with the deal before she decided on a mother. Barb was easy to convince.

I rested up all day in anticipation of our outing. Barb propped me up as we walked through the store and scanned the crowd for familiar faces. She'd been briefed on the routine to follow if we encountered someone I knew. If we couldn't avoid them, she was to say, "Terri's still recovering from her cancer surgery, so we need to go."

Perusing the tiny and frilly dresses, coats, sleepers, and bonnets was thrilling for a mother of boys like me. All the items had been marked down twice, and we were spending Barb's money, so my shopping zeal knew no bounds. My energy level did, though, and I needed to take frequent breaks, sitting on a vacant shelf. We coordinated soft pink gowns, blankets, and jackets with satin bows. We couldn't decide between the pink or the white ostrich-feather bonnets, so we got them both. Two hours and a couple of hundred dollars later, we returned home with a wardrobe befitting a teensy princess. I was exhausted but glad to discover that I could still find temporary solace in shopping. That outing was the most fun I would have all winter. And that night, Barb was awakened by a call from the orphanage. Maria Elena was hers. I added "being around to watch this little girl grow up" to my list of reasons for living.

irradiated winter

The minute I started to recover from surgery, it was time for radiation. I wanted to postpone the treatments to stockpile weight and energy, but the doctors insisted that radiation would work best four to six weeks post-op. Five weeks had already passed. Skipping radiation altogether was highly tempting. The side effects were grisly, and Dr. Prescott had warned that the radiation itself could cause new cancer in ten or twelve years. But as much as I dreaded sinking deeper into the role of patient, I couldn't ignore the experts who said that the treatments would greatly increase my chances of surviving. If I were lucky enough to be around in ten or twelve years, I'd deal with the consequences then.

I was determined not to fulfill the doctor's predictions about radiation's aftereffects. I decided I'd use all manner of alternative healing methods to breeze through the treatments. I'd show them. I almost believed my false bravado.

On Wednesday, January 20, Val took me back to the clinic at U of M, where we had met Doogie Howser almost two years before. Although I hadn't actually seen myself, I knew I looked as bad as anyone in the waiting room, and I hadn't even started radiation. A petite young woman with honey-colored hair guided us through the huge metal doors into a tiny examining room where, in time, we met the staff radiation oncologist, the chief resident, and a host of doctors in training. They lined up to gaze into my mouth and to pummel my surgical sites. After conferring, they announced that my wounds appeared sufficiently healed for me to begin radiation on Monday. First, they explained, I needed a "sim." Short for *simulation*, a sim was necessary to determine how to best position me during the treatments to zap as many cancer cells as possible and to protect the normal ones. The process would also involve crafting a custom-fitted mask to keep me in that position during each treatment.

Although Jeff and Val both accompanied me to the appointment two days later, neither of them was allowed into the actual sim room. It was already packed with people and paraphernalia. Green-gowned technicians scurried about amid shiny stainless steel equipment in a room so sterile that it made all the other examining rooms I'd been in look cozy. In the center of all this activity sat a metal slab table bolted to the floor. A short man with a brush cut told me to climb up and lie on my back. This bristle-headed attendant said sternly, "You can't move at all. The sim and the actual radiation can only succeed if you are perfectly still."

I hadn't lain flat on my back since the surgery; attempts to do so had made me gag. My request for a pillow was refused. Following orders, I cautiously lowered my head onto the rigid plane. My throat seemed to close up, and my newly configured neck and chest were stretched until the taut tissue felt like it would pop. Sharp, dry staccato coughs forced me to sit up and take a drink of water. Lying down again, I tried to breathe through my nose and inhaled a powerful whiff of Old Spice, apparently emanating from a member of the crowd milling above me. With my weight at its lowest point since childhood, I lacked my usual padding and the bones of my back protruded onto the unyielding surface. Being immobilized on that cold table took me back to the TB years and that frigid doctor who performed the needle-aspirations on my infected lymph node. Although the pain was indescribable, I never cried because I wanted Mom to think I could handle it.

At forty-seven, I was still trying to be brave and please people, so I strained to be still as the silent technicians took x-ray after x-ray. It seemed like an eternity but probably took about forty minutes for them to administer this appetizer of rads (units of absorbed radiation dose) in preparation for the rad feast that my body would consume over the next seven weeks.

I was allowed to relax momentarily while an important-looking man in the neighboring glass-enclosed alcove studied the x-rays. Then my body was rearranged by chilled hands, and another technician told me to return to absolute immobility. I closed my eyes. A female voice above my head announced, "Now we're going to put a sheet of plastic mesh over your face and neck to shape the mask."

Claustrophobia had never been high on my long list of neuroses. But sweet Jesus, this was too much. How would I breathe?

The voice answered my unspoken question. "We are inserting straws into each of your nostrils so that you can breathe while we fit the mask."

I felt the jabbing inside my nose and the slimy plastic encasing my face.

"I'm going to mold the mask very tightly to your face and neck. Please lie totally still."

I didn't believe I could endure much longer. My ability to hold body and mind in tight control was leaking out. Prior to my current estrangement from God, I would have sought divine assistance in a situation like this. But my spiritual resources felt tapped out, and there was nothing in me or in this bleak environment to revive them.

"Now we need to screw the mask to the table to be sure that it will fit on the actual treatment table. It's vital that you do not move at all."

Apparently there were holes in the corners of the table that corresponded to holes near the edge of my mask-in-the-making. I felt a tug at the hardening plastic, which was welded to my features and then heard the screws being threaded through the holes.

"Now that you're in place, we need to take more films," said the monotone voice.

This was as close to psychosis as I had ever come. My brain raged as I focused what little control I had left on keeping my muscles motionless.

Finally, they unscrewed me and removed the now hardened plastic mask, which belonged in a monster movie. It was not a flattering rendition of my face, but what mattered now was that I could move, my skin could breathe, and my nose was filling with air.

"Okay," said another green-garbed stranger, "now we need to put a mark on your chest so we'll know how far down on your body the radiation should go." I felt a sharp searing in the center of my chest, a few inches above my breasts. When the burning stopped, he held up a round mirror to show me the resultant black spot, about the size of a large freckle.

"This will fade away after radiation, right?" I asked.

"Oh no," responded the tattooing tech, "this is permanent. We need a mark that won't wash off." I looked at him in stunned disbelief that no one had bothered to mention this. As if replying to my stare, he said, "Well, it's just a little spot."

Each movement hurt as I was helped off the table. The thrill of liberation was tempered only by the knowledge that I'd always be branded with a reminder of that day.

Just in case the dot wasn't an adequate memento, I'd never forget the next preradiation ritual. After the sim, I had to meet with Dr. Lee, the chief resident, to learn what to expect from radiation and to sign the form verifying that I'd been warned. Jeff had to leave for a Rolfing session, but Val stayed with me. Dr. Lee, a small, serious man, handed me a sheet of paper that read:

> I am aware that the following symptoms and conditions
> could result from radiation treatment:
> Alteration in taste buds
> Damage to teeth and gums
> Destruction of salivary glands
> Damage to thyroid gland
> Swelling of tissue in mouth and throat
> Redness of skin
> Excessive mucus production in mouth or throat
> Decreased circulation to area
> Necrosis of larynx . . .

I stopped reading. In a strained stammer, I screeched, "NECROSIS OF THE LARYNX? Are you saying it dies?"

"Radiation can create a necrotic process in the larynx, and we'd have to remove it," said Dr. Lee, as if discussing removal of a wart.

Val looked on as my anxiety rendered me nearly hysterical. She kept repeating how rare necrosis must be, while I tried to decide whether to sign the damned form. Since I first learned that I had oral cancer, I'd often pondered whether life would be worth living if I couldn't talk. The loss of the ability to speak would not only ruin my career, it would deprive me of my life's greatest pleasure: connecting with others in deep conversation. Now I had even more experience with enforced silence and had heard the grating computer-generated voices of the laryngectomy patients in the ENT clinics. My musings on a nonverbal existence had made it quite clear that there were people on the planet for whom talking was not essential to life, and I was not one of those people.

Now I had to revisit the question of whether to have radiation, knowing it could cost me my voice. I signed the consent form without another word to Dr. Lee and fled the clinic as fast as my cramping limbs would carry me.

On the drive home, Val continued her campaign to convince me that my larynx would survive radiation. "He's an asshole for even telling you about the necrosis. That won't happen to you." Later, she called Dr. Lee to grill him about the likelihood of necrosis in cases like mine.

"I could see that your sister was upset," he told her, "so I looked it up. Necrosis of the larynx occurs in less than 1 percent of cases where the radiation is directed at that organ. In Terri's case, treatment will be focused on her mouth, and we can shield her larynx much of the time, so it's very unlikely. Tell her that we can erase 'necrosis of larynx' from the list if that will make her feel better."

Val told me what she'd learned from Dr. Lee. I really appreciated her thoughtfulness and the fact that she was still going so far out of her way to help me. I was also grateful for Dr. Lee's extra research, but it bothered me to be under the care of a physician who thought that deleting words from a list could expunge my fear. And given my ability to squeeze into the tiniest statistical segment, I wasn't completely consoled.

The plan was that I would receive thirty-four doses of radiation, one a day, Monday through Friday, from January 25 until March 11.

The doctors said that I should be okay for the first week or so, until the damaging effects started to take their toll. Then I should expect to feel terrible until the end of treatment and beyond. If I became too debilitated, I could take time off from the therapy, but that would reduce its efficacy. No one mentioned whether the weekend breaks, scheduled for the hospital's convenience, also diminished effectiveness. It wasn't until much later that I had the nerve to ask a doctor about the reasons for the "weekends off" policy, beyond the obvious staffing challenges of a seven-day week. She said that the hiatus gave healthy tissue in the radiated areas a chance to recover. I pictured the healthy cells going out for a few beers or watching a football game with the technicians and the doctors.

Treatment time in the radiation oncology department was assigned on the basis of seniority. As a new patient, I got 7:15 a.m., which meant the end of sleeping in. At 6:00 a.m. on Monday I put on my navy Michigan sweat suit, affixed my angel pin for good luck, and drank a can of Ensure. I gathered my lucky rocks, my tape recorder, and Bernie Siegel's *Getting Ready: Preparing for Surgery, Radiation, and Chemotherapy with Minimal Side Effects* tape, which was purported to reduce negative side effects via positive imagery. I wasn't sure I still believed in angel pins or lucky rocks or Bernie Siegel, for that matter, but they couldn't hurt. I donned my biggest down coat to face the bitter winter morning. This routine would repeat itself thirty-three times in the upcoming weeks with minor variations in sweat-suit color and breakfast menu.

Jeff drove me to my first treatment. He was quieter than usual that morning. Years later he told me, "Taking you to radiation always reminded me of going to my job in a Missouri ammunition plant during the Vietnam War. I needed the job, but I knew the bullets we made would soon be killing innocent people. I didn't know if the treatments would help you, and I knew they could hurt you. There wasn't any way to find out if the benefits would outweigh the damage. Besides, it was your body and your decision."

Having survived the simulation gave me some confidence that I could make it through the actual treatments. The sim also provided the specifics of what to fear. It was with great trepidation that I entered the windowless world of radiation oncology. There didn't seem to be enough air in this part of the hospital. What there was did not move and smelled like metal. A freckled brunette led me into the locker room where she instructed me to completely disrobe, to select a new outfit from the assortment of frayed cotton robes and gowns, and then to sit across the hall in the women's waiting area until my name was called.

Alone in the locker room, I actually deliberated over which gown and robe to wear. I coordinated their faded colors in an attempt to distract myself from the terror that was escalating by the minute. I devised a system of selecting which locker to use for my clothes. I started with locker number one and planned to move down one locker each day to count off the treatments. That way, I could celebrate a little victory every time I returned for my clothes. There were seventeen lockers, so I'd use each locker twice by the end of radiation. I felt better once I had a plan.

Adorned in harmonizing hospital style, I met Jeff in the women's waiting room. The inner waiting rooms were segregated by sex, ostensibly to protect the modesty of the patients, and then filled with opposite-sexed partners-in-waiting.

"Terri White," said a tall man. "I'm Tom."

Now I had to leave Jeff and go off with this stranger. Jeff later told me that Tom reminded him of Lurch, the zombie butler on *The Addams Family* television show. The fact that Tom came to be my favorite technician made Jeff worry what the others were like.

Enunciating as clearly as I could, I made small talk as I followed Tom down the hallway. We talked about football, and I made a mental note that he was an avid Wolverine fan. I wanted Tom to like me. I wanted it to matter to him that the plate which shielded my larynx was in exactly the right place, that the rads I would be absorbing went precisely where they belonged, that I received the 6,000 rads I was supposed to get, not 5,962 or 6,033. I wanted him to take the time to position me with the folded towel under my back and to set up my tape recorder so I could hear Bernie Siegel extolling the virtues of radiation. Maybe, if he liked me enough, I'd get a later appointment time.

We turned into the alcove leading to the treatment room, past a colorful weaving that seemed out of place, as if this radioactive suite were masquerading as an art museum. The room itself was bereft of aesthetic touches. Everything was made from gleaming metal: the walls, the sink, the shelves, the table, and the enormous robotlike radiation machine, which dominated the space and made me want to say good-bye to my new friend Tom and run out of there. The scene was pure science fiction. I've never liked science fiction.

Tom took me to a mirror and showed me how to insert six cotton rolls over my gums and a plastic mouth guard between my teeth. He said, "Watch very carefully. It's crucial that you put these in exactly the same way every time." My fear of failure kicked in as I tried to memorize the precise placement of each item.

My mouth stuffed and parched, the cotton having already soaked up my saliva, I followed Tom over to the table and climbed up the wide, steel stepladder. Here was another cold, hard slab where crying was not allowed. Sitting on the unyielding surface, I arranged the towel beneath my hips for padding and inched backward until I was lying down. My tape recorder rested on my stomach. Using an awkward amalgam of a charades game and an imitation of Demosthenes with the pebbles in his mouth, I managed to convey that I wanted Tom to guide my index finger to the play button, which I would push when the treatment began. I focused on breathing, enjoying my last few unfettered breaths before the dreaded mask curtailed my access to air. Then the personalized head restraint descended and covered my face. Even batting my eyelashes became impossible as Tom screwed the full-face muzzle into the table. *What the hell am I supposed to do if I choke or cough or something goes wrong?* I groaned to see if Tom and Debbie, the other technician, could hear me.

"What is it, Terri?" asked Tom. I was relieved that he responded, but concerned that he would have to demummify me to find out what I wanted. He might be annoyed to discover that this was "Only a Test," like those air-raid alert systems. He unscrewed the mask and handed me a pad and pencil so I could communicate with my mouth gear in place.

"Just making sure you could hear me," I scribbled, embarrassed.

"Yes, we'll be able to hear you all the time. If you need anything, just make a noise, and we'll answer." I could tell he wasn't happy about the delay and fretted that this experiment had cost me some hard-won, good-patient bonus points.

"We're elevating the table," said Debbie, "so you're at the right height. Now we're positioning the machine." I could sense the monster crouching above me. "Tom and I are leaving now. We'll be in the next room administering your treatment. We'll keep talking to you from there, and don't worry, we can hear you." I heard their footsteps crossing the floor, the door shutting, and then absolute silence.

Tom's voice burst through a loudspeaker, presumably from mission control in the radiation-free zone, "Okay, Terri, here goes. We're going to start the treatment. It will last fifteen minutes. Remember not to move at all. You'll hear a very loud noise."

He wasn't kidding about the noise. I pushed the play button and tried to focus on Bernie's soothing tones rather than the booming automaton. He was telling me how my friend, radiation, was stalking all those nasty cancer cells and asked me to visualize this drama. I was already attempting to rein in all physical movement, to direct my hearing away from the frightening roar, to hold my fear in check, and now Bernie expected me to control the pictures in my mind as well. I had always liked Bernie. I wanted to be an "exceptional cancer patient" like the ones in his books. So I struggled to generate fewer images of Hiroshima and more of rads conquering cancer.

I'd researched cancer-fighting images in preparation for this moment, but I hadn't chosen one. Carcinoma-chomping Pac-Men and tumor-zapping lightning bolts were popular but didn't appeal to me. Some patients recommended picturing piranha feasting on malignant cells, but that reminded me of my mother feeding live goldfish to her pet piranha, and I'd always found that upsetting.

Finally, I settled on an image my friend Lynn had suggested. She reminded me of the time I took her to the Womyn's Music Festival in central Michigan during the hottest August on record. We camped on the parched ground amid millions of mosquitoes and hundreds of militant women. One morning, we were awakened at 5:00 a.m. by the Festival patrol squad mounting a full-scale search for a man sighted on the female-only premises. As we dragged ourselves from our tent and marched in formation over the hard, steaming earth, Lynn assured me that, from now on, *she* would plan our vacations. Based on that experience, she proposed visualizing armies of strong women tracking down and annihilating trespassing cancer cells. She advised adding Harleys and automatic weapons.

Time crawled by in dry, noisy increments. I worked hard to keep my mind focused and my body still, but I failed. When my thoughts wandered away from pistol-packing feminist bikers, I tried to focus on the idea that my surgery had already gotten every deadly cell and that the radiation currently zapping me was just a precautionary measure. I struggled to envision myself in five years: alive, healthy, and feeling like a regular person, albeit "challenged" as to looks, speaking, and eating ability. Then the urge to cough overwhelmed all thoughts and images.

The tickle in my throat became so intense that I could not see how to avoid coughing. What rational ability I had left reminded me that coughing would mean starting the treatment over. Or worse, the movement of the cough might allow rads to reach my larynx.

Just when I felt I could not curb a cough any longer, it was over. Debbie and Tom scurried back in. The monster retreated into its corner, the table squeaked down, someone loosened my mask, and the stool appeared beside the table.

"Okay, time to go," Tom said.

I pulled the hockey equipment out of my mouth, tossed the cotton rolls in the trash, and handed the plastic guard to Debbie, who stored it with my mask for next time. There was a designated shelf in the storage area for me. My name and hospital numbers were printed in large black letters. I stood staring at my special space. Chills ran through me as I realized that I was taking up residence in this otherworldly house of horrors. My mind flashed back to all the situations in my life when I'd felt out of place. Here, I fit in.

I gathered my possessions, rescued my clothes from locker number one, signaled Jeff, and departed. As a special treat, we stopped at

Zingerman's, the world's most cheerful deli, for coffee on the way home. "I've got an idea," I said. "Do you think you could get me a little prize after each week of radiation? That way I'd have something to look forward to."

"You bet." Jeff smiled, revealing the dimples around his mouth for the first time in weeks. "No problem." He sounded relieved that I was asking for something that was doable and didn't involve gore. Jeff wasn't in my league as a shopper, but he wasn't bad for a man. On each of the next seven Fridays, I received beautiful gifts that we couldn't afford: a brass necklace laden with charms and semi-precious stones, a dozen peach roses, and a lacquered mahogany globe held aloft by the raised trunks of three pewter elephants. Jeff had always been generous, and his sweet rewards were the highlight of the radiation weeks.

Even with the stop at Zingerman's, we were home from radiation before 9:00 a.m. The day gaped before me. I pushed myself into my daily routine: eating, exercises, visualization, listening to tapes, writing, and worrying. All of this transpired under the watchful eye of Kathy, my hapless helper. I sometimes feigned sleep to escape her. My only other reprieves took the form of visitors, Roxicet, and *Wheel of Fortune.*

To make good on my promise to cruise through radiation unscathed, I felt I needed to add even more healing tools to my repertoire. I ground vile-tasting seaweed into my liquid meals because Jeff had heard it reduced negative side effects. Jeff's research had also revealed that acupuncture decreased radiation damage. He signed me up for a series of sessions with Robert Washington, a bearded, British acupuncturist who smelled of cigarettes. The idea of having needles stuck into me had about as much appeal as the radiation itself. But in hopes that it might help, I let the coughing healer poke holes into my skin.

As predicted, I felt all right after the first few radiation treatments. Now Kathy drove me to the hospital and took me to Zingerman's for postradiation coffee. While I understood that Jeff deserved a break and that he needed to rebuild his practice, I would have preferred him as a coffee date. But I did feel pretty cocky sitting there, in public, looking out at the snow, listening to 1930s music, drinking from a cup like a normal person. I repeated my oath to use the power of my intention to direct those rads to any residual cancer and protect my other tissue. I pictured myself sauntering into Dr. Prescott's office in March, wondering out loud what all that fuss over side effects had been about. He'd gasp in surprise at how great I looked and how well I could talk.

Preparing for my fifth treatment, my tongue was too swollen to fit under the mouthpiece. The hurried blond technician shoved my tongue to the back of my mouth and crammed the plastic guard in over it. I shoved the thought that the swelling might be a side effect to the back of my mind, but my tongue continued to grow. One night I said to Jeff, "I'm starting to sound like Dean Martin after cocktail hour." He laughed, but we both knew it wasn't funny. My throat also began to swell, making swallowing even more difficult. I sat for hours before an endless bowl of oatmeal.

Ten treatments down and twenty-four to go. I was losing energy. I no longer needed to fake fatigue, and almost every day included a fitful nap. My face grew pinker. Mucus issued from my mouth. Everything started to taste alike, as if my taste buds were only working part time. Still determined to do all I could to stave off ill effects, I doggedly wrote pages of affirmations: "Radiation is killing all cancer with no side effects. My normal cells are radiation resistant." I remembered from affirmation training that I was supposed to record any negative thoughts in a separate "doubts" column. There were so many doubts skulking on the edges of my awareness that I refused to grant them space on the page for fear they'd overwhelm my affirmative efforts.

Jeff was less available with each passing day. He was working more and, when he was home, he spent long hours at his computer doing God knew what. The sight of him hunched over that keyboard evoked the same isolation I experienced as a little girl watching my dad doze in his chair, surrounded by office work. I felt shackled by my dependency on Jeff, guilty that I'd asked so much of him already, angry that he wasn't more caring, mad that I couldn't do more for myself, and too tired to deal with any of it. I never quite knew what to expect from him. He sometimes snapped when I asked for help and other times he was his generous old self. Now when I approached him, I started to feel the way I felt coming home from school wondering whether I would find kind, funny Mom proffering snacks or the screamer who wanted my goddamned books off her counter. Jeff was more prone to pouting than shouting. I wondered if he suspected me of malingering, though he never verbalized that suspicion. We just couldn't talk to each other like we used to, and so we clothed ourselves in layer upon layer of resentment, going through the motions of living together.

Kathy, on the other hand, was only too willing to do everything for me. She tagged after me like an abused pet, constantly trying to please. By three weeks into her stay, it was obvious that Jeff and I were caring for Kathy more than she was caring for us. Luckily she got a real job and left us. We hired my secretary's mother to take me to radiation and cook a few meals each week, so much of the burden fell back onto Jeff.

§

On February 16, 1993, I retrieved my clothes and slammed the seventeenth locker. I had completed the circuit once. I was halfway home!

I was ready for a celebration—or so I thought. Then a wave of exhaustion forced me to collapse onto the wooden bench in the locker room, considering the possibility that I was too worn out to traverse the lockers again.

The next morning, I sat in the waiting room across from a woman about my age with a deep-purple burn on her neck and chest, wondering if my skin would soon look like that. My radiated areas were getting redder all the time. At least she could hide her scorch marks with a turtleneck. Only a burka could conceal mine. The swelling in my throat had once again rendered me speechless, so I wrote in my notebook, "What if I end up looking like that?" I held the notebook so that Jeff could see it, but the woman could not.

"Oh, I'm sure you won't," he said out loud. I was mortified that the poor woman might realize we were talking about her, so I dropped the subject and swallowed my fear.

Fear was about all I could swallow by the fourth week of radiation. My mouth and throat were so swollen and sore that my menu reverted to Ensure, milkshakes, and liquefied cereals. Everything was tinged with the metallic taste that had taken up residence in my mouth. The "flap" over the titanium bar, which replaced my missing jaw, was so enlarged that it covered two of my remaining lower teeth.

Dr. Bradford, my new ENT surgeon at U of M, said I had "the worst case of mucusitis" she had ever seen. On occasion, I would stand over the bathroom sink, open my mouth over the bowl, and watch the viscous strands cascade out. My stomach curdled at the sight, but it held a perverse fascination. I was compelled to stare at it in the same way that you have to look at an accident on the side of the highway. What was going on in this body? It had become a total stranger, doing things I have never heard of, not even in nursing school. I had turned into a freak, living in a secret world, alienated from reality, and detached from my friends, my God, and even from my own anatomy.

Only eight treatments remained. It was all I could do to drag myself to the hospital each day and then collapse into bed. When we drove past Zingerman's on the way home from radiation, just the thought of coffee made me nauseated. Even water made me choke. I was losing weight. Doctors lectured me about the importance of nutrition for healing. I knew all that, but much of the time I was too tired to eat.

Unable to utter a sound, the phrase "necrosis of the larynx" echoed in my head. The terror of these words intensified when I tried to lie down and the sound of air swooshed past my enlarged vocal cords. As soon as I reclined, the creepy whistle squeaked from my throat with each breath, and I started to cough. The noise and the pulling in my throat made sleep impossible. I propped myself up on four or five pillows. If I started to doze, I was awakened by more mucus. Never had I been so tired.

At 4:30 a.m. on the Saturday before my last week of treatment, I realized that I was feeling even worse than usual. I stayed in bed for a few minutes hoping the sensations, unlike any I had experienced before, would pass. I felt detached, somehow unhooked from my body. Was this what dying felt like? Stumbling toward the bathroom for water, dizziness stopped me. Leaning on the wall for support, I dragged myself into Jeff's room, shook him awake and wrote, "Something wrong with me."

"What's the matter?" he asked.

"Don't know. Slipping away. Go hospital!"

"Oh, you're just tired. Get some sleep, and you will be fine in the morning," he said, tucking me into my bed and returning to his room.

This was the first time Jeff had outright refused to help me. That SOB, couldn't he tell I was dying? I was way too frantic and furious to sleep. It felt like if I did fall back to sleep, I wouldn't wake up. I took my temperature, which was slightly elevated, waited a few minutes to see if I felt better, and then dragged myself back into his room to try again. He still refused! What was going on with him?

Thank God we had company. I clung to the wall as I made my way into the guest room to awaken our houseguest, an old friend of mine who was a nurse. She agreed with my assessment that medical attention was necessary. Jeff exuded disdain as he drove us to the ER.

The speed with which the triage team hooked me up to an IV forced Jeff to reconsider his diagnosis. The resident arrived quickly and ordered a battery of tests. After a couple of hours of lying on the gurney, listening to my case and my imminent hospitalization being discussed, I seemed to feel a bit better. By the time consensus was reached on my diagnosis, I was definitely more connected to my body. Dehydration had been the culprit and IV fluids the solution. With stern warnings about the importance of eating and drinking, no matter how painful it was, the doctor discharged me from the emergency room.

§

On March 11, 1993, my eyes opened to see a beautifully wrapped package near my pillow. The blue, gold, and red antique cloisonné fish inside, my final radiation gift from Jeff, broke through my resentment and reminded me how hard he was trying. Two hours later, I slammed the door on locker number seventeen, inserted my emaciated body into the Michigan sweat suit with the angel pin, and shuffled out of the ladies' radiation oncology locker room for the last time.

fallout

R adiation was over, but its residual effects were just beginning. On the Sunday after the treatments ended, I dragged myself into the bathroom once again to clear the mucus out of my mouth and brush my teeth. As usual, I tried to keep my gaze focused on the faucet, but I caught a glimpse of metal glistening in my mouth—is that the titanium bar? I ran from my bathroom in search of Jeff, hoping he would say, "It's nothing."

Jeff peered into my mouth and said, "It does look like something's going on in there." He stuck a flashlight into my mouth. "Yeah, the bar is definitely exposed, but we don't know what that means. Don't get hysterical before we know what's happening."

Dr. Gilbert, who was kind enough to let us call him at home on weekends, told Jeff that the hole in the flap was caused by radiation and wasn't necessarily a big deal, but did increase the opportunity for infection in my remaining jawbone.

"He said to keep your mouth extra-clean and not to worry," Jeff reported.

Right. The Vile Bitch Upstairs reminded me of the maxillofacial prosthodontist's warning about an infected jaw. How could I keep my mouth clean enough? I imagined millions of microbes marching through the hole in my flap to attack my defenseless jaw remnant.

Rigorous oral hygiene sessions were added to my unrelenting schedule of tortuous meals, painful exercises, and futile attempts at attitude improvement. This cancer business was a full-time job, leaving no room for fun. I wasn't even sure I still knew how to have fun. My usual guiding principles of being good and trying to please people were wearing very thin. Some days, I didn't even care about fighting off cancer. My daily activities were designed to improve a future that I was not at all certain I would attend.

I still couldn't talk, so Jeff's role expanded to include being my link to the world. I looked on helplessly as Jeff spoke to my friends on the phone. I whimpered in frustration at the inaccuracy of his reports and then wrote corrections on my pad. He told people I was doing better than I was. I wanted them to know how bad things were so they'd visit more.

The opposite was true when "we" talked to my kids. I wanted Jeff to convince them that I was fine. On March 25, we called to wish Justin a happy twenty-first birthday. I did my best to croak out, "Ahby Buuday" and gave Jeff the phone to complete the conversation, which was outlined in my notebook.

"Your mom is doing fine," he read from my notes, but soon found them difficult to decipher. "What the hell does this say?" he asked. Before I could write the answer, he continued, "She still can't talk or eat much, and the bar is still exposed and she's pretty scared about that, but I think she might be getting a little stronger. She has a lot of exercises and stuff to do, most of which she hates."

"DON'T TELL HIM THAT!" I scrawled in big, angry letters. "Ask him if he's working. Did he get my check?" Jeff glared at me, threw down the notebook, and continued telling Justin the truth. I felt so helpless. I was torn by conflicting urges—the scared child in me afraid of not getting her needs met and the mother in me wanting to protect my kids.

When he got off the phone, I went into the bedroom to write about my conflicting feelings and to try to make some sense of them. Having blown off the worst of my rage in hate mail to Jeff in my journal, I returned to the kitchen and handed him a watered-down version of my message. Always somewhat moody, Jeff's reactions were understandably more erratic during these difficult times. He sulked for two days.

My parents arrived on March 28, just in time to provide a diversion from the mounting tension. Mom and Dad jumped into action, doing the laundry, getting the dryer vented properly "so the goddamned house wouldn't burn down," grocery shopping, tracking down spoons thin enough to fit around my swollen tongue. Then there was the whole matter of attending to me: figuring out what to feed me, keeping me cleaner than I felt I needed to be, messing with my hair, irrigating the wound which continued to drain on my chest, and making sure I did my exercises.

None of these tasks mattered very much to me. Couldn't someone just hold me and let me cry and tell me I was going to be okay? But I kept quiet about my feelings, reminding myself that this must be hard for my parents. I did my best to be grateful for their help and to enjoy this rare opportunity to be an only child again.

We revived our ongoing gin rummy tournament, but I didn't care enough to satisfy my dad, who approached these contests as if he were mapping military strategy for a world war. Despite his frustration that Mom and I didn't take the game more seriously, he enjoyed having the upper hand. After he beat us for the fifth time in a row, I became exasperated and mouthed "Oh shit!" How nice that my parents could witness my first words.

The biggest noncancer project of the winter was picking Barb up at the airport when she returned from Mexico with Maria Elena. On April 1, Jeff, my parents, and I got up at midnight to meet their 1:30 a.m. flight, which didn't arrive until 2:45. I held posters aloft as the plane emptied its travel-worn passengers. Finally Barb appeared, leaning on her brother, as they somnambulated down the Jetway. Peeking out from the tangle of blankets in her arms were the biggest, brownest, brightest eyes I'd ever seen. Maria was wide awake and smiling. The gorgeous, copper-skinned baby was passed from person to person. I waited my turn. I hugged Barb with care, still guarding my surgical sites, then gently cradled her baby against my good breast.

"She's so beautiful," I muttered to Barb.

"Isn't she? I am glad to finally have her home," Barb said. She described their ordeal with immigration. "It is so sweet of you to be here. You look much better than when I left," Barb said and then moved on to the next person in line. Suddenly she turned back to me, looking shocked, and exclaimed, "You talked!"

§

As long as I was having surgery or undergoing radiation, I felt like I was doing something for my health. Having reached "the end of treatment," I couldn't just sit there stretching my mouth with tongue depressors and waiting for cancer to return. The urgency of my search for healing was intensified when an infection showed up in my mouth in mid-April. The ever-vigilant Bitch berated me, "I told you to brush more and floss better and use that special mouthwash more often! Now the infection will get into your jawbone, and it'll never heal because of the radiation. I knew you'd screw this up!"

Back on antibiotics, I reached a level of despair so pervasive that I wondered if I could keep going. And then came another setback. One night while watching television, I noticed a familiar tingling in my tongue. I tried to dismiss the sensation, sipped a hefty dose of Roxicet, and went to sleep. The feeling persisted the following day, and I asked Jeff to call Dr. Bradford's office.

"Oh, I'll bet that's just a residual effect of the radiation," Tammi, my nurse practitioner, assured him as I listened on the extension. "Try not to worry about it. She could have radiation-related symptoms for up to two months after treatment."

I really liked Tammi, and her opinion let me cling to a slim wedge of hope. Depleted as I was, I knew it would be dangerous to let go of that hope. My intuition told me what science now proves, that hope heals. So, I tried to think about other things. Maybe I would take my parents up on their offer to fly me to Florida. The drab Michigan winter was lingering as long as my symptoms. A little sunshine couldn't hurt.

Flying to Florida by myself seemed both dangerous and appealing. I hadn't even been to the store alone. What would people think of all the scars that underlined my face and neck, the redness and puffiness from the radiation, my altered gait, and my primitive speech? How would I eat? What if I choked? Still, it felt like an awfully normal thing to do, and with clothing as camouflage I might almost pass for a regular traveler. I could wear a turtleneck and a big hat. I could take plenty of Ensure and skip the airplane food. Jeff would put me on the plane in Detroit, and my parents would collect me at the other end. Besides, if the tingling in my tongue meant that the cancer was back, what difference did it make what people thought? I'd better grab adventure while I could.

In flight, I decided that as long as I was up in the heavens, I might as well reflect on whether or not I would like to stay there. Since that night before my first surgery, when it dawned on me that some part of me might want to die, I had tried to dismiss any hints of a death wish. Now two years and another bout of cancer later, I was terrified by the recent onset of symptoms, but still unsure I wanted to live. My grip on life was too tenuous to ignore any possible threat—even a subconscious one.

With my journal wedged between my water glass and bags of uneaten peanuts, I ran through another cost-benefit analysis on staying alive. I still wanted more time with my kids. Even though things were a little rocky now, I planned to work on the marriage as soon as I felt better. Jeff and I had connected in such a sweet way in the beginning—surely we could get back to that if we really tried. And I wanted so much to be a grandmother. The fact that I was currently on an airplane hinted that I might have a somewhat normal life again. Living won, but the number of reasons for giving up surprised me. Scrawled at the bottom of the list of reasons to live was "I'm too scared to die." Presbyterian promises of judgment day notwithstanding, it was the pain and expense of a prolonged death that scared me more than the end result. As I pondered the pros and cons, I began to see that unless I could face the possibility of death, I could never be fully alive.

The more I wrote, the clearer it became that I had to explore the darkest places in myself and try to find help in facing what I found there. It all felt murky and confusing, and I sensed a deep core of self-loathing, rage, and envy roiling within me. After all the workshops and therapy I had done, it was annoying that I wasn't fixed. I should be all loving and brimming with self-esteem by now. The Vile Bitch piped up to remind me of how far I was from that ideal: "You still worry way too much, you don't stand up for yourself nearly enough, you compare yourself to others way more than you should, your self-care sucks, and oh by the way, you are lousy at marriage." In a desperate attempt to escape her and reconnect with any kind of spiritual help, I wrote: "Dear God-Jesus-Diva-Higher Self-Great Spirit-Angels, Please tell me what to do."

As if taking dictation from an inaudible source I would later call my Guides, my hand began to write. First I made a "<" mark, as if to separate my own ideas from this new source of wisdom and wrote, "Maybe you should see Elizabeth," ending the message with a ">." Wow, I got a response! I assumed the message referred to Elizabeth Alberda, the healer a friend had recommended. I had no idea where this advice was coming from or whether I should follow it, but it was clearly a source other than the Bitch. Whatever its origin, this guidance gave me a little hope. I felt inspired to write affirmations: that my tongue was feeling better, that I was cancer free, and that I would live to be eighty-seven. I still don't know why eighty-seven. It just seemed like the right number. By the time I finished writing and had downed two cans of Ensure, we were on the ground in Fort Lauderdale.

My parents had stocked up on cottage cheese, Jell-O, Cream of Wheat, and other chew-free foods, so we ate mushy meals at home or went to restaurants where I ate various versions of clam chowder. Every night at cocktail hour, Dad had his martini and Mom her Vicodin. The one sip of alcohol I'd had since radiation set my mouth on fire, so I opted for Roxicet. I allowed myself a slug slightly larger than usual because I was on vacation. We watched a lot of TV.

On *Roseanne,* the grandmother came to visit, and I got tearful because I wouldn't live to see my grandchildren. I've never had easy access to my tears, so there was some relief mixed with the sadness. The next night, we watched *Breakfast at Tiffany's,* which I'd seen twenty-three times, and Audrey Hepburn's beauty triggered grief about the loss of my looks. I didn't express these feelings out loud, but as usual, Mom was at the ready with a beauty tip.

The following morning, she urged me as she had so often to "do something with that hair." Figuring that I couldn't look any worse, I let her take me to her budget salon. I emerged sporting the short bangs Mom had always favored. "You have such a lovely forehead," she said as she had in each of our bang-length conversations. Returning to their mirror-lined condo, I accidentally glanced at my reflection. The phrase "Godzilla meets the Dutch boy" came to mind.

My self-image was not boosted as I braved the beach on the last day of my visit. I basted myself with a thick coat of sunscreen in response to my doctor's urgings to keep my radiated skin out of the sun. I borrowed Mom's bathing suit, which hung on me due to my weight loss and the fact that part of my left breast was on permanent loan to my mouth. I donned the most thorough beach cover-up I could find and scampered crablike across the sand, trying to minimize my exposure to the sun and to the eyes of the other bathers. But I could still see them. I winced in regret at the sight of a slender, deeply tanned, platinum-blonde woman in a miniscule orange bikini. How many times had I compared my cellulite thighs to svelte specimens like her? And what would I now give to have my old face and body back?

The hot sand and broken shells hurt my tender feet, but the warm salty sea frothing over my wounds made it worthwhile. I prayed that the waves would wash out any lurking cancer cells as well as the chemicals that lingered in my system. I floated on the gentle waves and stood to let the rough ones crash around me. Against doctor's orders, I raised my face to the sun and basked in it. In that one moment, it didn't matter what I looked like. I became part of the ocean, my heart beating to its rhythm. In that moment, I was whole.

power zoo

The healing moment passed. Once I was back from vacation, I had to decide what to do about the tingling in my tongue. I'd had all the radiation my body could withstand. In those days, chemo was only used palliatively for oral cancer, so I had exhausted traditional treatments.

What now?

The message to see Elizabeth had been clear on the flight to Florida, but it drowned in a sea of options once I got home. I had my choice of three different cancer support groups, a vast array of therapists, all kinds of nutritional approaches, energy healers of every ilk, Mexican clinics, German drugs, and on, ad infinitum.

I discussed the possibilities with anyone who would listen and got all kinds of advice. Jeff was still adding to the list of alternative alternatives. One day he produced an article from some esoteric publication about a nearby "live foods" program, and the next he suggested a guy in Seattle who, for a mere $400, would study my case and research every remotely relevant remedy. I appreciated all the help, but none of my advisors had ever been in my place. My confusion was almost as frightening as the cancer had been.

It was up to me.

I meditated and waited for answers. None were forthcoming. I wrote in my journal, hoping intuitive guidance might appear as it had on the plane. I needed to hear more from that internal source before I would trust it, but only my usual inner chatter poured onto the page. I tried to contact my emaciated inner child, whom I had abandoned since my recurrence. She seemed reticent to trust me but finally indicated that she wanted the pain and fear to go away. She asked that I stop blaming her for everything and show that I love her.

Unlike the guidance that had come to me on the plane, this seemed to originate in a dark place within me. While it all felt very weird, this was the closest thing to direction I had. After a lifetime with the Vile Bitch Upstairs, I wasn't going to become a beacon of self-love overnight. I had no idea where to begin. And none of this brought me any closer to knowing which healing methods to pursue.

Needing a break from this introspective confusion, I asked Barb and Maria to come over. Much to my delight, Barb said that my speech was clearer than the last time we'd talked, and because she was used to how I sounded, we could actually converse. After a lovely visit, I hugged them good-bye, watched them drive up our bumpy dirt driveway, and turned to go back into the living room. Suddenly, I was stopped in the foyer and from somewhere inside me I heard, "Go see Elizabeth." Whoa! Where did that come from? It was more a knowing than a voice, but either way it didn't sound like the Bitch. Although keeping these inner messengers straight was getting tougher all the time, I was pleased to get a clear directive.

I made an appointment with Elizabeth. Taking one decisive action stimulated me to make others.

I researched various therapists and selected Claudia, a psychoanalytic social worker who worked with cancer patients. She was a kind, intelligent woman about my age with neatly trimmed brown hair peppered in gray, a narrow face, and soft brown eyes. She offered one sentence that made the entire session worthwhile. "If you work with me, our goal would be that in five years you will look back on this time and see that you have grown in ways that would have been impossible without the cancer." I loved it that she believed I would be around in five years to "look back" at anything, but it was clear in one session that I was not cut out for the psychoanalytic approach. I wanted someone to interact with me, not a Freudian blank screen on whom I could project my issues. The prospect of delving into past problems overwhelmed me. And maybe I was just plain afraid to venture into a psyche that I suspected was complicit in causing cancer.

I decided to defer emotional healing until I saw Elizabeth; in the meantime, I'd focus on my physical well-being. From my survey of nutritionists, I selected Jason because he hadn't mentioned giving up coffee in our phone interview. While Jeff was running out of steam for all things medical, he seemed to have endless enthusiasm for alternative approaches. He eagerly offered to accompany me to the appointment with Jason. Still craving his support and not comfortable going out on my own, I accepted even more eagerly.

Jason, a thin, somber young man, invited us into his depressing apartment where we sat around a scratched table while he assessed my eating habits. His jaw dropped in horror as I spoke of milkshakes, meatloaf, and mashed potatoes with lots of gravy. He proposed a list of alterations in my lifestyle that I knew I could never implement. I agreed to the easy ones, like drinking distilled water, avoiding poultry, and eating millet, a.k.a. birdseed. Jason also suggested alcohol abstinence. That one would be easy as long as alcohol burned my mouth. After that, we'd see about quitting drinking, which felt like a bigger decision than I could handle at the moment. I would also defer implementing some of Jason's other ideas, like eliminating sugar, until a later date, possibly another lifetime.

Jason and Jeff eagerly compared notes on approaches to cancer treatment. I looked on, wondering which of my horrendous habits had caused cancer and how I would ever eat well enough to prevent more of it. When they chanced upon their shared interest in "live foods," the speed and volume of their speech escalated.

"You know," Jason told Jeff conspiratorially, "cooking destroys digestive enzymes and other essential elements of good nutrition. Raw foods are so much healthier, and they've shown great results with cancer patients." Oh God, I thought. Just what I need: Jeff getting more ammunition. I appreciated that he cared, but he had so many suggestions that it felt like I was always letting him down.

"Absolutely," Jeff agreed with his new best friend, "and Terri doesn't get the enzymes in saliva since her salivary glands don't work. I've tried to tell her."

Despite my determination to beat the radiation odds, I'd woken up one morning to an incredibly dry mouth, and it has stayed that way. Since then I've needed to have water with me at all times. Speaking is even more difficult when the dry lining of my oral cavity adheres to itself, trapping words inside. Every night, I am awakened several times by a dehydrated mouth and a bladder full of the water consumed to lubricate it. The prosthodontist warned that the dryness would make me more prone to tooth decay. And the mechanics of eating were complicated by the dearth of saliva for food to mingle with and slide down on.

Adjusting to a mouth that perpetually wore the little sweaters of a hangover without benefit of a party was tough enough. I didn't need to hear that the food I worked so hard to get down wasn't nourishing me.

The bonding between Jeff and Jason accelerated further with the discovery that they were both believers in the Rife generator, an electric gadget that had supposedly eradicated tumors and been suppressed by the medical establishment. Jeff, who fancied himself as something of an inventor, proudly described the do-it-yourself model he had assembled for me and anyone else he could convince to try it. It didn't seem like a good time to raise my questions about the efficacy of sticking my feet in pans of water containing electrodes that made my legs buzz from the thighs down. Though it was hard to believe that this quirky procedure helped, I'd been following Jeff's prescription for twice-daily Rife sessions. We were so hard up for intimacy that we enjoyed a strange togetherness as he hooked me up and operated the controls.

Jason's version of the generator was more sophisticated and didn't involve putting my feet in water. Before I knew it, I was lying on a table in his dimly lit sunroom, listening to the sonorous buzz of the machine and the animated buzz of Jeff and Jason's conversation. Finally, Jason declared me adequately Rifed. With my cells vibrating, I lied, telling Jason we'd be in touch, and we took leave of his drab domicile.

Some of my doctors and many cancer patients spoke highly of cancer support groups. Studies showed that women with breast cancer who joined such groups lived longer. Still, I was reluctant to join a club for which cancer was the only admission criterion. In spite of the ongoing burning in my mouth, I wanted so much to believe that the disease was gone from me forever. But Jeff and Val were willing to go with me to the group at St. Joe's, and I hoped it would do them some good.

And so on a Tuesday evening in early May, I looked around the circle of twenty people and saw that I was the only one on whom cancer had left a visible mark. One woman wore a hat over what may have been a bald head, and the tall man to my left was rather thin, but from the looks of the group, it could have been a PTA meeting.

Luckily, it was more fun than the PTA. The stories were more honest, the laughter more high-spirited, and the connections between people more powerful.

We were directed by the two warm, jovial leaders to go around the circle and introduce ourselves: name, diagnosis, treatment saga, and prognosis. I was relieved to be the only oral cancer patient, so I wasn't exposed to any visual aids of what my future might hold.

A neatly groomed engineer in his early fifties described in detail his plans for his funeral, as well as letters he'd written to his children. These were to be distributed on significant occasions in the life of each child: graduations, twenty-first birthday, wedding day, birth of a baby. This made me unspeakably sad. I wanted to shake him and yell, "Whatever happened to positive thinking?" Instead, I wondered if I should be writing letters. I felt that I'd stumbled into a secret society in which people were dealing with concerns like mine. The sense of belonging was not entirely welcome.

Next, the family members and friends who accompanied each patient spoke of the travails of caretaking someone you loved but could not cure. Except for a slight catch in her voice, Val was as matter-of-fact as ever in describing her role as manager of my cancer journey. As she spoke, she put the finishing touches on a stunning needlepoint Christmas stocking. At a subsequent group session, Val would admit that she'd been scared I'd die and also that my illness had activated her grief for our brother Greg. Many years later, she would let me know just how hard my illness had been on her, how responsible she'd felt for saving me, and how alone she had felt with that responsibility. But that night, my sister seemed as unflappable as ever and spoke with welcome certainty about my survival.

Jeff's emotions were more obvious. He teared up and stammered through his story. "My first wife died suddenly at forty-three. I still don't know why. So it's scary for me that Terri has cancer. I try to help, but I don't always know what to do." Other caretakers in the group expressed empathy. Their eyes told me how lucky they thought I was to have such a beautiful, sensitive man looking out for me. While I knew I was lucky, right now I was mad. Since my big surgery, I had been pleading with Jeff to talk about my cancer in the past tense, but he still said, "Terri has cancer."

Walking to the parking lot after the meeting, the three of us were silent, caught in our own thoughts. Mine included recognition of how vulnerable both of my primary caregivers were; Val had already lost one sibling, and Jeff had already lost a wife. In addition to wanting me around, they had their own reasons for needing to save me.

On that balmy spring evening with the magnolia and cherry trees beginning to bud, I struggled to express my feelings to Jeff and Val. I choked up a little as I thanked them and told them how much I appreciated everything they'd done for me over the past two years. Jeff squeezed my hand, and Val said, "No problem." We agreed the group was useful and that we would return. I complimented Jeff on opening up with strangers and then expressed my dismay at his verb tense.

"Yeah, it was good to hear other people admit that the caretaking wears them out too," he said, walking slowly toward the car. He paused, opened the car door for me and said, "I think I'm afraid to say 'had cancer' because I'm afraid it's not really gone."

§

The next day I had my appointment with Elizabeth. I drove down one of the few dirt roads within Ann Arbor's city limits to find her redwood home nestled among tall trees, with altars of rocks and flowers adorning the yard. As instructed, I let myself in, left my shoes on the mat in the foyer, and went downstairs. The smell of musk, the sight of day lilies and Native American art, and faint flute music greeted me. This was quite a change from the waiting rooms I'd been waiting in lately. Elizabeth obviously understood what traditional health care was just beginning to discover—a healing environment promotes healing. I sank into a macramé chair and took a deep breath. I felt better already.

After a couple of minutes, the door opened and a burst of energy emerged in the form of a pretty woman about my age, wearing a batik print skirt with almost-matching sweater and socks. She exuded warmth, freshness, and a natural sense of herself.

Elizabeth showed me into a large, rose-colored room decorated with plants, drums, candles, and shells. We sat on pillows on the taupe carpet and talked for an hour. She listened attentively to my story then declared, "You are the picture of deprivation."

No one had ever described me that way. It was not the way I wanted to be seen or to see myself. But the moment she said it, I knew it was true.

"There were no boundaries between you and your mother when you were an infant. This is not uncommon. You started very early to take her pain into your body. It was so painful that you moved up into your head and developed your intellect, becoming bright and articulate, ignoring your body."

I gasped at her accuracy. Maybe I really had been codependent *in utero*. I clasped my knees to my chest. It was as if Elizabeth had stripped off the powerful, competent image I had worked so hard to show the world. I feared she might see other secrets. But her manner was so loving that I felt safe with her, even with my entrails exposed. She seemed the ideal companion for plumbing the dark reaches of my inner world,

"Is it too late to save myself?" I asked, sounding about six years old.

"It is never too late," Elizabeth said in a gentle tone. "You can do it, but you have to separate from your parents if you are to heal and become your own person."

I'd already done years of work in the name of "separating" from Mom who, despite our issues, had been my best friend until I got divorced from Tom. If I was still so hooked on her, maybe I wasn't capable of growing up.

"I'm sure you've done a lot of work on this already, but there's more to be done for you to be truly independent," Elizabeth said, moving closer to me. *I am independent,* I pouted to myself. It was amazing how quickly I became a needy child in Elizabeth's presence. She gazed at me with steady blue-gray eyes.

Maybe Elizabeth was right and I had never let go of my mom. Suddenly I sensed that my own survival hinged on doing this inner work.

"Where do I start?" I asked.

"We should start with an extraction, followed by a soul retrieval. When you're stronger, we can do some bioenergetics to help you get back into your body."

"I'm not sure I know exactly what you mean," I said. The only "extractions" I knew of were dental, and "soul retrievals" sounded too bizarre even for a seasoned seeker like me.

"In the shamanic tradition, it is believed that disease originates in the energy body. Extraction works on the energetic level to remove any intrusion that would eventually filter down to the physical body. An intrusion is an unwanted pattern that originated in another person but now lingers in your energy body. Does this make sense to you?" Elizabeth asked.

"Sort of," I replied, wondering what the hell I was getting myself into.

Elizabeth smiled. "This is all a little hard to put into words because we are talking about the nonphysical realm. But I've done this with lots of people, and the results are amazing."

I nodded for her to continue. "When the physical body experiences severe trauma, such as abuse or an accident or, in your case, cancer and its treatment, part of the soul exits the body in response to the threat of annihilation." Maybe this explained why I had lost touch with my spirit.

"The soul can also be depleted when significant people unconsciously usurp parts of it. Regardless of how portions of your soul departed, the retrieval is a process for getting it back, making you more whole. It involves using totems that the shamans call power animals." Elizabeth paused.

"Well, I get it that holes in my soul don't help healing," I said. "But that's about all that's clear right now."

She laughed. "Maybe that's enough for today. If you want more information, you can read *Soul Retrieval* by Sandra Ingerman."

The time had come for a decision. Should I venture into this strange realm with my new cosmic chaperone? There was something about Elizabeth that allowed me to quiet my usual cynicism. I was stunned by the speed and accuracy of her assessment. Her presence communicated that she'd always have faith in me. She might be the only person who really believed I could survive. Somehow I trusted her to guide me back to that belief when I waivered. And maybe I could find my way back to God in the process.

"Okay," I said, and we made an appointment for my extraction.

In the days before our next meeting, I skimmed *Soul Retrieval*. Elizabeth had also recommended contacting my "inner child," which I did by writing in my journal. I wrote to the youngster I was now calling "Tate" and told her what Elizabeth had said. As I wrote, I recalled the times that my mother thought she had cancer and how much that possibility had scared me, even though it never turned out to be true. Maybe I had absorbed Mom's fear of cancer along with her pain.

I uncovered resentment about how much of my childhood was spent caring for my "sick mother" and my siblings while my father was busy with business or golf. Since so many of my needs were not being met, some part of me had apparently decided to deny that I had them and to focus on the needs of others. I was disturbed to find myself still clinging to that resentment and to the hope that, someday, my parents would take care of me the way I wanted them to. These childish longings pulled me down into the hole of my own emptiness.

But I couldn't stay there. It was time to grow up and take care of myself.

I wore my radiation sweat suit to my extraction. After a warm hug, Elizabeth positioned me on the floor, making sure I had pillows in all the right places to allow my reconstructed body to lie comfortably. I summoned my experience with self-hypnosis and mentally put myself in a safe, quiet place. My muscles let go more completely than they had in months, and I sank into the thick carpet. Occasionally I could hear Elizabeth speak, but I didn't care what she was saying. Far too soon, I heard the drumbeat that was my signal to return to the room.

Although I hadn't spoken, Elizabeth had gleaned information about me from some "energetic level." She eagerly described her findings. "I uncovered a negative thought pattern that you probably inherited from past generations. I also found *six* power animals: a tiger, a mother elephant with three babies, and a turtle. Most people only have one."

"Oh," I replied, not at all sure how to respond to the discovery of this power zoo in my energy field. The process hadn't eradicated the pain in my mouth or my fear that a recurrence was causing it, but it had been somehow comforting.

I decided not to obsess about what it all meant, to try to accept this experience on a metaphorical level. I imagined putting the tiger in my mouth to eat any cancer and in my head to eat negative thoughts. The sweet mother elephant and her three babies, which I designated as Justin, Eric, and me, were placed in my heart. I envisioned the turtle in my belly to represent my connection to Mother Earth and giving birth to myself. While it all made some kind of intuitive sense, I felt a little confused and very vulnerable as I left the session.

Elizabeth's postextraction instructions included keeping to myself and staying in touch with my inner child during the next few days. It was challenging to navigate the abyss between the world inside and external reality. My correspondence with Tate became more regular and reliable. I apologized for neglecting her for all those years and asked how I could make it up to her. She requested love and food and flowers and walks and time near the water. She also asked that I stop putting everyone else's wishes before hers.

Back in Elizabeth's tranquil room, I prepared for the soul retrieval. Soft, soothing music played in the background. Once again, Elizabeth arranged me comfortably on the floor and told me that all I needed to do was relax. She then began to dance around me, chanting and shaking a gourd rattle.

I couldn't suppress a smirk, imagining what Michael, my decidedly anti–New Age second husband, would say if he could see me. I recalled the time a massage therapist had explained chakras, the body's energy centers, to Michael, and he informed her that his had been surgically removed. I felt somewhat skeptical myself, but my faith in Elizabeth and the truth in the insights she had helped me discover allowed me to push past my doubts.

When Elizabeth beckoned me back to awareness, she looked thrilled about what she had discovered. "In all the retrievals I have done," she said, "I have never seen anything like this. There was a glowing light and then Jesus appeared, holding a huge diamond. He wants you to have it for protection."

All I could say was "Wow." Elizabeth's mention of Jesus was startling, as she had never struck me as religious in the traditional sense. I was pleased to learn that Jesus was patrolling my soul and very relieved that He hadn't deserted me entirely.

The special connection I'd felt with Jesus as a little girl was warm and personal, and it didn't match the guilt-inducing way He was described by Rev. Rauth at the Grosse Pointe Woods Presbyterian Church. I could never figure out what I had done to deserve the "sinner" label that the reverend applied so liberally. I remember one Sunday when I was about eight and he was especially vehement in his condemnation. I felt pretty in my favorite coral, faux-silk dress, black patent-leather shoes, and white gloves, but I worried that this might be the sin of pride. I whispered a prayer to Jesus, "Whatever it is that I'm doing wrong, I will make it up to you because I'm going to be a nurse when I grow up."

It always seemed to me that what one wore to the GPW Presbyterian Church on Sunday mattered more than how one lived between services. So as a young adult, I'd abandoned my Protestant upbringing. I did join a church right after my brother died but found it too stiff and formal to nurture my connection with Jesus, so my attendance dwindled to His birthday and the day He arose from the dead.

Once my spiritual path veered off the straight and narrow, it took a lot of unorthodox turns. Several years after Greg died, I met a woman who "channeled" the spirit of Chief Joseph of the Nez Perce. Speaking in her "Chief" voice, she assured me that my brother was "far away among the stars" and doing well. She also told me to "return to

Christianity to see what Jesus has to offer." I found this interesting and purchased a cross, which I wore for a time.

A few years later, I joined the Mastermind group. In the first meeting, I prayed for a healthy relationship with a man. That evening, on my first real date with Jeff, he introduced me to *A Course in Miracles,* purported to be the channeled words of Jesus. Like me, his wide-ranging spirituality included a fondness for Jesus. When we moved in together, Jeff and I created a group to study the *Course,* and he also began attending my Mastermind group, both of which were a great comfort to us.

So Jesus was no stranger to me, but I had not experienced His presence in the way Elizabeth described. I was happy to see Him again and grateful for the safety that His protective diamond might provide. And of course I've always been a sucker for men bearing lavish jewels.

Elizabeth went on to describe the retrieval. "I found you as an infant, still attached to your mother by the umbilical cord. I severed the cord." I wondered if this had something to do with the fact that my birth was a month overdue.

Elizabeth looked at me with tears in her eyes. "A three-year-old part of you was attached to your father at the heart. It was hard for him to let you go. He believed he needed your heart energy. But now you need it back." She enunciated very clearly. "I also uncovered a seventeen- to twenty-one-year-old version of you who is *very* angry. She is full of rage, and her mouth is full of words that need to be said."

Elizabeth's words were clear, but much of their meaning eluded me. I resonated with the images of connection to my mother. But the part about my dad was baffling. I had always felt distant from him and had no sense of a "heart connection."

The angry young woman was a total stranger. My young adulthood was all about being perfect. I was such a good girl that my mother never had to give me a curfew but trusted me to be in on time. I was allowed to entertain my high school boyfriend in a hotel when I visited him at Northwestern, as long as he left my hotel by 2:00 a.m. While I never understood what we could do after 2:00 a.m. that we could not have done before, I always made him leave by 1:59

and remained a virgin until I married Tom. As soon as we were married, I wanted babies, in part to please Mom.

Anger was not acceptable for good girls like me. It was okay for Mom to yell and bang cupboards, and my siblings did their share of yelling back, but I never wanted to make her any more upset than she already was. I remembered what my therapist friend had said about unexpressed rage and wondered if mine had contributed to the cancer in my mouth and whether I would ever have the guts to let my anger out.

"It is important that you take the time to be quiet and integrate all of this," Elizabeth advised. "You will be very vulnerable for a while."

Elizabeth was right again. I felt fragile and awkward now that my energy body had had almost as much surgery as my physical body. Much as I wanted to be quiet and integrate, it was time to construct thick walls around Tate and take her to Columbus for our checkup.

§

"You look great," said Dr. Gilbert as he and Dr. Loud surveyed their reconstructive handiwork.

"You guys have a really warped sense of beauty," I replied. "The only time I feel pretty anymore is in your waiting room."

Dr. Gilbert bristled at my honesty and quickly resumed his exam. "Well, your flap is inflamed near where the bar is showing, but I don't think we want to do anything about that at the moment. We may have to close that exposed area at some point, but it's okay for now."

It occurred to me to ask just how they would go about "closing" the growing gap in my flap, but I figured that further surgery was involved so I kept quiet. Besides, if, as I suspected, cancer was once again rampaging through my oral cavity, the whole bar business would be secondary. But Dr. Prescott did not find anything that looked to him like cancer. He speculated that my symptoms might be the result of the problem with the bar or nerve pressure from surgery or radiation.

"Keep irrigating that wound on your chest twice a day, apply antibiotic cream, and cover it with gauze," Dr. Prescott told me. "It will heal one of these days."

Once outside the clinic, the fresh air washed me in relief. Their opinions did not prove that I didn't have cancer, but they also didn't determine that I did. For that I was beyond grateful. "I want to find the best cup of coffee in Columbus," I told Jeff. He drove slowly down High Street so I could scout each establishment with my "restaurant radar." My internal signal went off in front of a marginally trendy-looking eatery nestled among seedy bars and pawnshops caged in those gigantic metal baby gates.

"That's it!" I said, pointing at Rigsby's. In the parking lot, I did a shot of Roxicet to ready my mouth for its big adventure.

Large, bright, abstract paintings covered the red-brick walls of what turned out to be the only five-star restaurant in Columbus. In the gleaming open kitchen, multiple chefs were chopping vegetables, whisking sauces, and filling the air with the rich fragrance of garlic and caramelized onions. Near the long, marble bar, a skilled pianist played "Satin Doll" on a baby grand.

Jeff and I didn't have much to say to each other, but there was a lot of delicious sensory input. The coffee exceeded my expectations. Drinking from a real cup was still challenging for me, but I savored each sloppy sip. Having succeeded with coffee, I dared to take on soup. I slowly managed to ingest the beige onion purée, much to the delight of my taste buds, which were just now beginning to wake up from radiation. Next, I decided to tackle the risotto. What was $10.95 for mushy rice when I had just had a good checkup? Besides, Jeff would always eat it if I couldn't. Another victory! I mashed up a few bites of the savory mushroom and Marsala risotto and washed it down with bubbly water. Riding high, I moved on to the crème brûlée, which I handled like a pro.

Now that I could eat a little, I decided it was time to work on my diet in case I lived long enough for nutrition to make a difference. Jeff started promoting "live foods" again. He was ready to clear his calendar for two weeks at the end of June so we could take part in a residential training program at a live foods center. I needed to see the place before I would consider it.

The day of the open house at what we now called "food camp" dawned bright and beautiful. We drove along winding country roads, relishing the burgeoning greenery and blossoms and hoping that the food we were about to eat didn't come from the rundown farms we were passing. Then I realized that food camp *was* one of the rundown farms.

The shabbiness extended to the buildings and the rubble-covered grounds. I had seen less depressing back wards in state hospitals. In sharp contrast, the inhabitants were loaded with zeal and stories of miraculous healings from eating raw.

One especially gaunt, exuberant fellow gave us a tour: the residential quarters with hard, narrow cots where we would sleep for two weeks, the bookstore with its fifteen books, the colonics center whose purpose was obvious, and the wheatgrass greenhouse with windows so dirty that photosynthesis was the real miracle. The pinnacle of the tour was the kitchen, where a swarming mass of smiling people were busy not cooking.

And then there was the grand buffet. I took a plate and fell into line behind Jeff. There were platters of raw vegetables, big tossed salads loaded with sprouts, nut loaf, and rocklike dehydrated crackers better used as weapons than snacks. I had seven lower teeth. Ensure and smoothies were still the mainstays of my diet. Most of the dishes on this crunchy smorgasbord came with cayenne or other peppers to introduce a little flavor into the bland repast, so anything I could chew would be too spicy for my radiated mouth. The Bitch nagged, "You'd better at least try something. This might be the thing that saves you." But there was no way I could eat any of it. I sat sipping tea and feeling like I had at junior high dances, while everyone else, especially Jeff, wolfed down heaps of food.

By the time we left, Jeff was feeling the curative powers of eating raw and was ready to enroll in camp. "I don't know whether depression or starvation would get me first, but I know I wouldn't make it out of there alive," I told him. "I'd rather go to San Francisco and visit my kids."

In truth, I hadn't given up on food camp. I wanted to be able to tell one of those miraculous healing stories myself some day.

A few days later I went alone to a new oncologist to check out the continuing symptoms in my mouth and to get a refill for Roxicet.

Ellen Calveris didn't act like a doctor. With her plain, brown hair tied back in a long ponytail and her long, loose, flowered dress and Birkenstocks, she didn't look the part. Most unusual was the way she talked to me—as if I were her friend or, at least, her equal.

"I didn't know much about oral cancer," she said, in a gentle voice. "So I read up on it last night in preparation for your visit."

Her honesty increased my faith in her. It had been two years since I'd heard a doctor say, "I don't know," although clearly many of them hadn't.

"From what I can gather, even if the symptoms you currently have are not cancer, it is very likely that future symptoms will be." If I'd had a supporter with me, I would have stopped listening at this point, but I was on my own. "Having had two occurrences, the chances of a third are extremely high," she said.

I didn't feel the panic I would have expected these words to spark. Dr. Calveris's soft, even manner seemed to calm me.

"The surgeons will want to take extreme measures," she continued, "because you're young. You will have to decide how much to let them do. It is a quality-of-life issue."

Bit by bit, her message took root in my awareness. This kind woman was telling me that I was not going to make it. She wasn't just quoting statistics; she had reviewed *my* case and sounded more definite than any other doctor had. Her combination of gentleness and certainty disarmed my defenses. I suddenly believed I was going to die.

I let her finish and asked for a refill of Roxicet, and then I fled, past smiling volunteers in the quaint gift shop and into the parking lot shaded by budding trees, which unlike me, were bursting with new life.

My first impulse was to call Jeff, as I had in each of the previous crisis moments. No, I needed to be with this news alone for a while. After all, I would be dying alone.

Now that all my efforts at regaining health had proved futile, it was time for a big, strong cup of coffee. I found a trendy café, chose a small table near the pastry case, and stared blankly out the window. I reveled in the taste of the blackish brew and a large, luscious chocolate éclair as I pondered what to do with what little was left of my life. There was a curious freedom in not having to try anymore.

Suddenly, clarity seized me. I rushed to the pay phone and dialed Jeff's office number.

"Fuck food camp," I told him. "We're going to California."

What I didn't realize at the time was that California *is* food camp.

sausalito salvation

M uch as he would have preferred to go to food camp, Jeff supported my decision to go to California to discuss my impending death with my children. He'd known since we first saw Dr. Dudar that my odds weren't good, so he wasn't as shocked as I was at the new doctor's prognosis. And he understood my need to deliver the news to my kids in person.

We would need a place with a kitchen because I couldn't eat restaurant food. As usual, Val had a solution. A friend of hers was moving in with his fiancée and offered us his apartment in Sausalito, my favorite town on the planet and the scene of my first honeymoon.

The apartment was a twenty-minute ride across the Golden Gate Bridge from Justin and Eric's place in San Francisco. I was pleased that my sons chose to live together and couldn't wait to see their apartment. Though they claim to have fought as kids, I remember them getting along very well. Because they divided their time between Tom's house and mine from the time they were three and seven, the two of them were their most consistent family unit. Thank God they had each other then and that they had each other now.

One afternoon before our trip, I took my journal into the orchard, sat under an apple tree, and tried to soak up nature and the reality of my new prognosis. Even though I hadn't worked for months, it was rare for me to slow down long enough to enjoy the beauty of our secluded setting. Being still, my attention suddenly shifted from the sky and clouds to my internal landscape. I felt a hole open up inside me in the area of my solar plexus. What was this? In ways that are difficult to describe, I got an odd sense that there *was* a part of me that wanted to die, and it was located deep in this hole. How could I be so frightened of death and also welcome it as an escape from fear? My vision was not broad enough to embrace both poles of this paradox. I couldn't tell how much of me wanted to die, but I needed to find that part and befriend it. I had no idea where to begin.

I started to write in my journal but suddenly looked up and out over the orchard to the line of tall walnut trees that bordered our property. The trees were brimming with birds, some of which had a call that sounded remarkably like "Terrrrrri." I took it personally and assumed something out there was trying to get my attention. I breathed deeply, smelling the recently mown grass, and listened. An unfamiliar sense of peace moved through me, and I knew that cancer was not going to kill me.

Returning to my journal, the words quickly wrote themselves: *I am not going to die from this cancer.*

Then more words came, telling me that it was not my time to go because I had work to do. The message instructed me to stop reproaching myself for not being able to adhere to any one system of healing. It said that God had made me dissatisfied with existing cancer treatment regimens because I needed to create my own recipe for healing, and that I'd learn to love my eclectic ways. I was reminded of how, ever since I'd studied William James's *The Varieties of Religious Experience* in college, I'd borrowed elements from many approaches to craft my own spiritual quilt.

I sat back against the apple tree and wondered if others might someday use my process, whatever it was, for finding their way through the ever-expanding plethora of healing options. Maybe this was the work I was going to stay on Earth to do. Perhaps I'd describe it in that memoir I was going to write.

The belief that cancer wouldn't kill me, along with my renewed sense of purpose, lasted several hours until the persistent pain in my mouth and Dr. Calveris's words in my head ate away at my confidence. By the next day, I was convinced again that cancer was going to kill me—soon.

The flight to California was easier than the one to Florida because Jeff was there to help. I imagined people around us wondering what a handsome guy like him was doing with such a funny-looking woman. I wanted to tell them that I used to be pretty.

Val's friend met us in Sausalito. He led the way to his apartment, winding up the hillside past perfectly landscaped houses. The same sun had been shining back in Ann Arbor, but it was somehow brighter here. We passed magnolias the size of maple trees, giant tufts of pampas grass growing wild, and calla lilies everywhere. The pain in my mouth was almost forgotten as I attempted to absorb whatever it was that made this place so beautiful.

Bud opened the door to the top-floor unit of a brown-shingled apartment building. The small studio felt like an upscale tree house decorated by Crate and Barrel. Beyond the pines and poplars was a view too wonderful to be real. Rows of masts bobbed in the breeze on Richardson Bay, white sails pulled their crafts through glistening blue water, and an occasional kayaker paddled peacefully along. Across the Bay were the green hills and the glamorous homes of Tiburon and Belvedere. I tried to convey my gratitude to Bud, but there was no way to thank him enough for letting us use this tiny sanctuary. It pleased me that Bud, who was very handsome, looked right at me when we talked, as if my appearance did not offend him.

Bright sunshine woke me on Monday morning. It took me a moment to realize where I was. I went to the window to check on the view—still beautiful. We enjoyed a slow, lazy breakfast of soft cereal, coffee, and carrot juice made with the juicer Jeff had lugged from Michigan.

I discovered a Bloomingdale's catalog among Bud's trendy magazines. I probably couldn't afford anything in it but browsed to prevent further atrophy of my once powerful shopping muscles. I was on vacation.

Ralph Lauren fingertip towels were on sale for five dollars each and monogramming was free! After much deliberation, I settled on six towels for our Ann Arbor bathrooms: three beige ones with Jeff's monogram in brown letters and three burgundy ones with mine in ivory. Thirty dollars, plus shipping and handling, seemed a small price to pay for the immortality that towels bearing my initials implied.

Pleased with my savings, I set about finding a venue in which to discuss my impending death with my kids. I called Tiburon's Center for Attitudinal Healing, which conducted cancer support groups. It turned out that they held one group for patients and a separate one for families, which wouldn't allow me to talk to my kids in a safe place as I had planned. I felt defeated.

"We can handle it ourselves," said Jeff. We planned The Death Talk for Thursday afternoon. We agreed to try to keep things light with the kids until then, starting with their visit that afternoon.

My usual excitement at seeing my children was tempered by the realization that our visits were numbered. I couldn't keep from crying when I saw them, their lumbering frames and enormous feet filling the small apartment. Eric's hair was long, his face hadn't seen a razor in a while, and he looked tired. "Hey Mom," he said, with a hug so long and tight that breathing became difficult. He had not seen me since right after the surgery, almost six months before. My looks had improved since then, but I could tell that his sensitive artist's eyes still had trouble taking in my appearance.

"Momma," said Justin, "how ya' doin'?" and he hugged me nearly as long as his brother had. If he was reacting to my new visage, it was not obvious. Justin had an almost shaved head, a unique distribution of facial hair, and an expanded array of tattoos and piercings since the last time I had seen him. "Casual" is the nicest way to describe my sons' style of dress. They might have frightened me in the proverbial dark alley, but they were my babies, and my heart could not have been fuller at the sight of them.

We decided to explore Sausalito in search of food. The drive down Bridgeway—quaint shops, flowering bushes, pines mixed with palms, sculptured elephants, a huge fountain, and unique homes from funky to fabulous—reminded me how much I love Sausalito, not least because it offers my favorite view. The blue water, rippling to the beat of the neighboring Pacific, stretched to San Francisco. The triangular tip of the Transamerica building pierced the skyline. Chunky freighters chugged past the rocky protuberance of Alcatraz and out to sea. Smaller craft cruised around the verdant mound of Angel Island. I thought, *God, what I'd give to live in this place.*

Over lunch, the kids got Jeff laughing until he cried, and then they laughed at him laughing. Nothing made me happier than to see them happy together—I had found a good father for my kids. Jeff and I had created a real family together, and that would be the toughest thing to leave. But I decided to enjoy it while I could. I began chuckling myself. This was dangerous, as I couldn't eat and laugh at the same time, but it seemed worth the risk. About midway through my clam chowder, I heard a clicking sound in my mouth. I would postpone worrying about that as well.

Not only did the noise continue, but the next day my mouth started to hurt. It was a different kind of discomfort than the tingling, burning, shooting pain I had been having for months. This pain was in the area where the bar attached to my lower jaw, and it was more intense. I began to brood over what it meant and what to do about it. Jeff and I engaged in endless conversations about potential causes. The possibilities we knew about included cancer, an infection of my remaining jaw, and problems with the titanium pseudo-jaw or the flap.

Feeling like a foreigner in a land of fun, I now resented the kayakers skimming the surface of the bay. I was furious that my vacation, maybe my last vacation, was being ruined by *more* goddamned health problems. I was about to express my fury when I noticed the look on Jeff's ashen face. He cowered on the couch, his body rigid.

"I think we should go home," he said. "I don't want to be thousands of miles from your doctors with a serious problem going on." He had a point. But we had six more days in California, and I wasn't giving them up without a fight.

My symptoms were worse the next day. I could hear the clicking whenever I moved my jaw, not just when I was eating, and the pain was more intense. Jeff called Northwest Airlines to find the next available flight to Detroit.

"It's almost totally booked because of the Fourth of July," he said, holding his hand over the receiver. "There are two seats left on the 9:00 a.m. flight tomorrow, and I want to take them. It'll cost $500."

I shook my head "no" as vigorously as my reconfigured neck would allow and said, "Please, please let's talk about it some more. Let me look for a doctor out here." I was less concerned about the money than I was about missing the talk with my kids and the Cole Porter review I had gotten tickets for in San Francisco on Friday night. Jeff slammed down the phone and stomped into the bathroom. I felt very alone with my small victory.

The next two days were spent calling my doctors in the Midwest in search of referrals in the Bay Area. I asked Jeff to do the actual calling because my diction was still too mangled for strangers to decipher on the phone and because I wanted to keep his mind off travel plans. While he was on the phone, I fixed my gaze on the pink clouds and the still waters of the Bay, as if intense staring might compensate for lost time with the view. Through a convoluted series of callbacks, secretaries, and messages, by the end of the day on Thursday we had learned that doctors Bradford, Gilbert, and Prescott recommended I go to an emergency room.

I was not happy to hear that my symptoms required immediate attention, and I hated the emergency room idea. The chaos, chill, and wait time of trauma centers are always daunting, but going to a new hospital around the first of July when medical residents start their rotations is downright dangerous.

"I can just imagine the look on the face of a terrified resident peering into this mouth on the first day of their otolaryngology residency. No way," I said, as we discussed our options for the umpteenth time. Jeff agreed and headed for the phone to call the airline.

"Not so fast," I stalled. "We haven't tried Dr. Watson. Let's see, it's already past five there. I'll call in the morning."

Jeff stared at me as if I'd lost my mind. "You're going to call Watson?"

"Well, why not? He certainly owes me a favor."

Jeff didn't like the idea, but it was time to go to the city to pick up Eric and Justin for The Talk, so he let it go.

The four of us clustered in the cozy living room. The tone of the gathering was gloomy despite the sun shining brightly through all the windows. Justin sprawled over one end of the loveseat, his long legs draped over the coffee table, his hands clenching into fists. Jeff sat stiffly in the only comfortable chair. Eric languished on the floor, staring at the ceiling, his brow creased and the rest of his face hanging on him like a drab old coat. I borrowed one of the director's chairs from the kitchen. Words and laughter usually flowed freely when we were all together. Now we sat inside the silence, barely breathing.

I had asked Jeff to start things off. "I guess you know what we're here to talk about." He spoke in carefully measured words.

"Not really," said Eric, his voice as glum as his countenance.

"Well, you know that your mother has been having more of that tingling and burning in her mouth . . ."

"No, I didn't know that," said Justin in a flat tone tinged with irritation.

"I didn't either," said Eric.

Perhaps I had neglected to mention it to them.

"It's been going on for a couple months," Jeff said. "Her doctors can't find anything, and they say it could be due to the radiation or the surgery. So we don't know that it's cancer."

"Then what's the problem?" asked Justin, sounding eager to escape this grim terrain and return to our typical repartee.

"For one thing, Watson said it wasn't cancer last fall, and he was wrong," I responded, unable to keep quiet any longer. "Also, I went to see a new doctor a couple weeks ago. She said that even if these symptoms aren't cancer, the next ones most likely will be. With the kind and amount of cancer I had, and the fact that it recurred, it's pretty certain to come back. She said the surgeons would want to be aggressive because I'm young, but that I'll have to decide what I want done based on quality-of-life issues."

No one moved. The only sound was an occasional sniffle. My mouth was even drier than usual, and my breath burned in my chest as I watched my message settle over my somber sons. I wanted so much to erase, or at least diminish, their pain, and there was nothing I could say or do. I could not imagine how I would cope with their grief. I wondered if it might be easier to die at that moment than to agonize through months or years of good-bye.

As if reading my mind, Justin said, "Don't give up, Mom. Those predictions don't apply to you. You're different. You can make it. I know you can." He was the only one who wasn't crying, but the tears were in his voice, along with anger. His legs vibrated. I knew his bravado came from wishful thinking, but still, it helped. It amazed me to notice how susceptible I still was to the opinions of others when my own hope floundered.

"I don't plan to give up," I said, struggling to get the words out. "I just wanted you guys to know what's going on. It's strange, but this prognosis gives me a certain kind of freedom. If survival is such a long shot, I don't have to try so hard. I can lighten up on myself a little bit." Even as I uttered these words, I wondered if I could live them. "So, I plan to do pretty much what I want from here on. And part of that means spending more time with you guys."

"It's about time you gave yourself a break," said Justin, "but don't give up, okay?"

"I won't," I assured him.

"Do you promise?" asked Eric quietly.

"Yes, I promise." I pulled myself out of my chair and hugged my kids, signaling the conclusion of The Talk.

We played dice and Boggle, had dinner, and then lapsed into a shared celluloid coma by watching mindless movies. As we drove Justin and Eric home, the lights of San Francisco across the bay from Sausalito created a spectacle as breathtaking as the daytime view. It looked like some cherubic contractor had used Christmas lights and borrowed stars to construct a twinkling fairyland. The night was clear and the full moon reflected off the inky water. I was grateful to be there to see it with the three men I loved most.

Jeff had allowed me a reprieve for the meeting with the kids, but my mouth still hurt and clicked the next morning and he got back on his "Let's go home" campaign. I was running out of excuses to stay and confidence that we should. But I had that one last tactic. I called Dr. Watson's assistant who had helped me during my first round of cancer. She promised to check with the doctor and call me back. The phone rang at noon.

"Terri, this is Cindy from Dr. Watson's office," she said, sounding as cheerful as ever. Could she not know how Watson had failed me and how angry I was? "Dr. Watson says you should see Dr. Thomas Irvine. He's the head of otolaryngology at UCSF. Dr. Irvine practiced here for years and they are old friends. Tell him Dr. Watson sent you."

Finally something was going my way. But even as my spirits lifted at finding a nearby doctor, I knew it would take a flat-out miracle to get in to see a department chief at a university hospital on the Friday afternoon before the Fourth of July weekend. Except in emergencies, I had never gotten an appointment with my specialists without weeks or months of lead time. Buoyed by my success in communicating with Cindy, and not wanting to ask Jeff for help, I called the clinic myself. The hours I had spent in phone purgatory at other academic health centers had prepared me for a long, tortuous wait and much punching of buttons to get to a real person, so I was startled when a live voice answered. My astonishment increased when the voice indicated that Dr. Irvine was in and that she would ask if he could see me, and it peaked two minutes later when she returned to the phone and said, "Can you be here at 1:30?"

"Absolutely!" I stammered having no idea how far UCSF was from Sausalito. Given all this divine intervention, I figured we would make it to the clinic on time.

Dr. Irvine did not seem alarmed by my symptoms. He regaled us with good old boy stories of the good old days in good old Ann Arbor with good old Dr. Watson. He wrote a prescription for an antibiotic, told me to be seen as soon as I got home, and bid us a friendly farewell. If my hip had not still been tender, I would have skipped down the hall.

The medication cost $80 at the Sausalito Pharmacy. Apparently nothing came cheap in Marin County. I started to worry about the money we were spending but decided that with plenty of drugs and three whole days of vacation stretching before me, it was not time for fiscal fretting. Besides, it was time to enjoy the $230 worth of theater tickets I had bought.

I justified this extravagance with my love of theater, the likelihood of imminent death, and my pride that I had taught my hip sons to appreciate Cole Porter.

Fueled by Roxicet and the joy of having a son on either side of me, Porter's music took me to a place where pain and cancer and death were irrelevant. I knew all the lyrics, and I crooned along:

> Every time we say good-bye, I want to die a little.
> Every time we say good-bye, I wonder why a little.

High and smiling, I looked over at Eric. He burst into tears. My own tears answered his, and I was no longer part of the chorus.

Long before I was ready, it was time to leave the picturesque town with champagne in the air. I had never before been in love with a place. I wandered, forlorn, around the small apartment, saying good-bye to the bathroom, the bed, the kitchen, and saddest of all, the view. I prayed to God that I would see it again.

"You know," Jeff startled me out of my prayer, "you've done more healing this week by looking out that window than you've done in the health-care system in the last six months." I nodded in agreement. He put his arm around me and steered me down the hall.

Locking the door behind him, Jeff said, "I don't know how we're going to swing it, but we have to find a way to keep this place." I'd never loved him more.

bar none

On the UCSF doctor's recommendation, I saw Dr. Bradford as soon as I got home. Sitting in the crowded, window-less waiting room at U of M's "Oto" Clinic, the fortitude I had used to keep Jeff from aborting our vacation melted into fear. Would these be the symptoms that signaled the inevitable return of my cancer?

I relaxed a bit at the sight of Dr. Bradford's blonde curls, big smile, and starched white coat. After peeking, probing, and palpating me from the neck up, making me choke in spite of her gentleness, Dr. Bradford could not say what was causing my mouth pain or the click-ing. She suggested an MRI. I was not enthused. I didn't even want to be in a doctor's office. I wanted to be sitting at the kitchen table in Bud's apartment, drinking coffee and gazing at sailboats.

My only experience with an MRI was the one I had on the eve of the big surgery. The terror of that time had blunted my memory of the test. I knew I had felt claustrophobic during the long hour I spent inside the just-bigger-than-body-sized metal tube, into which I had been inserted like a human tampon. But I trusted Dr. Bradford, and I could not let my current mouth problems go unchecked any longer. I might still have a jaw if Watson had done an MRI instead of testing for lichen planus.

Once back inside the dreaded cylinder, the claustrophobia reap-peared. The technician warned me not to move. My mouth was dry.

I wanted to cough. I conjured every hypnotic induction I could recall to make my mind transport me away from the hideous chamber. I was jolted from my tenuous trance by a loud clanging noise emanating from the machine that encased me. I tried to convince my body parts to cooperate using the same warning the technician had used on me, "If you move, we'll have to start the whole thing over."

Just when I thought we must be done, the technician's voice reverberated within the steel tube, as if it came from another galaxy, "Okay, Terri, we're ten minutes into the test. Only forty-five to go."

There was no way I could sustain the gagging stillness for that long. I frantically started to count the seconds, but got distracted trying to figure out how many seconds there were in forty-five minutes. It felt as though the world's most powerful sponge had been at work in my mouth. Then it dawned on me: I had had working salivary glands during my last MRI. The urge to cough was so powerful that I was sure I would choke to death if I did not indulge it. I would have traded my house for a glass of water.

At long last, I was moving, being ejected from the tube to the welcome words of the technician saying, "All right, Terri, we're done."

I croaked, "Wa-a-a-ter," and received some in a small Dixie cup.

Anxious anticipation of the test results devoured massive amounts of mental energy. And being home from vacation meant that my interior dictator resumed tyrannizing my inner world. The Vile Bitch was relentless in her efforts to goad me into exercising, improving my diet, healing the still-weeping wound near my heart, giving up Roxicet, writing a book that would save the world, and on and on.

I began to explore my resistance to these activities, all of which I knew were "good for me." I started with writing because that held the most potential for pleasure. In my journal, I started a treatise, "On why I am not writing," hoping I might glean some insight from the inner advisor I had heard from before. The answer came that I was not writing because I thought I was dying. Taking time alone and the quiet contemplation necessary for writing were too frightening. I felt heavy with exhaustion as I wrote, "I don't feel like meditating or exercising or eating fruits and vegetables or giving up coffee. And I don't feel like writing. There is nothing left of me to put on paper." It would take years for me to recognize this voice as the one that wrote "Speechless" in Taos, the part of me that saw death as the only way out of relentless responsibility.

Having unearthed and expressed the source of my resistance, I was able to write a short piece to send to my long-distance writing group from the Natalie Goldberg workshop. July's theme for the monthly writing exchange was "I Will Never Again."

I generated thirty-seven things that I had done for the last time. Among them: bite into a hard Red Delicious apple, feel eyes on me and think it's because I'm attractive, wear the sexy Lycra tops I'd bought in Taos, go braless with both nipples pointing in the same direction, put total faith in any doctor, be as pretty as my sister, and take life for granted.

I began taking short walks down Peters Road. My postsurgical gait was still slow and awkward, but I pushed myself to the part of the road where the trees created a lush awning overhead. Some days I made it as far as the river and watched the murky water slapping the rocks. When my energy was spent, I picked out an identifiable rock or tree to measure my progress, hoping I could go farther the next time.

I attempted to curtail my use of Roxicet, which I now sometimes secretly used for relaxation and the momentary buzz rather than because I was in pain. Even under extreme duress, my perfectionism would not allow me a chemical break from the mental suffering. My critical voice, which caused a lot of that suffering, warned that I might grow dependent on the red elixir or build up a tolerance to it so it wouldn't work when the really big cancer hit.

As I reduced my reliance on Roxicet, I sought relief by fantasizing about Sausalito. One July evening, I let myself recline for a moment on the well-padded chaise lounge on our deck. I watched fireflies in the orchard and stars overhead, which reminded me of the night skyline of San Francisco as seen from downtown Sausalito. I called Val to thank her again for finding Bud's apartment for us.

"While we were out there, Jeff said it was so healing for me that we ought to rent it for a while since Bud's lease is up," I told my sister. "It was really sweet, but now we're back in financial reality, and he's wavering. He's right. There's just no way we can afford it." I gently massaged the sore place on my jaw as we talked.

"Why don't you ask his landlord if you can have it on a month-to-month basis?" said Val, who was always creative where money was concerned.

"That's not a bad idea," I responded, although I was hesitant to make a real estate deal that so accurately reflected my prognosis. The landlord was amenable to a month-to-month lease, and Jeff told him we would think it over.

Focusing on the possibility of spending some of our near-term future in Sausalito let us avoid the subject of our long-term future, so we thought it over and over. The pros and cons of renting the apartment filled all the holes in our conversation. We agreed that the idea was totally impractical and that practical was not our style. We postponed making a decision and luxuriated in deciding.

My hopes for a future soared when Dr. Bradford reported the MRI had not found any cancer. Nor had the test revealed the source of the tingling and burning in my mouth or the cause of the clicking. Although she doubted that the expanding hole in my flap could be surgically repaired, she wanted me to see Dr. Gilbert because the flap and the bar were his handiwork. While I was in Columbus, I should see Dr. Prescott about my symptoms.

My parents had volunteered to go to Ohio with Jeff and me for my late July visits to Drs. Gilbert and Prescott. Seated in the back of their Cadillac, with my father at the wheel and my mother in the passenger seat, I looked at their mostly gray heads and recalled all the times we had driven US 23 to Columbus to visit Mom's parents when her hair was black and his was blond. It felt a little strange to be in the backseat again at my age. Unlike previous trips, Dad wasn't smoking a cigar, Jeff and I weren't fighting over territory as Greg and I had, and no one was threatening to throw up. It also felt different being with my parents since my sessions with Elizabeth. Could this handsome older couple really have been soul bandits?

Most of my childhood vacations were spent in Columbus visiting my mother's parents, Ma and Dad. I'd always felt that I was special to them, especially my grandfather, who had nicknamed me Tate. But on this drive to Columbus, the tightness in my chest was born of dread rather than anticipation about seeing my beloved grandparents.

After a night in the Residence Inn, we ate mush at the Bob Evans Restaurant, then dropped my mother off at her high school friend's house on our way to the hospital. Mom had been complaining of a headache all morning and did not feel up to attending my appointment. I told myself it was just as well. I knew I didn't have the emotional reserves to be supportive if my appointment upset her. As I watched her walk haltingly up her friend's driveway in her snappy hot-pink-and-black outfit, I flashed back to all the times I had taken care of her. A small seed of resentment rose up in me. Even now, when I needed comfort so desperately, Mom's needs came first. Some inner part of me was yelling, *Take care of me for a change!* But I couldn't pay attention to it now.

When Dr. Prescott finally strode into the examining room, my father stood and introduced himself. The two men traded Ohio State Buckeye banter. My dad managed to weave into their conversation the fact that the president of the OSU Alumni Association was his close personal friend. Dr. Prescott suddenly had all the time in the world, and we got much more than the six minutes of attention that he normally allotted each patient. Once the Buckeye brothers finished maligning my Michigan Wolverines, Dr. Prescott got around to examining me. He did not see any cancer.

The tension that had gripped me throughout the gridiron discussion relaxed. Dr. Prescott told us that if Dr. Gilbert decided to do surgery on the bar, he would stop in during the operation and take a few biopsies. I pushed past my usual reluctance to confront authority figures and said I would let him know if I wanted biopsies. If nothing more could be done to cure me of cancer, why would I want to know that I had it?

Dr. Gilbert and Dr. Loud greeted us like old friends. "This bar is loose," Dr. Gilbert said as he looked into my mouth. "It will have to come out."

I slumped in the plastic-covered patient's chair and gazed ahead without seeing. *This cannot be happening. I quit. Somebody else will have to take over this body. I've had it.* The voice clearly enunciated each declarative sentence in a flat, resigned tone. I was done.

Wrapping my arms around my midriff to brace myself against what I might hear, I returned my attention to the room. Dr. Gilbert was describing how he planned to remove the bar, wire my jaw shut for six to eight weeks, and then attempt to do another free-flap with my right hip. He explained that the wiring was necessary to immobilize my jaw until the bar could be replaced with bone. If it was not stabilized, my lower jaw would gravitate to the left, eliminating the occlusion of my remaining teeth on the right and, with it, any hopes for chewing. Dad, his facial expression unchanged, politely asked questions to clarify the physics of jaw stabilization and the mechanics of the bar coming loose. They went on to discuss disintegration of the jawbone around the screws that held the bar in place and the risk of infection in that area. They might as well have been talking about OSU football. I was beyond caring.

Jeff sat silently staring at the floor, his eyes squinted and his jaw clenched. He said nothing. He rotated his shoulders and rubbed a muscle in his neck. Now it looked as though he had gone away, perhaps to a place where he could ponder what more surgery for me meant for him. He would later admit wanting to run from another round of caretaking, but his sense of responsibility held him in the chair.

No one said anything. It was clear that Dad and Jeff weren't getting me out of this surgery plan, so I would have to do it myself. "What are our other options?" I asked.

Dr. Gilbert paused and then said, "Well, I am afraid there aren't any." He enumerated the possible responses to my situation and the fatal flaws in each. I allowed myself to believe that he was concerned for more than his reputation, that he liked me.

I was making this up, but it helped.

"Check with my office manager to schedule the surgery," he said as he and the now quiet Dr. Loud prepared to leave.

I was not signing on for this surgery but was incapable of anything beyond compliance. I nodded and asked for a Roxicet refill. Dr. Gilbert seemed so eager to make me feel better that I think I could have gotten the whole pharmacy.

As we filed slowly out of the clinic, Jeff pulled me aside, his hand cupping my elbow, and whispered, "Let's get that place in Sausalito."

I could not conjure the sights or smells of Sausalito. Now I would not get another chance at a real life. It was clear that I could not make it through more surgery. Another twenty-four-hour free-flap operation would certainly spell the end of me. And how could anyone believe that it would work? The first flap failed because the vessels had collapsed. And that was before radiation, which everyone said reduced the blood supply to the affected area and impaired healing. And my jaw would be wired shut for weeks? I had enough trouble eating as it was.

As usual, when the lack of a future drove me into the present, my focus shifted to spending money or sensory pleasures that could be enjoyed now. I suggested lunch at Rigsby's where I could have both.

Knowing that with or without surgery, my chewing days were numbered, I ordered soup, risotto, and crème brûlée without looking at the prices. I noticed that my eating prowess had advanced since my last meal there two months before. Now all my efforts to become a competent eater would be for naught.

I was not much of a luncheon companion. Jeff and Dad were talking about what Dr. Gilbert had said and whether or not I should go along with his plan.

During each lull in their conversation, I said, "I don't want any more surgery."

"Well, look at it this way," Dad said sounding upbeat. "You can at least be grateful that you don't have the kind of cancer that can kill you."

I stared at him, speechless. Could he believe what he was saying? Dad was explaining how lucky I was to have avoided the really lethal forms of cancer. I excused myself, asked Jeff to rectify the misunderstanding, and headed for the bathroom. Later, I would understand my dad's life enough to empathize with his need to cushion the truth with denial. But that day, the whole scene felt surreal, and each bit of data my brain was asked to integrate seemed more bizarre than the last.

§

Once the shock of Gilbert's proposal wore off, giving up seemed less of an option. This situation wasn't going to kill me, so I had to do something. But what? Should I have the clicking bar removed? Agree to biopsies? Should I let Gilbert take my right hip, knowing it could easily end up in the dumpster like the left one had?

Much as I loathed the idea of more surgery, I saw no alternative to the first operation to remove the bar. Leaving it in place meant the danger of infection where it was exposed and the destruction of my remaining lower jaw where it was attached. Once I decided on that surgery, I could not see beyond it. I would deal with the reconstruction options later. But what about biopsies?

After consulting everyone who would discuss it with me and getting the usual array of opinions, I posed the biopsy question to my journal. "Should I let Prescott biopsy my mouth?" Farther down the page I wrote, "Yes" and "No" with spaces underneath them.

I didn't think, I just wrote. I scribbled three points under "Yes" such as "At least you'll know if you have cancer. You need to know," and two under "No," including "Maybe you don't want to know." This wasn't the definitive answer I'd hoped for, but any response from the mysterious internal source might mean that the voice of my soul was speaking to me again. And three to two looked like a victory for the "Yes" forces to me. I called Columbus to confirm the surgery, complete with biopsies, which was set for Thursday, August 5. Then I began to recruit yet another support team for the event.

In the days before the surgery, I relaxed my vigilance, talking at every opportunity and eating as much Dairy Queen as possible before being muzzled by wired teeth. I even tackled the tuna fish sandwich and iced tea I had lusted after during my last hospitalization. Most of it ended up sprayed across the table or dribbled on the front of my T-shirt, but the bits that made it down were fabulous. Although the motivation was unconscious at the time, I was beginning to nurture myself. Somewhere, I knew that I had to stockpile my inner resources in preparation for another foray into the health-care system.

Eric arrived two days before we had to leave for Columbus. He and I lounged in the family room watching movies and discussing our favorite actors and directors. We sat around the kitchen table with Jeff, drinking coffee and talking about books we liked, our favorite passages from *A Course in Miracles*, and news of what Eric and Justin were up to in San Francisco. I could have gone on like this for weeks, but it was time to go.

My brother Bill drove down from Grand Ledge, and Marge came over from Louisville to meet us in Columbus. I organized a Last Supper at Rigsby's. I was determined to enjoy my last meal with a free jaw. We were a boisterous group. Even Jeff, who looked pretty haggard, was laughing.

Only Jeff was allowed into pre-op with me on Thursday morning. He looked on as I made my standard presurgical request for lots of drugs and was told that I would not be allowed much in the way of preanesthetic relaxants. Since my throat was now constricted as a result of the big surgery, I needed to stay awake until they could get an airway down me. Failing that, I would have to have another tracheotomy.

I could not believe my ears. Why in the fuck hadn't anyone told me about this? I would have lived with the goddamned clicking bar until I died.

The ride into the O.R. atop the narrow gurney was lonely and long. I had never before been wide awake for this part. The operating room was cold in every sense of the word. An enormous, round light fixture, not unlike an alien ship, hovered overhead. I was hoisted from the gurney to the operating table through the synchronized efforts of several scrub-suited, masked beings. "1 . . . 2 . . . 3," they said in unison, and I was moving. I landed on another unyielding, frigid table and stared up at the blinding light. While I was clearly at the center of all kinds of activity, no one was talking to me. Finally, someone decided to include me in the conversation.

"Okay, Terri, now we are going to try to put this tube down your throat. Please relax and open your mouth as wide as you can."

I opened my mouth, and the lights went out.

§

I awakened just enough to realize that I could no longer open my mouth. What did that mean? Where was I?

Some hours or minutes later, I awakened again. I was in a room similar to the one where I'd spent last Christmas. Jeff and Eric were sitting near me. I opened my eyes and grunted for attention.

"Hi, Mom," Eric said in that tender voice that always made me want to cry. "The operation is over. You did great."

"They got the tube down," Jeff jumped in eagerly. "You didn't have to have the trach. Gilbert says it all went well. They took out the bar. Prescott looked you over and did the biopsies. He didn't see any cancer. Then they wired you shut."

Oh, so that was why my mouth wouldn't open. My parched tongue was imprisoned in a cage, secured by barbed wire that jabbed the insides of my mouth. I moved in and out of awareness over the next few hours and moved surprisingly quickly toward healing over the next few days. Marge, now in her second year of medical school, spread her belongings over the bed next to me and began running things as if she were chief of staff. I was afraid the nurses might be offended, but Marge was as charming as she was bossy, and no one complained.

On my last night in the hospital, Eric sat on the neighboring bed painting an illustration that had to be overnighted to *Time* magazine the next day. I worried that he wasn't getting enough sleep. It felt weird to have him taking care of me. He seemed so grown up.

With Jeff's wound-care expertise and Marge's medical training to go home to, I was allowed to leave the hospital on Sunday. The biopsy results were not due until Wednesday or Thursday, but I knew they could come sooner. There were many strange inconsistencies in the biopsy business. Some doctors said it took up to a week for the results to be accurate. Others seemed to know within a day or two, and sometimes surgeons got results while the patient was still on the operating table. I realized that there were medical reasons for some delays but suspected that many were due more to administrative obstacles than to scientific necessity. I wondered if results would languish in a lab for a week if it were bits of the surgeon's mouth instead of mine under scrutiny.

Marge did her best to defend her colleagues and to distract me. She kicked Jeff out of the house for hours at a time, telling him he had to take care of himself. As industrious as ever, Marge took on wound care, creative liquid meals, and emotional support.

By Wednesday, Jeff and I were as wired as my jaw, and even Marge was looking weary. Finally, Jeff called the hospital. He was told that someone would call him back.

I came unglued. Obviously the assistant had the results but wanted to let Gilbert break the bad news to me. We all gathered at the kitchen table and watched the phone.

After hours, it rang.

"Terri, this is Dr. Gilbert," said a sweet voice. "Your biopsy results are fine . . ."

I handed the phone to Jeff and sagged into the chair. Maybe God was still looking out for me after all. The ice floes in my bloodstream began to melt. I was a puddle of relief.

everybody's talkin' at me

Of course the biopsy results did not come with any guarantees, but for the moment, I had a life. But before I could live that life, I had to decide what to do about the next surgery. I told Val about Dr. Gilbert's proposal, and she sent me to see an oral surgeon friend of hers. Val's pal was a very sweet guy who agreed to see me free of charge and connected me with a bigshot oral surgeon in Miami who wrote the book on reconstruction using cadaver jaws. Dr. Carothers, the Florida expert, had invented a method that had significant advantages over Dr. Gilbert's—it would not cost me my remaining hipbone, and it offered the hope of teeth in my future. My dad had tooth implants similar to the ones Dr. Carothers would use and, though I never fully understood his reasons, Dad really wanted me to have a full set of teeth. He offered to fly me to Miami and to go with me. It would be the first time I'd traveled with my Dad since he took me to New York when I was sixteen. That trip was as special as it was unexpected because we had never before spent even an afternoon alone together. Val volunteered to come to Florida with us.

We stayed in my parents' condo in Pompano and left early for Miami, hours ahead of my 9:00 a.m. appointment time. As always, even on trips to the post office, my father drove as if we were already late, speeding and cursing the other drivers. "Goddamn old people," he growled at our fellow travelers, most of them younger than he was. We arrived at the University of Miami early enough to wait even longer than usual.

The cadaver jaw expert had a fairly prominent jaw himself, which he stroked knowingly while Val recounted my oral-cancer story. Dad chipped in from time to time with data gleaned from his dentist golf buddies and his own experience with dental implants. Silenced by my oral hardware, I contributed a written addendum only when the facts needed correcting.

Dr. Carothers explained in a gravelly voice that Dr. Gilbert had done my reconstruction all wrong and that another free-flap attempt would be a big mistake. Instead, he would remove the rear portion of my right hip, extract the bone marrow, implant the marrow in a cadaver's mandible and then attach the corpse jaw to what was left of mine. I was surprised to learn that his approach also involved sacrificing part of my hip, but it was a smaller, less essential part. At most points in my life, the thought of chewing with a previously owned jaw would have been repellent. But I had become so inured to the bizarre rearrangement of my body parts that the idea did not faze me. Dr. Carothers went on to explain how he would add dental implants once the stiff's jaw had settled into my mouth.

He then led me into an examining room, where I became an exhibit for a pack of mostly male medical students. Pointing to my mangled chest, Dr. Carothers said, "You should never take the flap from the front on a woman. See what it has done to her breast. You always take tissue from the back." My shame at having all those young men peering at my misshapen breast was outstripped only by fury at realizing that I could have traded that deformity for a scar on my back. I was furious at Dr. Gilbert.

Back in his office with Dad and Val, Dr. Carothers surprised us by saying that the approach he had been promoting was too expensive and complicated to perform on me right away.

"Let's put in another titanium bar and see how it goes. If things go well, we can do the reconstruction and implants in a year or so," he suggested.

"If things go well" was code for "if I didn't die." I wanted to lob the plastic mandible on the desk at Dr. Carothers's inflated head. We all knew that he was explaining the impracticality of wasting a perfectly good cadaver jaw on one who might so soon be a cadaver herself, but we pretended he was just expressing a scheduling preference.

"Why would this bar work better than the first one?" Val asked.

As if entering the finals in a match of medical egos, Dr. Carothers went on to enumerate the ways in which his bar would be superior to Dr. Gilbert's. My father's face lit up when he began to detail the engineering differences between the bars. My only goal was escape. The fastest way to achieve that was to shut up and let others plan for me. The operation was set for October 28. In closing, Dr. Carothers said he didn't think I needed to keep my jaw wired in the interim. That was the only good news of the visit, although it made me wonder how Dr. Gilbert could be so wrong.

Over lunch in our red vinyl booth overlooking the parking lot of the Red Lobster, Val and Dad conducted an animated yet scientific analysis of the various approaches now available to me. They ordered a carafe of white wine. I wished for a big slug of my drug, but settled for iced tea and my signature clam chowder. I was sucking the gooey, white soup through a straw, trying not to catch clams in the wire nets covering my teeth, when Val noticed I hadn't mumbled anything in a while.

"So, what do you think?" she asked.

"I don't care," was my clenched response.

"What's the matter?" she queried. My father sat quietly by, sipping his wine.

I pulled out my pad and wrote, "What difference does it make? Carothers made it pretty clear that he doesn't think I'll make it long enough to need a new jaw."

Their words of reassurance rushed out, tripping over each other, declaring that I had misinterpreted Carothers's desire to delay installing a new jaw. "Given the statistics," Dad said, as if discussing a team's win-loss record rather than my likelihood of living, "it just makes sense to wait." Val told me, for the hundredth time, that I was going to be okay. I was comforted by her claims, but not convinced. I suspected she wasn't as sure as she sounded.

The conversation shifted to the incredible coincidence that my first cousin had just been diagnosed with oral cancer, identical to mine. More amazing was the fact that she had been referred to Dr. Watson even though she lived eighty miles away. I mentioned that my cousin had grown up drinking the same unpasteurized milk that had caused my bovine tuberculosis, and that one doctor had told me that he thought my cancer was related to the TB. Given that my father's idea of alternative medicine was a female physician, I deliberately neglected to identify that MD as the staff physician at the Ayurvedic cleansing camp I'd attended.

My father stiffened beside me. "Don't ever tell your mother he said that," he said in a taut voice. "My life would be a living hell if she knew." Although it had been forty years, apparently Mom still blamed him for the damage done to me by his mother's milk.

My insides twisted. This was my big chance to have my father's attention, and I had messed it up. I felt like I had the day Dad took me with him to play a couple holes of golf and I talked when he was putting. He was furious.

After the first wash of childlike humiliation passed, I began to reflect on what had just happened. Why was I feeling guilty? How could he think of himself in the face of what I was going through? "Living hell" would be the nice way of describing my life. Now I was furious. Maybe that angry teenager Elizabeth found was still in there after all. I was tempted to run to the phone and tattle to Mom, but instead I sulked into my chowder. Val redirected the conversation to safer ground—whether or not to tell my cousin about my experience with Dr. Watson. We decided against it.

As soon as we returned to Michigan, I went back to Val's oral surgeon friend to have my jaw unhooked as Dr. Carothers had suggested. When the last of the wires had been clipped and I could open my mouth, I revisited the kind of relief I felt when the nasogastric tube was pulled from my nose after the big surgery and I could breathe again. To celebrate, I headed straight for Dairy Queen and lathered my tattered gums with a large cup of vanilla soft serve.

I scheduled free-flap surgery with Dr. Gilbert for November 4, exactly one year after Dr. Watson found the lump in my mouth. Now

I had two operations on the books and several weeks to decide what to do. I decided to go to California and defer my medical decisions.

Back in our tiny getaway home, I studied the Spiegel catalog in search of accessories to complement the furniture Bud had left. I consulted Jeff on the décor, but only as a formality. He could not have cared less. I picked out a hunter-green-and-white striped comforter, and then dishes, cutlery, towels, and accessories to coordinate with that color. I had free rein, as long as nothing cost very much, to refurbish all four hundred square feet of our studio. My pleasure in the process reinforced my belief that, for me, shopping is a spiritual path. Though I flinched a little with every check I wrote, I vowed to live long enough to get my money's worth from each purchase.

When we weren't shopping for lamps or futon covers, Jeff and I explored Marin County. One day we wandered through Muir Woods, where dappled sunlight laced through the redwoods, and I expected to see elves cavorting among the ferns. Jeff stopped to examine every burl and banana slug while I forged ahead, trying to build up my strength. On another glorious late-summer day, we drove north on Highway 1 to Stinson Beach with my kids. My favorite road in the world, the highway skirts the ocean and is flanked by rocky cliffs and tawny hills, curved like a woman's body. Sitting on the deck of a café with my guys, relishing carrot soup and chocolate pudding, it was hard to imagine that I'd ever had problems.

The annual Sausalito Art Festival began. From our apartment, we could look down on the park full of peaked white tents. I was not all that interested in attending the congested event, especially by myself, but Jeff had an appointment with his first California Rolfing client, and I had to vacate the apartment. His starting to get work in Sausalito meant we might be able to spend more time there, and I was all for that.

So, on the Saturday of Labor Day weekend, I found myself hiking down streets lined with luxury cars heading for the Festival. I walked gingerly since my new hip was not accustomed to hills, and I stopped often to breathe, drink water, and survey the view. The beauty of the place was almost too much to absorb. Other than my flights to and from Florida, this was my first solo foray into the real world since my big surgery. Who could have guessed a year ago that I would make my comeback in this incredible spot?

Even before cancer robbed me of my beauty, I had a bad habit of comparing how other people looked on the outside to how I felt on the inside. As soon as I got through the turnstile of the elegant fair, the contrast between the beautiful Marin art lovers and me triggered a downward spiral in my mood. I felt like a homely child who couldn't find her mother in a big crowd, afraid that I might burst into tears at any moment. I sat in the shade of the refreshment tent, sloppily sipping a can of strawberry Ensure. I watched the patrons and matrons of the arts savoring Napa Valley merlot and champagne, and I wished to God that alcohol did not burn my mouth. I needed some chemical relief from the shame and envy burning in my gut. After my snack, I slipped back into the milling swarm and tried to focus on the paintings and pottery on display. But I couldn't keep my eyes off the perfect-looking people.

One booth did capture my interest. The display consisted of mirrors and ceramic wall hangings similar to those in other booths except that each piece bore statistics etched in artsy script:

> In 1988, Americans spent $74 billion on diets, $20 billion on cosmetics, and $300 million on cosmetic surgery; a recent study shows 81 percent of ten-year-old girls are dieting; cosmetic surgery is the fastest growing medical specialty.

Apparently I wasn't the only one feeling unattractive. I was disturbed by the facts and slightly incredulous, especially that all those women were choosing to have surgery. The only way I could imagine using the words "cosmetic" and "surgery" in the same sentence was "I took my cosmetics off before surgery."

I summoned my courage and pressed through the horde to ask the artist the source of her data. "*The Beauty Myth* by Naomi Wolf," she told me. I would buy that book as soon as I could. For now, I'd had enough art. I limped to the Waterfront Cafe, where Jeff was to retrieve me.

Relaxing at a round marble table a few feet from docks housing stunning sailboats, I breathed in the sparkling air and took stock of my surroundings. The other tables were full of fit joggers in vibrant-colored Lycra and white-clad yacht owners wearing Top-Siders without socks. I drank my latte very carefully to prevent its trickling down my chin. The big surgery had rerouted the nerves in my neck and chin in such a way that sensation was blunted. Jeff and I had developed what we called the "spousal alert system," whereby he would subtly touch a place on his face to indicate the location of wayward food or beverage on mine. I was on my own here, so I prophylactically patted my chin with a napkin at frequent intervals.

My thoughts returned to the Festival. I was troubled by the juxtaposition of all those beautiful people and the data on the beauty industry. How ironic that, as a recently disfigured woman, I was spending time in Marin County, where looks mattered as much or more as they had in Grosse Pointe. Once I fled that superficial suburb, I lived most of my adult life in Ann Arbor, where diversity of appearance and everything else was encouraged. I had refused to follow my mother's first commandment for exterior maintenance, to "do the most with what I have." Even back when I was good looking, I didn't want to be loved on the basis of my looks. I had never learned to apply makeup or style my hair. I wanted people, probably especially my parents, to see who I really was and to love me for that.

What did it mean that all these women were willing to suffer through painful surgeries and spend so much money just to look "better"? Perhaps this was a manifestation of the kind of self-loathing I had always sensed but was just now discovering within myself. Back when I was pretty, I focused on my breasts being too small, my thighs too fat, and my hips too thick. My appearance seemed such a trivial issue when living and talking and eating were in jeopardy. Now I could see that, all protestations to the contrary, I *had* cared how I looked. I still did. I would have to learn to live in this new body. Perhaps if I could find a way to love myself, looking the way I did, I might have something to teach others.

I had started recording ideas in my journal. Hunched over the red notebook, my attention was so riveted to the page that I didn't notice Jeff standing above me. He cleared his throat. "Oh, hi," I said, looking up.

"Well, you made it. In fact, you look really good. How was it to be out on your own?" he asked.

The words to describe my afternoon all wanted to be uttered at once, and my speech was still somewhat halting. I sputtered in excitement. I took a breath and forced the words to queue up in orderly fashion. I told him about the Festival, the beauty myth, my insights, and my new sense of purpose.

"It feels so good to be writing!" I told him. "Maybe I can write a book about this."

"That's a good idea," he said, smiling. "You can call it 'Butt Ugly, But Happy.'"

We threw back our heads and laughed. I could laugh because Jeff had told me many times that he did not find me ugly. I wasn't ready to honestly appraise my appearance, so I told myself that there was no truth behind his joke.

It was true that our sex life had dwindled to rare, carefully planned and executed encounters. But there were plenty of explanations for that. Sex had never been the strongest part of our marriage. Certainly, the past year's assaults on my body had left me feeling anything but sexy. And we had both been preoccupied with other things, most of them low in erotic content. Our new nurse-patient relationship did little to inspire arousal. Having to survey my extensive suture network and irrigating the wound on my chest made Jeff understandably reluctant to climb aboard this disaster area. And given his fear of disturbing my rebuilt mouth, I had to settle for pecks on the cheek or soft, squishy busses on my lips. I especially missed the kissing. But I was so grateful that Jeff was sticking with me, I felt I had no room to complain. Most men would have bolted after one look at the new me. Instead, Jeff was giving me what I had always wanted and what I could only hope to some day give myself. He was looking beyond my appearance and finding me loveable.

inside for answers

September had always been one of my favorite months in Michigan. The heat of August had abated, and October's foreshadowing of winter had not yet begun. Still, the moment I stepped off the Jetway into Detroit Metropolitan Airport, the dull gray atmosphere of the Motor City eclipsed the pink glow I had brought with me from Sausalito. The carry-on bag that I had managed easily throughout the trip was suddenly too heavy.

I loved fall in Ann Arbor. It was football season and the start of school in a college town. Our chestnut-brown house on Peters Road was especially appealing at this time of year, surrounded by trees tinged in red and gold. But I wasn't eager to return to a life full of unmade decisions. I wanted to retrace our route to the airport and catch the next plane back to San Francisco.

My desire to face real life was further diminished by the discovery of a notice from my health insurance company in the huge stack of mail that awaited us. The statement detailed the costs of the big surgery nine months before. Its bottom line: "You may owe $7,800," apparently for Dr. Gilbert's failed reconstruction efforts.

Along with the threat of this huge debt, I needed to resolve the quandary about the surgeries that were only a few weeks away. I also had decisions to make about the open wound on my chest, the weird pressure that had just started in my left ear, alternative healing methods to prevent cancer, my office, my work, and how the hell I was going to support myself. Foggy with jet lag, the weight of these dilemmas pushed me deep into depression. I could only see what I had lost. In 1992, my gross income had been almost $100,000, and I had only worked eight months. In the first eight months of 1993, I had earned almost nothing.

I continued to pay for my expensive office; to give it up would be to admit that my professional life was over. The bit of work I had scheduled for the fall hardly constituted a career. And all of it was with loyal, established clients who could adjust to my new appearance and the fact that I might disappear again at any time. Many could not. One therapy client who had lost a host of family members to cancer sent me flowers and a sweet note telling me she appreciated the work we were doing but couldn't risk another loss. How would I ever get new work looking and feeling like this? Who was I if not a "consultant" or "speaker" or "therapist"? What good was I if I was not helping somebody?

When I talked to friends and family about the surgical dilemma, they all had ideas about what I should do—all different, of course. How would I ever get enough data to ferret out the right answer? If Jeff had an opinion, he kept it to himself, saying, "It's up to you." I tried writing questions in my journal, then making the < mark that had preceded the answer like I did on the plane to Florida, but there was no response. When I told Barb that I was consulting my "Guides" about the decision, she told me I was spending too much time in California. The variables in this conundrum lay before me like a disassembled jigsaw puzzle with hundreds of pieces all so similar in shape and pattern that I couldn't pick out the ones that formed the edges.

Compared to this one, the decisions to have the earlier surgeries looked easy—did I have the cancer removed or let it keep growing in me? This time what the doctors called "function" was at stake—eating and talking, rather than my life. Experience had taught me that operations don't always deliver on their promises. I wasn't eager to sacrifice my hard-won gains in eating and talking. Another major surgical procedure meant more hospital time, more pain, more wounds, and more opportunity for complications. And radiation-impaired healing.

Twice each day, when Jeff irrigated the open suture line near my heart and tended to the site of the recent bar removal, I was reminded that I was still not recovered from the surgeries I had already had. And if the strange pulsing in my ear were cancer, my future would be too short for liquid diets and silence.

Even if my body made it through another operation, what about my soul? It was becoming clear to me that physical survival and healing were two different things. Healing seemed to be the process of becoming whole on all levels—mental, emotional, spiritual, and physical. I felt so empty after all the technical tinkering with my body. My time in Sausalito and with my kids had just begun to make me feel a tiny bit like my former self. I knew I didn't have sufficient emotional reserves to carry me through another descent into the anonymity and hollow coldness of the hospital. I was just emerging from the role of patient, and I wasn't eager to return.

The deeper I sank into this mire, the more muddled it became. If I decided to have surgery, which one? Was the perfect solution still out there waiting to be discovered?

I liked Dr. Gilbert, and in spite of Dr. Carothers's critique of his work, I desperately wanted to believe that he was as skilled as he was reputed to be. Doubting him now would be to doubt myself for choosing him in the first place, and I could not afford to do that. It had never occurred to me to blame Dr. Gilbert for the failure of the free-flap. He was so sincere, and he had tried so hard. I now understood why malpractice suits seldom happened to physicians who make the effort to know their patients as people.

But however much I liked him, Dr. Gilbert's free-flap efforts had failed. And whether or not his current strategy to replace the bar with my right iliac crest worked, I would lose my last hip bone and its supporting musculature, and with them any vestige of my formerly small waist and my only comfortable sleeping position. I had slept on my right side ever since the big operation surgically removed all the other acceptable options. When I shared these concerns with Dr. Gilbert at my most recent visit, he had pointed out that they paled in importance next to issues of eating ability and facial appearance, which would both be adversely affected when "your jaw floats over to the left and you can only consume liquids." I knew he was right. But when I looked at his perfectly formed, perfectly functional, perfectly groomed face and body, I also knew that he could not fathom the impact of another bulging hip or the inability to rest in one's own body.

Dr. Carothers's approach would not leave my right hip unscathed either, and I didn't like him. At least Dr. Gilbert thought I was worth his continued efforts, whereas Dr. Carothers was basing his treatment plan on the likelihood of my demise. I wanted to be surrounded by doctors who believed in my chances. Lacking dental insurance, I would have to pay for most of the complicated and expensive procedures Dr. Carothers was proposing. There was also the added expense and inconvenience of having surgery in Miami. At least we could drive to Columbus.

The Vile Bitch Upstairs relished this kind of high-stakes decision and rehashed the details of the debate around the clock. "You heard those doctors. You'd better make the right choice or you'll be sucking down mush for the rest of your days. You look bad enough as it is. The last thing you need is more disfigurement."

Thank God I had an appointment scheduled with Dr. Bradford. I wanted her to check my chest wound and the problem with my ear. Then I would explain what Dr. Carothers and Dr. Gilbert were proposing and pray that she would break the tie.

Dr. Bradford examined me and found nothing abnormal. "We do worry about ear problems," she warned me, "so keep track of those symptoms." As to the wound on my chest, she said, "Just leave it alone. It will heal someday." Speaking in tandem, Val and I explained the reconstruction predicament and asked her opinion.

"Well," she said, thoughtfully, "if I were going to attempt another free-flap, I would use your tibia. We've found that the leg bone works better than the hip." Just what I needed, another option.

"Another approach," she continued, "would be to . . ."

No more approaches! I screamed silently. *No more fucking approaches!*

". . . just do nothing," Dr. Bradford concluded.

"What?" I said.

"There are dangers, of course. Your jaw could gravitate to the left without anything there to stabilize it. If that happened, your eating and appearance would be compromised. But it's also possible that your jaw might stay where it is, even without a bar or a bone holding it in place."

I thanked Dr. Bradford profusely for her suggestion. I felt a little more peaceful by the time she left the room. Seconds later, Tammi, the nurse practitioner, returned to give me a prescription. "You know, those sensations in your ear could be a side effect of the radiation." I thanked her for the benign possibility. As soon as the nurse was out the door, Val smirked.

"What's so funny?" I asked.

"If you show up here with an ingrown toenail when you're ninety, they're going to blame it on the radiation," Val said.

§

Of course I loved the idea of doing nothing, but was I being wise or just scared? I didn't want to look back on this decision being more disfigured and unable to chew. The Bitch would have a field day! I had gathered all the scientific data I could handle. It was time to consult a different kind of knowing. A cancer-survivor friend raved about a teacher whose If I Should Wake Before I Die workshop sounded like just the thing.

Getting ready to spend the weekend with a group of strangers was daunting. The Saturday morning of the gathering, I gazed into my underwear drawer at the Jockey for Her undershirts, shaped like the ones worn by paunchy, beer-drinking men watching sports on TV, except mine were peach and pink rather than sweat-stained beige. I'd worn them since the big surgery and found comfort in the secure snugness of the soft fabric clinging to my marred chest. But I wasn't ready to expose my mismatched, mutilated breast to the public. So I dug deeper in the drawer and retrieved a well-worn, lightly padded bra that would create the lumpy illusion of a symmetrical bustline.

I couldn't get into the bra. The range of motion in my left arm and shoulder were too restricted. The Bitch chastised me for not having done more of the postmastectomy exercises last winter. My hands couldn't meet behind my back to hook the graying bra. Then I remembered watching Ma, my maternal grandmother, drape her brassiere around her waist with the hooks in front, fasten them, rotate it 180 degrees, and insert her arms through the straps as her pendulous breasts filled the large cups. I felt unspeakably old as I carried out the inherited ritual, but it did the job.

I was also rusty at outfit selection and tried a lot of options before settling on a big sweater over tights. I checked to make sure that this look camouflaged my bulging left hip. What little skill I'd ever had at applying makeup had atrophied since December. It was hard to see the point of trying to beautify this new face. And putting on makeup meant looking in the mirror. I hurriedly applied a little eye shadow and mascara, hoping these minor improvements might draw attention away from my mouth and chin. I knew that if I looked at my face too long, I'd lose my nerve. I couldn't help noticing the way the skin of my lower right cheek wrinkled like thick brocade when I tilted my head.

My fear of facing new people mounted as we neared the workshop venue, but I relaxed a little once inside. If Disney ever built a New Age theme park, it would look like this. Painted and carpeted in a creamy white, the place was overrun with angels, crystals, drums, plants, stuffed animals, and healing homilies in purple and gold calligraphy. Flute music, patchouli incense, and herbal tea rounded out the ambiance. I sat in a soft chair, snuggled under the pink cotton afghan I'd selected from the largest pile of lap blankets I'd ever seen, and stared at the candles and lilies that adorned the altar. There was something about having so many blankets to choose from that made me feel safe.

Gwen, a PhD psychologist and leader of the workshop, looked about fifty, though I knew she was over seventy. A palpable radiance emanated from her petite body. With her stylish blonde coiffure and coordinated outfit, she should be lunching at Saks rather than leading this diverse pack of forty seekers in "awakening to higher energies."

Gwen instructed us to hold hands in a circle to "call in the four directions and the souls on the other side who will help us in our work today." The other attendees, most of them high-end aging hippies, invited departed friends and relatives, power animals, Jesus, Buddha, and all sorts of spirit guides to join us. I got light-headed standing up for so long, and my mouth was desperately dry as the guest list dragged on. I felt shy about speaking but finally summoned my brother, deceased friends, and grandparents. Once participants from all realms were assembled, I collapsed in my chair and grabbed my water bottle.

Then we went around the circle introducing ourselves and saying what we hoped to get out of the workshop. I said, "I've just finished treatment for oral cancer and have big decisions to make. I hope to find clarity here." Everyone seemed to understand my words, which emboldened me to talk more as the day went on and even to venture into humor. God it was good to make people laugh again! Before long, I had to curtail my comments for fear of looking like a showoff.

On Sunday, Gwen guided us through a structured meditation that had us free-associate on different parts of our bodies and ponder a body part that we didn't like. I thought about the unhealed spot near my heart. I saw a wounded bird, cradled in a hand, that needed lots of love before it could fly. After the meditation, Gwen told us to write about what had come to us:

> Red heart . . . pink muscle . . . empty whole [I meant
> to write hole] . . . confusion of the part of my mouth
> that belongs in my chest . . . disorientation . . . it's not
> me . . . revulsion . . . must get through revulsion.

I had no idea what this meant but got the sense that healing my chest wound was going to involve more than saline rinses and antibiotic cream. Gwen said, "The body part you selected represents your dark side. You have to love it or it will leave you," referring to the body. I was not sure that I could ever love my body enough to keep it from leaving.

The next day, Gwen called on me to do individual work. I told the short version of my cancer story and shared my dream of writing an inspirational memoir. After consulting her inner source of wisdom, Gwen informed me that my purpose in this life was to learn to love myself. Again, I was filled with doubt that I was up to the task. I asked Gwen what to do about my surgical dilemma. She referred me back to my own inner guidance and went on to work with the next person. Shit.

Being home alone with my choices after two days in the warmth and safety of the group, my isolation was striking. I tried to take Gwen's advice to seek an inner source of direction, but writing questions in my journal failed to elicit much intelligence. I got that the decision about surgery was "a major test of my ability to tune in to higher wisdom for guidance," but if the voice of wisdom had more to say, the Bitch drowned it out.

Maybe Elizabeth would know what I should do.

Like Gwen, Elizabeth referred me back to myself. Why wouldn't anyone tell me what to do? She did offer to teach me to take shamanic journeys on my own so I could contact my power animals and spirit guides for help in determining my path. She explained, "We talked about how extractions and soul retrievals work on the energy body, which is an invisible blueprint of the physical. Shamanic journeys venture into the same realm, so you can unite with all aspects of yourself and become more whole. It is totally safe and very pleasant."

Not only was this stuff getting stranger by the minute, I hesitated to dig up more inner characters. I could barely keep track of the ones I'd met. But given the hostility I'd gotten from some of them, I did want Elizabeth to come along if I was going to explore this terrain. Maybe these journeys would lead me back to my spiritual side.

Elizabeth positioned me on the floor of her healing room and began to beat a drum. My bare arms nestled into the soft pile of the carpet. She told me to focus on the slow, steady rhythm and to see my invisible inner self leaving my body through my chest or the top of my head and entering the earth. There, I would find the "lower world," where my power animals resided. Still skeptical, I visualized my soul as a Casper-shaped cloud and watched it exiting my body through the crown of my head. My spiritualized self traveled to South Dakota, of all places, where I got into the elevator at a cave-turned-tourist-attraction that Jeff and I had visited. The elevator took me deep into the earth and let me out onto a mesh metal catwalk that snaked through the dank cave. I had always hated walking on see-through surfaces while in my physical body, and my spirit body proved equally squeamish. I'm not all that crazy about tunnels either, but I urged myself to get flat on my belly and crawl through the tight channel in the rock.

After edging along through the cool, slimy surface of the tunnel, I emerged into a dense, lush jungle. The sun was bright, and everything seemed green, but my vision was too murky to make out the specifics of my surroundings. As instructed, I had come prepared with questions for my power animals. I looked around for an animal and finding none started to shout out my questions anyway. "Why does my ear ache?"

The answer echoed through the trees from no discernible source, "There is no ear ache; you're okay." Whoa, that was weird.

"What should I do about the wound on my chest?" There was no response. Did the silence mean that I was to do nothing with the wound or that the mysterious voice had stopped speaking to me? I tried a question that Elizabeth had suggested. "What is the core belief that keeps me from using my full healing potential?"

"The belief that you don't deserve it," was the reply. The notion of deep-seated undeservedness fit with the Bitch's theme that I'm never enough. Maybe this jungle did hold answers for me.

Suddenly, I sensed animals in the vicinity: an elephant, a tiger, a turtle, and a giraffe. Just as I began to investigate this supernatural wildlife preserve, Elizabeth's voice beckoned from the distance.

"When you are done in the lower world," she said, "see yourself ascending to the upper world to take your questions to your spirit guides. Maybe a power animal will give you a ride. I will let you know when we are out of time by speeding up the drum beat."

Flashing once again on how bizarre this all was, I hopped aboard the elephant, who sprouted aviator ears like Dumbo and flew me up into the clouds. There I found Jesus, sitting on a throne next to Barbara Oleshansky, my dear friend who had died nine years before of a mysterious form of hepatitis. I was delighted to see both of them, but since Barbara was Jewish, I was a little surprised to see them hanging out together. As in life, Barbara spoke right up without waiting to be asked, "Stay away from medical types," she said. Having died in a hospital where the staff was unable to diagnose or treat her ailment, Barbara seemed a credible, if biased, source of advice. I had missed her so much in the years since her death that I wanted to spend time catching up. But knowing that my session with Elizabeth must be almost over, I figured I had best get on with my other questions.

"What is the meaning of the ear ache?" I repeated.

"It is to get you to listen to your inner voice," was the response, which may have come from Jesus or from Barbara. Being new at this, the images were very hazy, and I wasn't sure who was saying what.

"What should I do about my chest wound?"

"Give it sunlight, warmth, love, and vitamin E. Visualize it healing." Again, the source of the reply was unclear.

"What is the core belief that keeps me from using my full healing potential?"

"You don't believe that you are my child, but you are." This time it was clear that Jesus was speaking.

The drums in the background sped up. I boarded the elephant, flew back to the underworld, and retraced my path out of the cave and into my body, which was right where I had left it on the floor.

"How was it?" Elizabeth asked in a soft voice.

It took me awhile to find the words to describe the excursion. When I did, Elizabeth looked stunned. "I have never known anyone to come up with such specific answers on their first attempt," she told me. While I felt far from clear, Elizabeth gave me so much encouragement that I set up another appointment.

A week later, my second trip into the lower world was speedier and the images were more distinct once I arrived. Enveloped by the leafy jungle, I could discern pink, yellow, red, and white tropical flowers and colorfully feathered birds. The moist air was ripe with the fragrances of the blossoms and the cacophonous voices of the birds. Waterfalls gurgled in the background. I asked if there was anyone present who could heal my chest. An alligator appeared, chewing on raw meat. He sauntered over to me and spit some of the masticated mixture onto my wound. That was a more definitive solution than my doctors had offered; it built my confidence in this underground clinic enough for me to ask the big question.

"Should I have surgery on my jaw?"

A chorus of "no's" emanated from all around the forest. My power animals came into focus. The tiger growled "No." The elephant trumpeted "No," with his trunk high in the air. The turtle grunted a slow "No" and told me that he was involved in the healing of my chest, which was why it was taking so long. The tiger nuzzled my arm, signaling that it was time to head for the upper world. With a quick movement of his head, he invited me to climb aboard. Once I was seated on his back, he became a high-speed flying tiger and delivered me to my destination in record time. Jesus was waiting for me there. On his chest was that bleeding heart symbol that I had seen in Catholic depictions of Him. I was reminded of the wounded-bird message I had gotten in Gwen's workshop. Jesus let a drop of His blood fall into the unhealed suture line near my heart. I was very grateful for this divine remedy but heard the speeding drums and knew I had to go. In our debriefing, Elizabeth explained that hearts open to healing by first being broken, and I saw that my physical lesion symbolized a much deeper wound.

Once back in the real world, I was as confused as ever. The surgery dates were fast approaching. Should I listen to some of the world's top medical experts or a menagerie of imaginary animals? It still felt pretty strange, but I practiced shamanic journeys at home to get into the habit of tracking down my inner wisdom and learning to trust it. I started with easy questions like, "What should I do for my healing today?"

One day while wandering the underworld, I encountered the elephant, wearing a jewel-encrusted headdress. He rocked me in his trunk and said, "Cradle yourself." On my visit to the upper world on the same trip, I encountered one of my favorite clients, who had recently died of cancer. While alive, he had a wealthy wife and traveled in socially prominent circles. "Do not envy people just because they look good," was his advice.

The next day I repeated the query, seeking guidance for the day's healing. Down below, the turtle whispered, "Listen to the still, small voice within." I climbed on his back, and he slowly ferried me to the upper chambers. There I met an angel dressed in white. She said, "Love yourself." A group formed a circle. Jesus was there, as were most of the deceased people I'd ever known. It wasn't that I could see them exactly; I had a sense of their presence.

I felt a measure of guilt connected to each person and scolded myself for not doing enough for them when they were alive, especially Greg. He was sitting next to Jesus in the spirit circle. "No one is to blame for the way my life ended. Tell everyone that I am fine now," my brother said, sounding more peaceful than I'd ever heard him. "Tell Mom and Dad I love them." Logically, I knew that my failure to return Greg's last phone call had not killed him. I wanted to believe the adage that suicide can't be prevented when the person is determined. But I still couldn't entirely shake the belief that I might have said something to make him want to keep living.

Greg joined the others in the circle in saying, "Forgive yourself" and "Love yourself." Barbara, a hedonist even in heaven, said, "Have fun!" The first AIDS casualty in my acquaintance, a friend since junior high school, spoke up. "It's great here," he said. "Live fully as long as you do and don't be afraid to join us."

These journeys brought me more comfort than my forays into the health-care system did. I fantasized about relying exclusively on my burgeoning inner guidance and deserting doctors all together. But I was not ready for so radical a shift. I did begin to follow some of the advice gathered on my inner travels. I sat bare-breasted in the sun on our private deck to warm the wound on my chest. The hole seemed to be getting smaller. I looked for new ways to love myself as suggested by the angel and the spirit circle. This felt very foreign to me, like writing with my nondominant hand. Taking care of others came so much more naturally. I awkwardly pursued self-love, allowing a little more time for the things I enjoyed, like reading, writing, and movies. I made an effort to find foods that were both soft and tasty.

Unmade decisions were lying in wait ready to ambush any budding peace of mind. I decided to start with the easier issues and work my way up to the surgery predicament. I granted myself a postponement on selecting preventive healing methods until after the operation question was answered. I weaned myself from the fleeting comfort of my old friend Roxicet. As I sucked up the last of the precious red liquid and squirted it down my throat, I consoled myself with the knowledge that I could always get more if I needed it.

The slight improvement in my chest wound encouraged me to follow Dr. Bradford's advice to leave it alone. I entrusted its healing to Jesus and the alligator, and I stopped the irrigations, creams, and bandages. The sore stopped dripping after ten months.

I decided to let go of my office. While holding on to it all these months had kept my hopes for resurrecting my career alive, that hope had become too expensive in dollars and worry. Jeff helped me move my hypnotherapy Lazy Boys and teak office furniture into our lower level, which I tried to assure myself would only be an interim site until my business took off again. In truth, I doubted that I would ever again have such a fancy office or such great colleagues with whom to share it. I cried as I said good-bye to my officemates and the swanky setting that had made me feel so good about myself.

Once the move was complete, I was relieved to be free of the expense. And my fiscal concerns were further reduced by two phone calls. The first was from Dr. Gilbert, who offered to forgive me the $7,800 that my insurance was refusing to pay. How could I even consider going to another surgeon when he was so nice?

The second call came from my father. I answered the phone in the kitchen and sat at the oak table as I talked, enjoying the atypically warm evening air through the open sliding door. I noticed something odd about Dad's voice. Was he on the verge of tears? The only times he had sounded like this were when his mother was dying and when Greg died. Even more unusual was that Dad was calling instead of Mom.

"You have a benefactor," he said. "Do you remember Ginny Brown?" I said that I did. Ginny was a neighbor in my parents' condo complex whom I had met briefly. "We've been keeping her informed on your situation. You know that her only daughter was killed a few years ago?"

"Yes, I remember."

"Ginny called us tonight. She said, 'I've been thinking. You know I don't need much to live on. I wish I could give my money to my daughter, but I can't. Terri has been so brave, and I know how much that apartment in Sausalito means to her. I'd like to pay for it for six months.'" His voice faltered again. He steadied it and continued. "She didn't want us to tell you where the money was coming from, just that you had an anonymous donor. But your mother and I felt you ought to know."

This was the most generous gift I had ever received. And from someone I barely knew! Now it was my turn to talk through tears. I thanked Dad. I told him to thank Ginny. I thanked God, assuming He was in on this because that very afternoon, for reasons I still don't understand, I had reached my arms to the heavens and told Him I was open to receive His gifts. And just in case they had played a role, I thanked the power animals and spirit guides as well.

Jeff had been eyeing me with curiosity throughout the conversation. When I got off the phone and filled in the blanks in what he had heard, he grinned and hugged me. We rehashed this miracle hundreds of times. Maybe our luck was shifting. After Jeff went off to bed, I went out on our deck to thank God in person. Now that we were speaking again, I thought He might be willing to part with a few answers.

As I had earlier in the day, I spread my arms as far as they could reach and tilted my head back as far as it would go. I looked up at the heavens and called out, "Dear God, what am I supposed to do about my jaw?"

Nothing. All I could hear were the crickets. No thundering voice from above, not even a still, small voice in my head.

I was disappointed but could not drum up much anger at a God who had given me such a great day. I went to bed imagining six whole months in my dream town.

When I woke up the next morning, the answer was clear. I would not have surgery. The source of the clarity was a mystery, but it did not matter. I was siding with my power animals. I wrote questions in my journal to confirm this intuition with the internal advisors I was now referring to as my Guides. For the umpteenth time I wrote, "Should I have surgery? If so, which one?" As usual, I placed the < mark below my questions and waited.

"NO! NO! NO!" wrote itself. The Guides went on to tell me to exercise the muscles on the right side of my mouth, to pray like crazy that what was left of my jaw would remain aligned, and then added the > mark to signify the end of their response.

I visualized myself as an old woman, chewing happily on a soft cookie. Wrinkles hid some of my scars. This future version of me had bright, sparkling eyes and a big, crooked smile.

Doubts besieged me as I set about canceling surgeries and changing travel plans. I worked at subduing these second thoughts and at maintaining my resolve. We would use the airline tickets my folks had given us to get to Miami for Dr. Carothers's operation to go to Fantasy Fest in Key West with friends from Detroit.

Driving a rented white convertible, Jeff looked like a model in an ad for tropical vacations with his shiny silver hair and smooth bronze skin. We cruised down the highway that linked the Florida Keys like so many charms on a sparkling bracelet, turquoise waters on both sides. I was grateful to be here for a party rather than an operation. And I was grateful to be alive.

"Do you think I did the right thing?" I asked him.

"Oh, I think so," Jeff said, and we rode for a while in companionable silence.

Key West buzzed with booze and celebration. It was difficult to find our friends in the raucous, wildly costumed mob outside the elegant yellow Victorian bed and breakfast where we had agreed to meet. Then I spotted them at the bar, two beefy ex-priests in matching Annette Funicello costumes.

In that moment, I knew I had made the right choice.

healing hiatus

ow what?

Despite the Bitch's persistent badgering that I was making a big mistake, I followed my intuitive guidance to steer clear of scalpel-wielding surgeons and forge my own path to healing. This was the first time in my life that I trusted myself enough to fly in the face of expert opinion. It would be a long time before I fully realized the significance of this shift from living a life goaded by the Vile Bitch Upstairs to one guided by my internal wisdom. At the time, I was scared and confused. Yes, I was grateful not to be heading back to the operating room, but it was frightening to be out from under the care of doctors. Every time I had another twinge, pain, or burning sensation—and there were many—I rushed back to the health-care system. Otherwise, I was on my own. And, if I wasn't a patient, who was I?

I felt very far away from the competent professional I had been, and there was no way that I had the strength or energy to work as I once had. I felt lost in some vague middle space between versions of myself, with no idea of who the next iteration of me would be. And it wasn't clear that I would be living long enough to reinvent myself.

Lots of doctors had told me that 90 percent of oral cancer recurrences happen within two years. My two years would be up on March 11, 1995. I decided to give myself a break from trying to rebuild my old life until then. I would do the work that showed up, but would not worry about marketing or money. That hippie doctor in Chelsea had made it sound like another recurrence was inevitable. What was the point of drumming up new clients only to say good-bye again?

Besides, I deserved a little rest. I would enjoy my sponsored six-month respite in Sausalito. And I'd do whatever I could to regain my health, to get along better with Jeff, and to reestablish my connections with Jesus and God. I called it my "healing hiatus."

So I made reservations for our next trip to Sausalito and then set about crafting a healing plan. With a steady stream of suggestions still pouring in, the question of how to choose among the options for gaining weight, energy, and stamina; building up my immune system; and finding a little peace of mind kept growing more complicated. And the Bitch with her "You better do them all" diatribes wasn't helping. Perhaps this was a job for my newfound inner guidance.

After meditating on my healing alternatives in my loft on Peters Road one snowy morning late in 1993, I was prompted to reach for my journal. As I stared at the blank page, something stirred in me, and I wrote, "I will come up with a plan for myself." The writing continued:

The steps in my process are as follows:

1. List all the options I know about.

2. Decide whether or not to research other options.

3. Go through the list and eliminate the ones I know I don't want to do—trust my intuition.

4. Choose the ones that appeal to me and rank them.

5. Do the most appealing ones first. Take on one or more now and create a plan to integrate others later. Do not turn life into a medical treatment. Allow time to make living worthwhile.

6. Pick a date on which I will evaluate each approach and reconsider the others. Until then, *forget* the ones I'm not doing!

7. Do the ones I've chosen and ignore the Bitch even if I skip a day.

While I didn't follow it to the letter, I tried to use my new system to review the current alternatives, which included but were not limited to:

Take molasses (contains iron)
Meditate twice a day
Eliminate alcohol
Eat more to gain weight
Read *A Course in Miracles* and do daily lessons
Take shark cartilage
Exercise
Do a three-week dietary cleanse
Keep seeing Elizabeth
Call Silent Unity to make prayer requests
Look at myself in the mirror more often
Get 714X shots to mobilize immune system against cancer cells
Make gratitude lists every day
Give up coffee
Get coffee enemas (Jeff's current favorite)

I decided against researching additional options.

My intuition was clear that giving up coffee was a bad idea, and I wasn't ready to tackle my drinking. Yes, alcohol was a risk factor for oral cancer, but the thought of never having another drink was overwhelming. I had given up enough already. And since alcohol still burned my mouth, I was only having an occasional glass of watered-down wine. That couldn't hurt. Drinking molasses, on the other hand, did not appeal to me, so that idea failed to make the cut.

As directed, I went inside to consider the other options. I knew I wanted to keep seeing Elizabeth because I always felt so good after our sessions, and she seemed to be the only person who was consistently convinced that I would survive. I had been calling Silent Unity to ask for healing for years. That was easy. I knew I needed to consume more calories because my weight was still too low, but chewing was such a challenge that I opted to add an extra can of Ensure to my daily diet.

As part of my effort to evaluate each approach, Jeff and I drove to Jackson, Michigan, to see a specialist in 714X, an immune-system booster that operates through the lymph system. The doctor demonstrated injecting the compound into a node in my groin. After the demo, Jeff was about as eager to administer the shots as I was to receive them. When we got home, I called the inventor of 714X, who upon hearing my cancer history assured me that I would die without his treatment. This warning gave me pause, but the thought of coaxing Jeff into giving me a hideously painful shot each morning didn't strike me as a great way to start our day.

Jeff did want to help, so I agreed to a series of coffee enemas. This kept him busy constructing an inverted slab over the toilet for me to lie on and jerry-rigging a complex network of tubes. The meaning of "having coffee together" would never be the same.

My dad had given me a copy of *Sharks Don't Get Cancer*, courtesy of one of his golfing buddies. I tracked down the doctor who had done the seminal work using shark cartilage to treat cancer. He informed me that his most up-to-date research indicated that bovine cartilage was more effective. Taking the cartilage would involve consuming the contents of twenty-four capsules per day, reminiscent of the twenty-six pills a day I took as a kid with bovine tuberculosis. If, as the Ayurvedic doctor in Canada had indicated, my cancer was related to the TB, a cow-based remedy seemed the ideal way to complete the circle of life-threatening diseases.

In addition to seeking inner guidance to help with treatment decisions, I was always on the lookout for signs from the universe. The bovine cartilage doctor had spent his childhood summers in Dexter, Michigan, minutes away from our house on Peters Road, and he currently lived on Lyon Street in New York. Eric and Justin had lived on Lyon Street in San Francisco. The only pharmacist in the entire country who dispensed bovine cartilage had just moved to Sunningdale Drive in Grosse Pointe, the street where my family lived from 1957 to 1978. Clearly, the universe wanted me taking this stuff. I wrote a check for $425 for a month's worth of pills and mailed it off to my old neighborhood. Every morning for the next several months, I counted out twenty-four capsules, pulled apart the sticky gelatin halves, and emptied their contents into a blender with soymilk and Carnation Instant Breakfast. As I drank the unappealing smoothie, I tried to affirm the healing power of bovine cartilage.

Even with all these efforts at healing, I continued to be plagued with frightening symptoms. Maybe I should have known that I would never be "over" cancer, but nothing had prepared me for what a relentless stalker its specter would be. I discovered that once you've had cancer, the truth of mortality can return in a heartbeat. Driving home from lunch with a friend one afternoon, I felt a lump in my mouth and my life flashed before my eyes. Close inspection in the bathroom mirror revealed a lentil.

In early February, my tongue started tingling one evening when Jeff and I were watching *An American in Paris*. I got in to see Dr. Bradford right away. She didn't see any cancer. The numbness continued and was joined by shooting pains in my neck. These symptoms brought back body memories of times when I'd had similar problems that the doctors said were nothing. Of course, this was cancer. What else could it be?

I went to see Elizabeth, who managed to dig up a learning opportunity in any disaster. She encouraged me to get friendly with death so that it wouldn't be so frightening and loaned me *The Tibetan Book of Living and Dying*. The first teaching in the book was that we should all waste less time on accomplishments and spend more time quietly contemplating our own death. She led me on a shamanic journey during which I asked the questions, "Am I dying?" and "Why did God give me a cancer that is so hard to detect?" In the upper world, a huge ball of light appeared and a voice said, "Look beyond cancer," whatever the hell that meant. I hoped that it meant I might live beyond cancer. Then I got an intuitive sense that God had given me this challenging assignment because He thought I was up to it. I was reminded of Mother Teresa's comment, "I know God won't give me anything I can't handle. I just wish He didn't trust me so much."

My symptoms lingered, so I started conducting do-it-yourself shamanic journeys at home. One gray, frozen Ann Arbor day, I retreated to the underworld where it was hot and humid. The elephant led me through a lush jungle with vibrant flowers and gurgling waterfalls where my power animals were assembled. They promised to protect me from interior and exterior enemies. In the upper world, a voice that I took to be Jesus's explained that the tingling and pain were yet another reminder that I had a choice about whether or not to live. I wasn't then and am not now sure that I had a choice about it, but I continued to listen. He said, "If you stay alive, you will help others prepare for the journey of death by showing them that there is nothing to fear. Heaven can be found on Earth, and if you stay on the planet, be sure to live in a place as close to heaven as you can get." Most of this was confusing to me, but I knew He was talking about Sausalito. He concluded by saying, "Go slowly to see, hear, and feel. Be in love with yourself." In the following weeks, I noticed that the tingling was diminishing and my faith in the kind inner voices was increasing.

We were spending more and more time in Sausalito, and I had begun to fantasize about gradually relocating there. Jeff was intermittently on board with this idea. He loved all the natural beauty of the Bay Area as well as the spiritual diversity that California has to offer. When he was there, he could see us staying, but when he returned to Ann Arbor, he felt planted in Michigan. It was hard to know what he actually wanted. I, on the other hand, felt a very strong pull to Sausalito. If I was going to be dying soon, I wanted to see my kids more than once or twice a year. But that wasn't the only reason. In some strange way, it felt like my odds of survival were better in Sausalito.

That spring, we took a couple of trips from Sausalito, which made it feel even more like home. We drove to San Diego with Eric and Justin to do a weeklong workshop with Gwen, the spiritual teacher whose workshop I'd taken last fall. We stopped on the way to visit Hearst Castle on March 11, 1994, my first survival birthday. Walking to the car after the tour, a huge wave of gratitude washed over me as I looked out over the Pacific. I was alive: breathing, eating, talking, and here with my favorite men.

Everyone in Gwen's workshop thought it amazing that two cool, young men were so interested in spiritual growth that they were willing to travel with their parents. I was so proud of my guys! A few weeks later, Lynn and her fiancé treated Jeff and me to ten days in Hawaii as a belated wedding present. We all bought matching flowered outfits at Hilo Hattie's and had a fabulous time.

By the fall of 1994, I was strong enough to make a road trip to California and to stay there by myself. Jeff and I stopped in St. Louis for Lynn's wedding, and he drove with me as far as Boulder, Colorado, and then returned to Ann Arbor for work. I arranged a complex relay of travel companions to accompany me the rest of the way. Moving my car and a carload of belongings to Sausalito would save money on rental cars and was an exciting investment in a new life. My friend Nan drove the final leg of the trip with me and stayed for a few days of fun—estate sale shopping, *Beach Blanket Babylon,* and eating ravioli in North Beach.

After Nan left, there wasn't much to do. Justin was now temporarily living in Austin, Texas, "for the music," and Eric was busy with his burgeoning illustration career. I had yet to make many friends in California. I missed Jeff but not the increasingly frequent fights we'd started having. We talked on the phone at least once a day and, while we could also get into long-distance dustups, we seemed to get along better this way. It occurred to me that we might both need time to ourselves. Maybe we had to heal as individuals before we could heal as a couple. A strong introvert, Jeff needed to catch up on his alone time after all the togetherness of the last few years.

Unlike Jeff, I had never liked being alone. That's why I worked so hard at making friends and one reason that I kept getting married. Even with the discovery of friendlier inner companions, time alone usually meant time with the Bitch. Especially since I wasn't doing anything she deemed productive. She wasn't a big fan of inner work and eschewed the Tibetan worldview on the value of contemplating one's death. "You are such a failure. Look at how your sister and all your friends are out making money and making a difference in the world. You're just taking up space. Why do you have to drag out this 'healing' business?"

As I listened to her diatribe day after day, I began to see that I agreed with her. One day when I couldn't reach Jeff or any of my Michigan friends on the phone, I sat staring at a game show without playing along and it hit me. Deep down, I believed that if I wasn't doing something worthwhile, I wasn't worth anything. If I wasn't helping someone, I didn't deserve my place on the planet.

I was able to sit with this knowing and the emptiness it engendered for a few minutes. Then the phone rang. As always, talking to Barb helped. I went back to watching television, this time in earnest. Over the next several days, I reverted to my standard tactic of getting busy. I volunteered at a foundation led by a local spiritual teacher and started to meet like-minded people. I formed a new Mastermind group with three of them, and we met whenever I was in town.

Although I was getting out a little more, I quickly ran out of steam, so I still had a lot of alone time on my hands. I puttered around the apartment, talked on the phone, watched movies, and did a decent job of creating distractions. But some part of me knew that I had to stop running from myself. It was time to learn to value myself for who I was, not for what I did. I still wanted the satisfaction that I got from helping others, but the well from which I had been giving had run dry. I began to sense the deep-seated deprivation that Elizabeth had seen in me. While watering plants one cool, misty Sausalito morning, I remembered the image of that emaciated waif I had found huddled in the dingy closet. I realized that she was the spokesperson for that deprivation. It was time to face the Girl in the Closet.

I sat down at the kitchen table with my journal and my coffee. I lit a candle because that's what we do in Marin. The fog hadn't quite burned off the bay, so I could see blue sky out of one window and gray out of another. This held my interest for quite a while. Finally, I picked up my journal and wrote in it as if anticipating a dialogue.

Me   Hello? What do you want?

GIC   . . .

There was a long pause, and then the words came.

GIC   I want to come out.

I was pleased to get such a swift response, but once she started to spew the venom she'd been harboring, I saw why I had postponed this conversation.

> **GIC**   I want you to pay attention to me instead of
> taking care of everyone *but* me! You started neglecting
> me when we were really little, stuffed all the bad feelings
> in this crappy closet, and then got busy to avoid them. I
> was all alone and really scared. Look what it took to get
> your attention!

She went on for pages and pages, several journal-writing sessions worth. She hated that I had dragged her up on stage in front of hundreds of people when she was so shy. It hurt her feelings when I compared her (a.k.a. myself) unfavorably to other people.

> **GIC**   Even after you got so sick and couldn't work,
> you didn't let up. You kept pushing me to do more and
> be busy all the time! We were almost dying, and I still
> couldn't do enough to satisfy you.

She was talking to me as if I were the Bitch! For most of my life, I had thought that the Vile Bitch Upstairs was all there was to me. Now I was beginning to see that her voice was one of many I could hear if I slowed down enough to listen. It was becoming difficult to keep my who's who of internal voices straight. But I knew the Girl was right. I'd used work and busyness to avoid her, the keeper of the feelings.

> **GIC**   Now you ask what I want! I want you to sit still
> and do nothing once in a while. And, by the way, you
> won't get paid work until you learn to do it my way. And
> I don't want you to look good. If you still looked good,
> you'd be out there pleasing everyone and ignoring me.

On a shamanic journey the following day, the Jesus voice put it another way. He urged me to find my heart and heal the split between the part of myself I showed to the world and the Girl in the Closet. He encouraged me to embrace the Girl and know that "she is you and you are her and you must unite to survive."

Although I was pleased with the progress the Girl and I were making, I wasn't thrilled with the idea that my survival hinged on getting along with this moody child. I needed to get out of my little apartment and off this internal battleground.

One clear, lapis-lazuli September day, I decided to risk strangers gawking at me and took an outing to Angel Island, which sits in the middle of San Francisco Bay. At various points in its history, the island has served as a hunting and fishing site for the Coastal Miwok Indians, an army post in the Civil War, a processing post for Asian immigrants, a camp for German and Japanese POWs, and a Nike missile base.

Perched on the hard bench of the Angel Island ferry, I stared at the glistening water and passing sailboats and listened in on the conversations of neighboring couples. I positioned my bejeweled left hand in plain view to show that, although I was alone today, I did have a husband somewhere. I sweated in a turtleneck because I was not ready to expose all my scars to public scrutiny.

Once on the island, I treated myself to an iced tea and set out to limp the twisty road that girdles Angel Island. I paused at each turn to get my breath and take in a new vista: the City skyline, the cayenne-colored Golden Gate Bridge, the rocky coastline of the Marin Headlands where I want my ashes scattered someday, grand houses and tiny cottages tucked helter-skelter into the hills of Sausalito. What better way to reconnect with God than to admire His handiwork?

Halfway around the island, my aching hip reminded me of another circular trek that I had hiked not so long ago. It had been less than two years since the flat walk around the nurses' station at the James Cancer Center had seemed insurmountable. And it wasn't just my mind that remembered my struggle to complete that circuit and get back to bed. The cool metal of the IV pole in the palm of my hand, the strap of the catheter bag around my leg, and the tug of tubes in and out of every orifice God created—and several He didn't think of—were all embedded in my body. My gait was slow and awkward, and I sat on each

222

bench along the way, but I walked every inch of the bumpy five-mile path back to the ferry. I didn't care who stared at me on the return trip.

I was sore the next day but felt so virtuous after that huge hike that I considered adding regular physical activity to my healing plan. It had been amazing to have an almost competent body and to do something so utterly normal. I had kept my distance from exercise since elementary school where Bernie Falk, the compact Italian gym teacher, made me shimmy up ropes. Now that I was in this fabulous place with its wonderful weather, I could go for a stroll a few times a week.

While I was updating my healing plan, I decided to start keeping a gratitude list. Every day, I added five things for which I was grateful: my kids, talking, that Jeff and I were still together even with all the challenges, the view from the window in Sausalito, coffee. I found that focusing on what I appreciated made me feel better. Now there is scientific proof that gratitude leads to happiness.

Coupled with my improved attitude, I was feeling a little more confident about my appearance. I wanted to get out more not only for exercise, but also to meet new people and have some fun—all of which meant it was time to face my face.

I moved "look at myself in the mirror more often" onto the active list of my healing plan. That meant I had to stop staring into the bathroom sink while washing my face and brushing my remaining teeth. I forced myself to look in the mirror long enough to put on a little makeup before I went out for walks or into the city to see my kids. The static in my stomach as I approached the bathroom told me that I wasn't ready to confront my reflection full on, so I devised strategies to soften the blow. I took off my glasses. If I held my head in a certain way, I could focus on the parts of me that hadn't been distorted. Looking myself in the eyes was the best approach. The surgeon hadn't ventured north of my mouth and, as my mother always said, my eyes are my best feature. My nose was fine and if I kept my mouth shut, my asymmetrical smile hid missing teeth and my partial, twisted tongue. Again a turtleneck covered the hollowed-out left side of my neck.

I was able to look at myself a little longer at each mirror session. I worked up to looking at my whole face rather than focusing on its upper regions. In time, I was able to peek into my mouth and glance at my uncovered neck. I stopped avoiding my reflection in store windows. I was just starting to feel a little better about how I looked when I received the photos taken at Lynn's wedding. The photographer had caught me from angles that I had never seen in the mirror. I looked hideous. There was a deep cavern under my chin on one side and swelling on the other. Puffiness in my left cheek gave way to an unsightly hollow in my neck that revealed an off-center Adam's apple. Worse, I wore a big open-mouthed grin, revealing my C-shaped tongue fragment curled around six sorry lower teeth and a gaping hole where the other ten should be.

How in God's name had I ever gone out in public looking like this? I thought I'd had fun at that wedding. Now I realized that the wedding guests, as well as everyone who had seen me since the surgery, had had to look at these grotesque sides of me. How had they kept from gagging? I felt retroactive embarrassment and never wanted to be seen again.

I called Jeff to tell him how upset I was about the photos. He said everyone takes a bad picture now and then. I wanted to kill him. He had never taken a bad picture in his life. How could he patronize me like that? Somehow my empathy for those who had to look at me did not extend to Jeff who, even with our increasing time apart, saw me more than anyone else did. I acted as if he had a legal obligation not to be repulsed. It was just too frightening for me to acknowledge that this handsome man who had been drawn to the attractive me in my sexy black sundress might be having trouble now that my looks were gone. Jeff said he could see my inner beauty, and I bought it. Case closed.

We were able to work through most of my anger in a couple of phone calls. I couldn't afford to stay mad at Jeff. I needed him. I'd sure as hell never find another husband looking like this. And I was so lucky to be free of cancer that I had no business complaining about superficial stuff. The treatment that made me look this way had saved my life. My appearance was here to stay, and I wasn't going to let it make a prisoner of me. If I wanted to spend time alone in Sausalito, I had to get out into the world.

If anything was going to make me feel better, it was discount shopping. After the worst sting of the photos wore off, I told myself that I needed to scope out local bargain opportunities and headed for the Marshall's in Corte Madera. After a couple blissful hours of perusal and selection, I was waiting in line with my cart of greatly reduced household accessories, lounge wear, and presents when an adorable towheaded boy of about four pointed up at me. In a voice louder than the store's public address system, he said, "You have a really big chin. You have a really big chin. You have a really big chin. . . ."

His mother, juggling purchases, her checkbook, and his little sister, said in a stage whisper, "Tyler, that isn't a nice thing to say. Tyler, that isn't nice . . ." and tried to interest him in his new cement truck. But the damage had been done. This was what I'd been afraid of since the operation. Even the solace of shopping couldn't smooth the dent in my denial that day. I crossed mirror gazing off the to-do list.

§

In its place, I added, "eliminate drinking." This was no simple decision. Questions about my drinking—Could I control it? Was I maybe a slight alcoholic? Was drinking getting in the way of my spiritual development?—plagued me even before I learned that alcohol was a risk factor for oral cancer. This obsessing and the Bitch's rants increased in intensity when I realized that each glass of wine could be pushing me closer to a recurrence. Since radiation, the burning had prevented much imbibing. But my mouth was starting to heal and with it my capacity to enjoy a cocktail.

Maybe using wine to dilute the Bitch's toxicity wasn't the healthiest way to go. Whenever I drank, I worried about when and how much to drink. Years before, when I tried drinking only on weekends, I started fantasizing about Friday night along about Tuesday. All these mental gymnastics took a lot of energy and interfered with my ability to make sense of my inner landscape. And drinking sure wasn't helping our marriage.

Also, I knew there was a history of addiction in our family. Alcohol and drugs had played a role in Greg's problems. People in my family drank, but most of them were so highly functioning that it was tough to tell if anyone had a real problem. Only after I got sober and Mom had been dead for several years did I realize that she might have been a little too fond of alcohol and prescription drugs. There were stories of drunks in her family history. My Woman's-Christian-Temperance-Union-founding paternal grandmother's adamant anti-alcohol stance could well have been a reaction to alcoholism on that side of the family. All in all, the odds were high that my sons had a hereditary proclivity toward addiction.

I wrote to my Guides about it then paused to quiet my mind and clear the way for a response. There wasn't much hesitation that day. The Guides were taking the Bitch's side on this issue. They assured me that sobriety was vital to my physical well-being and my progress toward inner peace and that I would come to know I'd made the right choice.

§

All of these factors, especially the advice of my Guides and the fear of a recurrence, played a role in my quitting. But in the final analysis, it was the way I feel about my children that got me sober. If cutting off my limbs might help one of my kids, I'll go shopping for a saw. If not drinking might set a good example for them, I would say good-bye forever to manhattans, chardonnay, and, God help me, champagne.

So I wrote, "eliminate alcohol" in my healing plan and called Jeff to tell him that I was planning to quit drinking when I got back to Ann Arbor the following week. He said he wanted to support me and would quit right now. This was the nicest thing anyone had ever done for me, and I will always be grateful to him. But what was the rush? I intended to have a lot of little going-away parties with myself before I left Sausalito.

Back in Ann Arbor, I had my last drink on December 9, 1994.

§

Facing the New Year and the end of my healing hiatus with no work on the books was also sobering. I consulted my internal guidance about my money fears and they assured me, "YOU WILL ALWAYS HAVE PLENTY OF MONEY." They were emphatic, using all caps on this topic more than any other. They pleaded with me to trust that I would be provided for financially, but I still sometimes have trouble doing that.

I was getting into the habit of consulting this inner wisdom on a daily basis. I wrote in my journal most mornings, starting with my gratitude list, explaining what was on my mind that day, and asking what, if anything, I needed to do regarding my concerns. Following my specific questions, I added the < symbol and then the answers seemed to write themselves automatically. When the words stopped flowing, I closed the section with a >. While I called the source of the advice my Guides, I had no idea where the information actually originated. I knew it was part of me, but I liked to think it was connected to some higher intelligence. Often their only advice was to turn the problem over to God—the hardest direction of all to one who thinks she has the answers and likes to be in control.

The Guides were right a lot, and I relied on them more and more. When they told me a symptom wasn't cancer, the biopsy was negative. They said I was done with cancer, and often I believed them. When I worried about my kids, they politely suggested that I mind my own business and let my boys grow up. They assured me that it was fine for Jeff and I to spend more time apart, but they wouldn't say whether we would stay together. Even when I got up the nerve to ask them point blank, all they would say is "You'll be fine either way." I felt so close to Jeff for quitting drinking with me and wondered why they were so evasive on this subject.

celebrating beauty

arch 11, 1995, came and went, and the healing hiatus wasn't over. I was beginning to wonder if it ever would be. My definition of healing was expanding to include any changes that allowed me to be more fully myself, and I didn't want that process to end.

Jeff and I were spending more and more time apart but continued to work on our marriage. We saw a couple's therapist whenever I was in Ann Arbor. Marin County being a New Age mecca, it was easy to find a Tantric weekend. We enrolled in an effort to resuscitate our sex life. We rendezvoused in Santa Fe for a weeklong Relationship as Spiritual Path workshop in 1997 and repeated the training the next two years. Apparently we were in the remedial group when it came to relationships. The workshops culminated in a self-designed commitment ceremony for each couple. My reluctance grew each time it was our turn to vow our undying love, and I really struggled with the third ceremony, held on a secluded beach on Maui. Jeff never hesitated.

On the surface, it appeared that our life was moving west. In 1997, we sold our Peters Road house and bought a condo in Sausalito. Jeff rented a duplex in Ann Arbor where he would continue his small Rolfing practice and where we would stay when in town. When he was in California, he continued to say how much he loved the area and seemed enthusiastic about moving. Wanting to increase his career flexibility, Jeff connected with my former mentor and trained to be an organizational development consultant. He created an OD networking group in the Bay Area and began to actively look for consulting work. But on returning to Ann Arbor, he still talked about how nice it was there. His oscillating started to drive me a little crazy, but he said he liked going back and forth and was in no hurry to relocate permanently, so I did my best to let it be.

One evening in 1999, we were in Sausalito, still discussing when he might move there for good. "You know, I moved so much as a kid," he said. "It got to the point that I didn't bother to make friends because I knew I'd just have to leave them." He paused, looking out the window of our condo on to Richardson Bay. "I'm not sure I have it in me to start over again." I felt a chill of terror. Wait. What was he talking about? We had agreed we were both moving to California; we just hadn't decided on a date. We'd bought a house together here!

"Maybe you could move back to Ann Arbor?" Jeff said in a hushed tone. Before I could respond, he shook his head and answered his own question, "No, you couldn't do that. Your life is here now." We quickly dropped the subject, sensing we were wandering into dangerous terrain. I mumbled something Marin-ish about how it would all become clear in time, but inside it felt like there was a hole in my gut.

In truth, I wasn't entirely convinced that I wanted him in California all the time. When he was back in Michigan, I missed him sometimes, but at other times I enjoyed being free of the mounting tension between us. It was kind of nice to do exactly what I wanted to do without having to convince him to come along or to feel guilty if he didn't. We still talked at least once a day. Jeff had long said that his ideal relationship would involve living separately, but I'd always thought that was just weird. Now I wasn't so sure. For the first time in my life I was on my own, and I was proud of my growing self-reliance.

More and more, I dared to get out and meet people. I enrolled in aqua exercise for older adults at College of Marin, even though I couldn't believe I was remotely old enough to qualify. My first-ever therapy client in Ann Arbor moved to the Bay Area, and so I had a tiny bit of work. I continued to volunteer with the spiritual foundation and coordinated all the volunteers for a big benefit with

Neale Donald Walsch. I went to Spirit Rock Meditation Center to hear Jack Kornfield's wonderful talks. This place was teeming with brilliant, creative, and famous people!

I was listening to NPR one day when they interviewed the funniest, wisest author I had ever heard. I tracked her down and was delighted to discover that Anne Lamott lived in Marin and taught writing at Book Passage ten minutes from our place. Although her class was full, Annie let me sit in the back of the room, and I began to schedule my trips to California around her classes. I also joined Annie's funky, little Presbyterian church, which could not have been more different than the one in Grosse Pointe.

I took up personal storytelling. As I made new friends, several of them told me I needed to meet a man named David Roche, a facially disfigured storyteller with a solo show entitled *The Church of 80% Sincerity*. "What should I do, call him and say, 'I look funny too. Let's talk?'" But fate, or serendipity as we call it in California, landed me at a class in David's living room. David has a congenital venous malformation such that part of his face is swollen and purple. He has even fewer teeth than I do. His appearance is startling at first but his warmth, wit, and authenticity quickly obscure it.

The class was full of interesting people, and David was very encouraging about my storytelling ability. After that first class, he said, "I'll do anything I can to support you," and I sensed that he only said things that he meant. But was I really ready to face an audience? I'd done a little work with established clients since my healing hiatus, but still hesitated to return to public speaking with my lopsided looks and a voice that sounded remarkably like Dr. Lambe's imitation. I doubted I could drag the Girl in the Closet back onto a stage to give speeches.

A few more storytelling classes convinced me that telling my stories for a small, receptive group, many of them my new friends, might be the gentlest way to test the waters on stage. One evening in David's living room, I was telling the story of meeting the Girl in the Closet on that walk down Peters Road. David said, "I'd like to hear from the Girl herself." I wasn't at all sure that I wanted to show this dark inner image to the group, but I wasn't too worried. The Girl had just started speaking to me. No way she was going to talk to strangers. To my surprise, David was able to lure her out, and the first story I told in public was all about the Girl. It ended in a conversation with her, and it turned out that she and I like a lot of the same things: "Big hats and feather boas, sitting by the water, and listening to Gershwin music."

Unbeknownst to me, one of the other storytellers in our first public showcase sent a video of my story to the founder of the Cancer as a Turning Point conferences. A few months later, I performed the story for 1,400 cancer patients, survivors, and their loved ones at the Marin Veterans Auditorium. I went on to tell that story at a lot of conferences and in a variety of health-care settings.

In our second storytelling showcase, I told the story of my wild weekend in New York with the piano player. Afterward, David said, "You're ready to do a solo show."

"Are you crazy? No I'm not! But I'll do one with you." We had a ball over the next few months creating *Facing the Holidays with David and Terri*. Turns out our chemistry worked on stage, and we riffed on tooth-free holiday eating, personal ads for the disfigured, and geriatric erotica. We each told a solo story. As I walked onto the stage to tell mine, we played "We Need a Little Christmas" from the CD I had gotten for Christmas 1992 from Johnny Mathis. I still feel the thrill of that night rising up in me whenever I hear that song. My kids were in the audience as were Val and Lynn and all my new friends in Marin.

Not only was David my inspiration in returning to the stage and my partner in teaching storytelling, but having a funny, disfigured friend was a huge gift. When I went out with David, I got to be the pretty one. He taught me how to deal with people staring and how to charm people before they judge you. David also showed me that even the best humored people get sick of being out in the world looking so different.

Jeff even got into the storytelling act. At first, he provided technical support at my performances. Then he attended a few classes. Finally, he participated in a men's showcase. A confirmed introvert, this was a huge leap for him. Three of our four sons were in the audience, and he made us all proud. But beyond the pride, I was thrilled because I took this as a sure sign that he was ready to move to California.

Jeff rented office space in Marin and continued to market his growing Rolfing practice. He formed a partnership with a successful OD consultant in San Francisco. I felt great relief when he ordered business cards with our California address. More encouragement came when we vacationed near the Trinity River. Jeff fell in love with the area and took up fishing! We found a cottage that we liked and, though we couldn't remotely afford it, talked about going in with friends to buy it.

In 2000, Jeff and I were invited to perform together in a Cancer as a Turning Point conference at Stanford University. I would share my saga as a cancer patient, and Jeff would speak from the caregiver's point of view. It took a little convincing, but Jeff agreed, and we set about creating a tandem story.

As we prepared, Jeff finally told the truth about what it had been like for him when I was sick: how repulsed he had been by my wounds, how often he wanted to bolt from the hospital, and how hard it had been to look at me after the operation. Every version of his story included his emphatic declaration, "I did not sign up for this!"

When we rehearsed our story with other people, they were concerned that I'd find his honesty upsetting. Proving the depth of my denial, I said and believed, "No, it's fine. I'm so glad he's finally getting this out. Now we can heal."

I was wrong. Late on the night of July 21, 2000, after a delightful dinner with Justin and his girlfriend during which we raved about our dream house on the Trinity River, Jeff and I met in my bedroom for a prearranged sex date. After a few clumsy attempts at ardor, Jeff said, "I've had enough of this." Postponing sex yet again felt disappointing to me, but we were both exhausted, so I agreed.

Jeff was referring to our marriage.

Our divorce was final in February 2001. When I tell the story of our breakup on stage, I say that Jeff left me for a "younger, blonder, more symmetrical woman." This is true, but it doesn't tell the whole story. My initial ambivalence about being married to Jeff didn't stop with the wedding. There were many wonderful times and lots of ways in which we were compatible. But we were fundamentally different in temperament and always had plenty of issues. I sometimes wonder if we might have split sooner if it hadn't been for cancer.

§

Now I really was alone. Yes, I had my friends, my family, and a little work. But who was I without a husband? This was the first time since I was sixteen that I wasn't dating at least one man. In order to figure out who I was if not a wife or girlfriend, I needed to settle on a name. Given my multiple marriages, I had accumulated so many last names that one day Eric said, "You know Mom, you could be your own law firm." It was time for a name that was all my own. I chose "Tate," because I felt so special when my grandfather named me that as a kid and because it was what I'd sometimes called my neglected inner child.

Terri Tate was asked to open for Holly Near at a benefit concert for a women's cancer organization in Santa Cruz. Holly had been an idol of mine for decades, and sharing a stage with her ranks among the biggest thrills of my life. A friend asked me to speak at a Patch Adams conference. I entered the Scintillating Sausalito Summertime Queen beauty contest, a delightfully bizarre pageant limited to "actual women over forty who love sequins, boas, and Sausalito." It took a lot of urging, and every ounce of chutzpah I could muster, to stand before an SRO crowd of yachting types in a slinky black, feathered dress and tell the story of my love affair with Sausalito. The previously raucous and well-lubricated audience went silent the moment I spoke my first line. I had them! And I won the contest. The next day, my picture was on the front page of the *Marinscope* newspaper under the headline, "Celebrating Beauty."

In January 2004, I performed my solo show, *Shopping as a Spiritual Path*, for the first time in Mill Valley, a town just north of Sausalito. *Shopping* chronicles the misadventures of my cancer journey, describes disfigured dating, and shows the shift from a life lived under the Bitch's reign of terror to one spent following the gentle direction of the Guides. I performed the show for cancer audiences across the country. I entered it in the San Francisco Fringe Festival where it won the Best of the Fringe award. This was a huge thrill; it meant that even real theater audiences liked my work.

And then I got a grant to make a DVD of *Shopping*. The show was taped as I performed for several hundred people at California Pacific Medical Center's Institute for Health and Healing Mini-Medical School. Preparing for the show backstage had felt a lot like pre-op and, were it not for my friend Jo Anne's urging and support, I might have bolted.

§

May 2007

I stepped between the maroon velvet curtains as the emcee said, "Please welcome Terri Tate in *Shopping as a Spiritual Path!*"

I was met with thundering applause. I couldn't see the audience well because of the stage lights, but I felt their loving excitement. They laughed and moaned at all the right times. The show went off without a hitch.

It ended like this:

"I am alone but seldom lonely. In fact, now I cherish my time alone. Things have gotten a lot more peaceful on the inner front since I bought the Vile Bitch Upstairs a gold watch for sixty years of faithful service and got her a condo in Boca. The minute I get the least bit stressed, she's on the red-eye back from Florida. But when she tries to take over, I remind her that we are under new management now. That loving board of inner advisors is always at the ready with compassion, wisdom, and encouragement. I just have to remember to ask.

"People are always saying, 'God loves you.' I was never sure what He saw in me. Now I'm learning to see myself through God's eyes. Or, to put it in shopping terms, I am learning to love myself as is."

The crowd leapt to its feet, applauding and cheering wildly. Basking in the glow of their love, I could not have felt more beautiful.

epilogue

One glorious morning shortly after I taped the *Shopping as a Spiritual Path* DVD, I was driving north on Highway 101 out of Sausalito. At the point where I could see the bay, Mount Tamalpais, and lush wetlands in one glance, a question popped into my head.

"Why did this happen to me?" The inquiry was born of curiosity rather than self-pity. The answer came quickly from that gentle voice I'd come to trust.

"You wanted your woundedness to show."

Startled, I had to ponder this for quite a while before I could see the truth in it. Perhaps depriving me of my looks was one of the desperate measures that the Girl in the Closet had to take to get my attention. Or maybe my oral cancer was the result of genetic factors, too much ice cream, environmental toxins, alcohol, inadequate affirmations, a brother's suicide, cigarettes, three divorces, not enough exercise, or an immune system that was compromised by the massive quantities of sulfa I took to fight TB. I will likely never know what combo plate of these and other variables made me sick, but I'm doing a decent job of not blaming myself for any part I may have played in causing my illness.

Then there is the other "Why me?"—the mystery of my survival. Which of the myriad healing paths I trudged contributed to my still being here? Perhaps my work to expose the Vile Bitch Upstairs like the Wizard of Oz healed something fundamental in me so that I could fight the disease. I'm pretty sure that trusting my Guides to solve the surgical conundrum rather than relying on external experts helped me heal. I'd like to think that all my inner work played a role in my survival. I know it's had a huge impact on the quality of this bonus life. And I do believe that our bodies possess self-healing mechanisms that we're only beginning to tap. But maybe it was the Czechoslovakian sea captain or the Rife generator or the radiation or the bovine cartilage or the laughter or all that support or Sausalito that tipped the balance. Or was it just not my time? Whatever contributed to my survival, I am certain that something mystical beyond the medical was at work, and the final decision was out of my hands.

A better question might be, what has all this taught me? I've learned something about forgiveness. Forgiving others for their failings seems to make it easier to live with my own. I'm not totally there yet, but I've come a long way in forgiving myself, specifically the Vile Bitch Upstairs. Looking back, I see that she caused me more pain than the cancer did. I feared meeting her on my deathbed with her long list of "not enoughs" more than I feared dying itself. But now I can see that, like her mentor, my mother, the Bitch was trying to look out for my best interests all along. It wasn't their fault that they were both terrified all the time.

I forgive Mom for teaching me that illness is the only legitimate route to relaxation and getting your needs met, as well as a fine way to be the center of attention. Now I can get attention from a loving audience, as well as from my fabulous friends and family. And I'm learning to ask for what I want and need without being sick to get it.

I forgive Jeff who did his very best, which was a lot, and I almost forgive myself for not appreciating him more.

And I'm pretty sure I've forgiven Dr. Watson. A few years back, I gave a speech at a conference in the same building as his office and paid him a spontaneous visit. Dr. Watson seemed surprised to see me on a lot of levels—being alive, looking healthy, and wearing a business suit. After a sweet, superficial chat about what was new, he said, with a tiny tear in one eye, "I'm going to move you into the success column." I was happy to set his record straight.

This journey has taught me something about acceptance. I'd spent a lifetime trying to adjust circumstances in order to make the people I love happier. It never worked. I haven't entirely abandoned this strategy even though it only leads to misery. I'm slowly learning that things get better when I get out of the way and let God do the work.

In embracing the Girl in the Closet, I symbolically accepted those aspects of myself that I had disowned—the clingy, needy parts that didn't fit with the powerful image I wanted the world to see. During a recent meditation, a new image of the Girl showed up—she's wearing a soft, fuzzy, pink sweater and her thick hair is done up in pigtails. She's gained weight and her cheeks are so chubby you can see them from behind when she smiles. I'm giving her a piggyback ride—she's bouncing along, arms around my cratered neck—telling me which way she wants to go. I don't mind carrying her or following her directions.

I've come to accept being on my own. I'm at peace with a career that is not as big as it was before cancer. And I've adjusted to life without a full set of lower teeth.

Much as I wish it were otherwise, I accept that I will never really be done with cancer. I recently had pain in my mouth that felt very much like my recurrence. It was my worst scare in decades, complete with an oral biopsy under a paltry local anesthetic and eight days of waiting for results. Oddly, I wasn't as panicked as I expected to be. I felt held by God in a new way and was able to sleep and spend quiet time finishing this book. I looked back on the twenty-five bonus years I've been granted and felt really blessed. There's still a lot I'd like to do in this lifetime, but I finally saw what Jeff meant when he said, "I'll be okay whatever happens."

And I've learned something about gratitude. It's my best defense against the Bitch and may be the one true path to happiness. I'm not New Age-y enough to say that I am grateful to the cancer, although if not for that disease, I doubt I would have ever stopped trying to make a big splash in the world long enough to listen to the little ripples within. I am grateful for twenty-one years of sobriety, which has contributed to my internal peace. This inner quiet has allowed me to discover that the Bitch isn't the only one in there, let me see the dire state of the Girl, and finally led me to the Guides, for whom I could not be more grateful. While I realize most people don't name their inner wisdom like I did, we all have it. Trust it.

More than anything else, I wanted to stay alive to watch my kids grow up and to become a grandmother, and these are the top reasons I'm grateful that I got to stick around. I was in the delivery room at 5:43 a.m. on March 25, 2003, when my precious granddaughter was born. Nothing makes me happier than hearing her laugh when her dad and uncle are being silly.

I'm learning to be grateful for moments like these:

- Breathing in the ocean air of the Pacific sans an NG tube

- Walking, even with a little limp, along the wetlands near my house when a blue heron takes flight

- Coaching a storytelling student to find a rich story inside

- Savoring salted caramel ice cream with a partial tongue

- Talking on the phone with my Michigan friend who understands every word

- Singing along with Bette Midler

- Getting the timing just right so the audience laughs a little harder at my joke

Gratitude abounds for the return of a little romance. One handsome fellow was kind enough to relieve me of my secondary virginity after I'd been out of the dating pool for years. I had a magnificent time rekindling a love affair that started in graduate school in 1974. I thought that one would last. Sadly, it did not. But it did give me the opportunity to relearn kissing, and for that I will always be grateful! I still hope to find love again in this lifetime, but I no longer believe that my happiness depends on it.

I am grateful that I was never obsessed with my appearance and have long believed that it's what's inside that matters. I know people who refused surgeries like the ones I had, opting for death over disfigurement. I understand this choice, but I never considered making it. Many of the richest moments in my life have happened in this newly configured body. I wouldn't dream of trading them for my preoperative looks.

I'm not always comfortable wearing my woundedness for the world to see. Every once in a while I am caught off guard by a chance glance at my reflection that reveals a new facet of my disfigurement. But the other day I was on the couch chatting and laughing with a close friend over Sumatra dark roast when I caught a glimpse of myself in the dining room mirror. And there she was smiling back at me—that woman I visualized after I skipped the surgery—the one with the bright, sparkling eyes and a big, crooked smile.

gratitude list

When Haven Iverson, my wonderful editor at Sounds True, read the manuscript of *A Crooked Smile*, her first question was, "Do you have any idea how extraordinary your support network was through your ordeal?" I do. Val, Barb, and Jeff were relentless and terrific in their caring. Also there when I needed them were my kids, my brother Bill, my parents, my nieces and nephews, Karen McNeil, Peter Wilkins, Tom White, Nancy Janssen, Marge Altman, Karen Packard, Shelley Tessmer, Linda Stott and the Mastermind group, the Grunners, Al Davenport, Carol Anderson, Linda Shubow, Elliot Altman, Johnny Mathis, Doris England, the McWilliams, Ginny Brown, Jason Porter, Karen Keeler, Elizabeth Alberda, Gwen Jansma, Elizabeth Kairys, the Markels, Mark Packard, the Carters, Mike Penrod, John Slater, and many more. And though I don't recall their names all these years later, I am grateful to the nurses, doctors, and other traditional and alternative health-care providers who took mostly wonderful care of me during the cancer era. My special thanks to Dr. Bradford, Dr. Sullivan, and Tammi Miller, RN, MS, who continued to support me for many years.

It took a big gang of people and a lot of grace to keep me alive and more of the same to bring this book to life. I wanted to write before I read Anne Lamott in 1994, but she was the one who showed by example how it was done and gave me something to aspire to as a writer. The fact that she wrote the foreword for this book ranks among the biggest thrills of my life, and I plan to be buried with a copy of it. When Annie stopped teaching writing at Book Passage, one of the coolest independent bookstores on the planet, she suggested that we devotees form a writing group. At first there were as many as twelve of us, but over the years the group dwindled to a steadfast core. Claudia Bluhm, Amy Ingersoll, Margit Liesche, Mary Cone, and I met at Book

Passage every Wednesday for sixteen years. These ardent reviewers have read so many versions of my memoir that I'm sure they're relieved to see it in print. Once I had the "shitty first draft" that Annie recommends, she sent me to Neshama Franklin for the initial edit. Neshama is incredibly well read and so facile with the English language that her endorsement encouraged me to press on. My friend Jo Anne Smith has been fiddling with the manuscript ever since and has provided endless help of every kind in the book's development. Like Jo and Neshama, Rob Weisbach, Renee Sedliar, Doug Childers, and Meredith Maran made it better. Another writing group, The Write Sisters, inspired me to persevere when I was still at work on the book twenty years after I started. And Marlena Blavin, usually a gentle woman, got fierce with me one night over Indian food and said, "Stop fussing about your love life and finish the damned book."

Thank you all.

Jan Adrian, the founder of Healing Journeys and my guardian angel is responsible for getting *A Crooked Smile* to Sounds True via a series of serendipitous events that are impressive even by California standards. I am forever in her debt.

What can I say about the new family I've found at Sounds True? Starting with Acquisitions Director Jennifer Brown, who was born in the same hospital where I had my first surgery, it's been a perfect match. Every change that Haven Iverson suggested was an improvement I knew the book needed or a fresh idea that I instantly recognized as right. And we had a ball along the way. Karen Polaski and Rachael Murray set me up for a daylong photo shoot, which not only resulted in a fabulous cover, but also fulfilled a lifetime of pin-up-girl fantasies. The delightful day that I spent with Brian Galvin and the brilliant and creative sales and marketing team taught me a loving way to see promotion. Leslie Brown managed the book's production with care, skill, and grace. Cynthia More is as elegant as she is diligent in publicizing it. Sounds True with its great people, spiritual mission, and organizational integrity is the publisher of my dreams.

I want to thank those who have brought joy to my bonus life. David Roche urged me to tell my stories and showed me how to hold my head high as I ventured into the world as a disfigured person. Bette Midler inspired me to get back on stage. In addition to the folks I've mentioned, massive gratitude goes to Judy Dobbs, Amy Metzenbaum, Susan Bowman and the Grandmothers, Nancy McGinnis, Patricia Arquette, Carol LaRue, Amy Byers, Doug's meditation group, Tura Franzen, Georgia Gasner, the Story Sisters, Susan Amanda Schratter and the Circle of Women, St. Andrew Presbyterian Church, Pam Joaquin, the Aries birthday gang, Claire Baker, Susan Irvine, College of Marin aqua aerobics, Janet Ryvlin, Sam Jackson, Joe Nevotti, Miss Kitty's Poker Club, Joyce Lillis and the Circle to Stage stars, Merijane Block, Brad Mossman, P. L. Thorndike, Cameron Tuttle, Alison Gibson, Nancy Simpson, the Death Salon, Deborah Carter, Brian Sharkey, Kevin Levey, my mahjong group, Marin Mastermind, Marin City Fellowship, and too many more to name. I am still blessed with a remarkable support network.

I am thankful for the memory of my brother Greg who lives on in me.

Finally, I am grateful to the forces that have allowed me to survive to be a grandmother to my precious Georgie and to extend my tenure as mom to Justin and Eric.

about the author

*T*erri Tate became a nurse to please her mother and because she was inspired by the *Sue Barton* books that she devoured as a girl. Due to her fascination with the mental and emotional workings of humans and her deep-seated aversion to gore, she specialized in psychiatric nursing. She worked on psych units at the University of Michigan Medical Center and then launched a private practice as a psychotherapist. She was the first hypnotherapist in the Ann Arbor phone book.

Terri broadened her focus from individuals to groups and organizations and became a nationally known speaker and consultant. After experiencing her lively, laughter-filled talks, audience members often said, "You should be a stand-up comedienne." And "You should write a book." Before she had the chance to do either, Terri was silenced by two bouts of disfiguring oral cancer, which threatened her voice and her life. But her sense of humor was never in danger.

She found her way back to the stage via storytelling, performing in local showcases and then delivering her one-woman show, *Shopping as a Spiritual Path,* to enthusiastic audiences from Berkeley to Boca Raton. *Shopping* won Best of the Fringe at the San Francisco Fringe Festival. Terri teaches storytelling classes privately and in organizations and coaches solo performers. She has published in professional journals and contributed to *I Am with You: Love Letters to Cancer Patients.* She presents TERRI Talks to cancer groups, health-care organizations, and general audiences. For more, see territate.com.

Terri lives in Marin County, California.

about sounds true

Sounds True is a multimedia publisher whose mission is to inspire and support personal transformation and spiritual awakening. Founded in 1985 and located in Boulder, Colorado, we work with many of the leading spiritual teachers, thinkers, healers, and visionary artists of our time. We strive with every title to preserve the essential "living wisdom" of the author or artist. It is our goal to create products that not only provide information to a reader or listener, but that also embody the quality of a wisdom transmission.

For those seeking genuine transformation, Sounds True is your trusted partner. At SoundsTrue.com you will find a wealth of free resources to support your journey, including exclusive weekly audio interviews, free downloads, interactive learning tools, and other special savings on all our titles.

To learn more, please visit SoundsTrue.com/freegifts or call us toll-free at 800.333.9185.